Death Records
of
Missouri Men

1808-1854

by
Lois Stanley
George F. Wilson
Maryhelen Wilson

Copyright 1990
By: Southern Historical Press, Inc.

All rights reserved. No part of this publication may be reproduced,
stored in a retrieval system, transmitted in any form,
posted on to the web in any form or by any means
without the prior written permission of the publisher.

Please direct all correspondence and orders to:

www.southernhistoricalpress.com
or
SOUTHERN HISTORICAL PRESS, Inc.
PO BOX 1267
375 West Broad Street
Greenville, SC 29601
southernhistoricalpress@gmail.com

ISBN #0-89308-440-9

Printed in the United States of America

It is fortunate for the researcher that Missouri newspapers began so early and that so many survived. The death notices are particularly important; the earliest pre-date the first short-lived recording of vital statistics (in the 1880s) by more than 70 years. Missouri's climate is not kind to soft old tombstones, and few survive from the pre-Civil War period. But the newspapers, first on crumbling, yellowing paper and now on microfilm, can fill many gaps in our knowledge of our ancestors.

Obviously the state was not totally covered at all times. The truly remarkable thing is that so many deaths were recorded. The earliest newspapers reported happenings from a wide area; as time went on, they picked up items from each other. Deaths across the state appeared in St. Louis' Missouri Republican; and many of those included here were taken from newspapers of which no traces remain. When the location of a death is not shown it can be deduced from the location of the newspaper in which it appeared.

This list includes notices for men, and boys of 12 or over; an earlier book (see facing page) listed women's deaths. In addition we included probate notices from countries whose early records burned -- notices which not only provide an accurate record of date and place of death but often include names of relatives who acted as administrators.

A few of these records have appeared in the Quarterlies of the St. Louis Genealogical Society and the National Genealogical Society.

CODE	NEWSPAPER	GENERAL AREA OF COVERAGE
BEA	St. Louis Beacon	St. Louis city and county.
BGDB	Bowling Green Democrat-Banner	Pike and adjacent area (Lincoln, Ralls, etc.)
BOLT	Boonslick Times	Published Fayette; Howard, Boone, Cooper etc.
BGRAD	Bowling Green Radical	Pike, Lincoln, Ralls, etc.
BOBS	Boonville Observer	Cooper, Boone, Howard, etc.
BORE	Boonville Register	"
BRUNS	Brunswicker	Chariton, Carroll, surrounding area
CAMP	Plebeian	Published Canton. Lewis, Scotland, adjacent counties
CANE	Northeast Missourian	"
COGL	Globe	Published Columbia. Central Missouri.
CGWE	Western Eagle	Published Cape Girardeau. Southeast Missouri.
COP	Patriot	Published Columbia. Central Missouri.
COMB	Commercial Bulletin	Published Boonville. Cooper, Boone, Howard etc.
FAR	Far West	Published Liberty. Clay Co. area.
FULT	Fulton Telegraph	Callaway county area.
GLWT	Weekly Times	Published Glasgow. Howard county area; Chariton.
HANT	Tri-Weekly Messenger	Hannibal. Marion Co. and surrounding area.
HANJ	Journal	
HIM	Independent Missourian	Published Huntsville. Randolph and surrounding area.
HERMWOCH	Wochenblatt	Hermann, Gasconade Co. Printed in German.
HOB	Howard Co. Banner	Published Glasgow. Howard, Chariton, adjoining area.
INJN	Journal	Published Independence. Jackson, Clay, Platte, etc.
INP	Independent Patriot	Jackson, very early. Large area of southeast Missouri.
JASO	Southern Advocate	Jackson. Large area of southeast Missouri.
JEFRE	Republican	
JEFS	Jeffersonian)	Jefferson City. At various times these newspapers
JEM	Metropolitan	covered large areas of central Missouri.
JINQ	Inquirer	
KCEN	Enterprise	Published Kansas City. Jackson County area.
LEXP	Express	Published Lexington. Lafayette County area.
MIN	Missouri Intelligencer	Very early. Published first in Franklin, then Fayette, then Columbia. Covered a wide area of central Missouri.
MODE	Missouri Democrat	Published Fayette. Howard and surrounding counties.
MOAR	Missouri Argus	St. Louis city and county.
MOH	Missouri Herald	Jackson. See INP.
MORE	) Missouri Gazette Missouri Republican	St. Louis. The area's earliest newspaper, which in the early years covered a great part of the state and which picked up items from other newspapers, state-wide, for many years. An enormously valuable resource.
MORP	Missouri Reporter	St. Louis city and county.
NERA	New Era	"
NMJ	New Madrid Journal	Southeast Missouri.
OSIN	Osceola Independent	St. Clair and surrounding counties.
PWH	Palmyra Whig	Marion and surrounding counties.
PLAR	Platte Argus	Platte, Jackson, Clay, etc.
POT	Miner's Prospect	Published Potosi (Washington Co.) Also reported from Franklin, Jefferson, St. Francois, etc.
SALT	Salt River Journal	Pike and surrounding counties.
SASE	Savannah Sentinel	Andrew County, northeast Missouri.
SCOMB	St. Louis Commercial Bulletin	St. Louis city and county.
SLAM	American	"
SLINQ	Inquirer	"
SWERE	Weekly Reveille	"
SLDU	Daily Union	"
SPAD	Advertiser	Published Springfield. Southwest Missouri.
SOV	Shepherd of the Valley	Catholic; St. Louis and eastern Missouri.
STCHMO	Missourian	St. Charles county and surrounding areas.
STCHRO	Chronotype)	
STCDE	Democrat	
STEGPD	Plain Dealer	Ste. Genevieve area.
STGAZ	Gazette	St. Joseph, Buchanan Co., northwest Missouri.
WAR	Visitor	Warsaw; Benton and surrounding counties.
WEM	Western Emigrant	Boonville; Cooper and surrounding counties.
WEPT	Western Pioneer	Trenton; Grundy and surrounding counties.
WESJ	Weston Journal	Platte and surrounding counties.

Most of these newspapers may be found at the Newspaper Library, State Historical Society of Missouri, Columbia. Some are available at the Missouri Historical Society, Jefferson Memorial, St. Louis. Both libraries have the Missouri Gazette-Missouria Republican (MORE) from the earliest days.

MOCHA	Missouri Courier	Published Hannibal. Marion and surrounding counties.

Death Records of Missouri Men

ABBOT, Amos died 10 April ae 63. Funeral from his residence,
    Chestnut between 6th & 7th, to Methodist cemetery.   MORE 11 Apr 1846

ABBOT, Josiah died 3 November in his 38th year of
    consumption. Left wife, 7 children.   STGAZ 10 Nov 1852

ABERNATHY, Batty, of Jackson Co., died of cholera 11 June
    6 miles west of Ft. Kearney. Left wife and
    two children.   MORE 7 Oct 1850

ABERNATHY, Rev. Blackstone L. died of cholera in Palmyra.   MORE 28 June 1833

ABLES, James of Polk. Co. died 11 June 60 miles west of
    Ft. Kearney, age 54.   MORE 7 Oct 1850

ACREE, Andrew Jackson died at Ft. Pickens 13 October.   MORE 26 Oct 1841

ADAMS, Mr. ___ -- B. H. White was convicted of his murder
    in Ray Co. (and sentenced to death).   MORE 29 July 1841

ADAMS, George, an old and respected citizen of Howard Co.
    died 10 February.   MODE 17 Feb 1847

ADAMS, George F. -- Chariton Co. Letters of administration
    granted to John Lane.   BRUNS 6 Sep 1849

ADAMS, Humphry -- Chariton Co. Letters of administration
    granted to John Cavanah 10 July.   BRUNS 19 Aug 1848

ADAMS, James died in St. Ferdinand "Saturday last" age
    about 44. Formerly of Virginia.   MORE 3 Feb 1852

ADAMS, Jesse, a soldier died at Bellefontaine. George
    Davenport appointed administrator.   MORE 15 Jan 1814

ADAMS, Levin died near Louisiana (Pike Co.) 2 March age
    about 64. Kentucky papers please copy.   BGDB 8 Mar 1845

ADAM, Martin Sr. died in St. Louis Co. 14 April age 80.   MORE 21 Apr 1835

ADAMS, William -- DeKalb Co. Letters of administration
    granted to Anne Adams 8 May.   STGAZ 1 June 1853

ADAMS, William died at Ste. Genevieve 22 July age 54.
    Kentucky papers please copy.   MORE 12 Aug 1846

ADAMS, William Whipple died at Marthasville, Warren Co.
    9 August age 25. Maine papers please copy.   BGRAD 10 Aug 1844

ADDERLY, Edward, a "worthy son of the Emerald Isle" died
    Monday night last.   MORE 23 Oct 1818

ADKINSON, John, killed by Indians.   MORE 18 Mar 1815

ADREON, G. W. L. died 22 April at the residence of his
    brother Dr. Stephen in his 21st year. In St. Louis
    only 2 days, left widowed mother in Baltimore.   MORE 11 Nov 1844

AELFRIND, Louis, a German age about 30, was found drowned
    near Ste. Genevieve.   MORE 18 Apr 1816

AGEE, Samuel, of Bowling Green Prairie, age about 32,
    died "Sunday Week."   BRUNS 4 Nov 1848

AGNEW, John Oliver, formerly of St. Louis, died 7 July
    in San Jose. -   MORE 18 July 1853

AKIN, Andrew Jackson died Sunday last age 25. (Letters of   SPAD 8 Nov 1845
    administration to John N. Akin.)

AINSLIE, John, of Boonville, drowned in the Missouri River;
    M. S. Ainslie offers reward to someone finding his
    body. He was 37.   MORE 8 July 1844
    (This death was reported in the issue of 24 June;
    drowning occurred 16 June. He was English, a man
    "of some fortune," and had lately returned from
    a trip abroad with his family.)

ALBRECHT, Henry fell from the dry dock and drowned yester-
    day. Left a large family.   MORE 8 Sep 1843

ALCOME, George died at his residence in Clark Co. age 75,
    on 2 June. Formerly of Kentucky.   MORE 18 June 1842

ALDEN, Charles H. died 6 March in Portland, Maine in his
    29th year. Left a wife in St. Louis.   MORE 23 Mar 1844

ALDRICH, Albert Henry age 18, eldest son of Nahum, a St.
    Louis merchant, died in Havana 18 March.   SWERE 7 Apr 1845
    (shown as Henry A., died of consumption, in
        MORE 5 April.)

ALESWORTH, Isaac J. died at the City Hotel in Brunswick
    Sunday. Of the firm of Brinker (Bunker?) and
    Alesworth, age about 37. Native of New York,
    came to Fayette 12 or 14 years ago, also had
    lived in Keytesville & St. Louis. Methodist.   BRUNS 13 Jan 1849

ALEXANDER, Nero C. of Immiteau Twp. was killed by a
    falling log. Left wife & 3 children.   JINQ 21 Oct 1841

ALEXANDER, Col. Wallace B. died last Saturday.   MORE 20 July 1826

ALEXANDER, Capt. William died at the National Hotel
    31 Oct. Of 5th Reg. U.S. Inf.   MORE 1 Nov 1838

ALFORD, Stephen W. age 25, son of Gen. Peyton, late of
    Gerard Co. KY, died in New London 24 Feb at
    the residence of Lewis Tracy.   BGRAD 11 Nov 1843

ALFORD, Thomas of Chariton Co. died of cholera 10 June
    at the crossing of the South Platte.   MORE 7 Oct 1850

ALLEN, Beverly of St. Louis died in the east; his body was
    to be returned to St. Louis for burial.   MORE 24 Sep 1845

ALLEN, Charles -- Montgomery Co. Final settlement by
    Wm. Cowherd and David P. Allen.   MIN 3 Oct 1835

ALLEN, David B. died 25 Feb in Howard Co.   COP 19 Aug 1842

ALLEN, E. H. died in Independence 11 February in his 29th
    year. Son of S.W. of Sylvania, OH and brother of
    W.D. of St. Louis.   MORE 12 Feb 1853

ALLEN, Jedediah, died in St. Louis "last night." Funeral
    from residence of his son Beverly.   MORE 5 Sep 1835

ALLEN, John Esq. died in Louisiana (MO) 5 October in his 73rd year. Revolutionary soldier. Born in Farmington, Conn. 20 March 1758, came to MO prior to the Purchase. — MORE 19 Oct 1830

ALLEN, John H. died 25 August, age about 30. — JEFRE 29 Aug 1840

ALLEN, John O., late of Vicksburg, died at the house of Mr. Wickersham. — MORE 5 Sep 1842

ALLEN, John P. of Warren Co. died 23 May age 29. — MORE 27 May 1849

ALLEN, Jonathan died in Pittsfield, Mass. in May; left several children including one in St. Louis. — MORE 9 June 1845

ALLEN, Dr. Joseph H. died in Troy 15 December age 30. Formerly of Shelby Co. KY — MORE 10 Jan 1832

ALLEN, Capt. Noah H., late of New Orleans, died in St. Louis "Thursday evening last." — MORE 22 Aug 1835

ALLEN, Richard M. Johnson, son of the Hon. C.H., died 16 May in his 19th year. — PWH 1 July 1843

ALLEN, Richardson died 17 Sep in his 74th year. — PWH 23 Sep 1843

ALLEN, Robert, many years a resident of St. Louis. Funeral from residence of brother-in-law, F.G. Warrance. Philadelphia papers please copy. — MORE 15 July 1851

ALLEN, William J. died Saturday. Tributes by I.O.O.F. and Sons of Temperance. — BRUNS 14 June 1849

ALLEN, William age about 50 committed suicide in Lincoln Co., near New Hope. — GLWT 17 Apr 1851

ALLEN, William of Scott Co. died 4 June of cholera 50 miles west of Ft. Kearney, age 20.
Felix of Scott Co. died 100 miles west of Ft. Kearney, age 17. — MORE 7 Oct 1850

ALLEY, J. W. -- Taney Co. Letters of administration to William Goff 5 August 1845. — SPAD 16 Aug 1845

ALLISON, Lt. John of the U.S. Army died 12 April at Council Bluffs. — SLINQ 19 Apr 1820

ALSOP, Thomas died "in this town" Wednesday last age 53, "a worthy citizen." — MIN 17 July 1824

ALVAREZ, Manuel Gregoire died in St. Louis yesterday age 43. — MORE 13 May 1837

ALVERSON, Jesse of Howard Co. died 22 April. — GLWT 1 May 1851

ALVERSON, Matthew M. died 16 December in his 29th year. "Served in the late war where he contracted the disease which terminated his existence." — MORE 26 Dec 1848

ALVERSON, William, lately deceased -- a notice of respects from the Sons of Temperance. — HIM 16 Nov 1854

AMES, Benjamin was killed at the racetrack by Daniel Brady (news report of Brady's conviction of manslaughter) — MORE 22 May 1841

AMES, Nathan, of Henry Ames & Co. Cincinnati please copy. — MORE 29 Jan 1851

AMES, William H., for many years a respectable merchant of St. Louis, died 5 December in Charleston SC. — MORE 3 Jan 1832

AMMONS, John L. of New Franklin died 27th July of paralysis. Age 61y 11m 14d. Native of New Kent Co. VA. — MODE 5 Aug 1846

AMOS, John died 23 January. Funeral from the residence of David Graham. Baltimore papers please copy. — MORE 23 Jan 1849

ANDERSON, A.M. died in St. Louis 11 June, late of St. Peter's. — MORE 13 June 1840

ANDERSON, Ambrose. St. Clair Co. -- final settlement by Joseph Whitley. — OSIN 13 Aug 1853

ANDERSON, Andrew, a deckhand, drowned off the steamboat Howard on the trip down from Chariton 28 Sep. A Dane, or German. Age about 30. — MORE 16 Oct 1837

ANDERSON, Jacob died 29 November near St. Louis, formerly of Campbell Co., VA — MORE 11 Dec 1832

ANDERSON, James, native of Scotland, later of Boston, died 27 December. — MORP 31 Dec 1845

ANDERSON, James M. died 29 January at the residence of his mother Mrs. Eliza Anderson in Shelby Co. — PWH 22 Feb 1849

ANDERSON, Rev. Joseph died in Lewis Co. 20 August in his 74th year. — PWH 9 Sep 1847

ANDERSON, Maj. Joseph L., a resident of Cooper Co., died 28 September. — COMB 1 Oct 1846

ANDERSON, William -- Chariton Co. Final settlement by Stukeley Mott. — BOLT 8 Oct 1842

ANDREWS, Carroll of Howard Co. died 22 September. — GLWT 25 Sep 1851

ANDREWS, Green, living in the forks of the Chariton, was murdered by Solomon Harlow at Chariton Ferry. Left wife and 8 children. — HANT 5 Aug 1852

ANDREWS, Green B. -- Chariton Co. Sale in Fayette by order of the Chariton Co. Court. Administratrix, Jemima Andrews. — GLWT 14 Apr 1853

ANDREWS, William, late of the firm of Andrews, Beakey & Co. Funeral from residence of Thomas Andrews on 3rd St., "two doors above the theatre." — MORE 3 Dec 1839

ANDREWS, William C. died near Fayette 21 May. — GLWT 5 June 1851

ANSON, George, a broker, died yesterday age 37. — SWERE 28 Sep '46

ANTHONY, Capt. Thomas, a sub-agent for the Indians, died Tuesday morning last. — MORE 3 July 1834

ANTLE, J., of Mercer Co., died of cholera 16 June 100 mi. west of Ft. Kearney, age 36. Left wife and five children. — MORE 7 Oct 1850

APPLING, James R. -- Montgomery Co. Letters of administration to Frederick Dryden 28 April. — FULT 1 June 1849

ARBOGAST, Marcellus died of cholera age 26. Formerly of Pittsburgh. — MORE 20 June 1851

ARBUCKLE, Samuel died in Lexington 11 April age 78. He was a resident of Ray Co. — LEXP 15 Apr 1845

ARCHER, William -- Montgomery Co. Letters of administration to Grief Stewart 22 November. — SLDU 28 Nov 1846

ARMITAGE, Abraham died 17 January, formerly a citizen of Pittsburgh PA. — MORE 23 Jan 1822

ARMSTEAD, Thomas P. age 38 died 11 March. Formerly of the US Army. Resided #39 2nd St. — MORE 12 Mar 1849

ARNOLD, Caeser, "a man of color" -- Chariton Co. Letters of administration to George W. Shaw 4 August. — MODE 11 Aug 1847

ARNOLD, sons of John, Chariton Co. Milton died 29 March in his 25th year and William died 4 April in his 23rd year. — MODE 11 Apr 1848

ARTHUR, John, a native of Lexington, KY apparently committed suicide by drowning in the Mississippi. — MORE 12 July 1810

ASBURN, James F. age 21 died in Warren Co. 31 July. — MORE 4 Aug 1853

ASBURY, Henry, formerly of Flemington KY died 29 August in Rocheport. — MORE 4 Sep 1850

ASBURY, Horace, of Johnson Co., froze to death 4 November. — KCEN 22 Nov 1856

ASHLAMAN, John died of cholera. Chariton Co.: administratrix, Catherine Aschleman. — BRUNS 24 May 1849

ASHABRAUNER, Absolom died at St. Louis Hospital 15 October. Resident of Cape Girardeau, in St. Louis on business. Interred in city graveyard. — MORE 17 Oct 1834

ASHBY, Abram, son of Rev. James S., died Tuesday last of consumption in his 21st year. — BRUNS 17 Mar 1849

ASHBY, James S. died of cholera 24 May. — BRUNS 21 June 1849

ASHLEY, William J. formerly of Carlisle KY died 25 Jan. — MORE 27 Jan 1840

ASHUR, George -- Chariton Co. Sale of property by the Public Administrator. — BRUNS 28 Oct 1847

ASPINALL, George of Aspinall and Bros. died yesterday. Funeral from his residence, 8th & Elm. — MORE 13 Feb 1846

ATCHISON, Henry, youngest son of the late Capt. George, funeral notice. Interred Rock Spring. — MORE 1 Aug 1851

ATCHINSON, James of Troy was thrown from a horse and killed 29 June. — MORE 7 July 1845

ATCHISON, Solomon, age about 20, was killed by the accidental discharge of a gun aboard the steamboat Lynx Saturday. Son of Solomon of St. Louis Co. about 12 mi. from St. Louis. — MORE 17 Mar 1845

ATCHISON, William died 2 October in his 32nd year. — SLDU 3 Oct 1846

ATCHISON, William Sr. died at residence of his son in Clay Co. 30 January. Late of Fayette Co. KY — LEXP 1 Mar 1854

5

ATKINSON, General Henry of the US Army died at Jefferson
    Barracks 14 June. Buried there.   MORE 15 June 1842

ATKISON, Capt. William died of cholera in St. Louis.
    Buried in Lexington.   BRUNS 21 June '49

ATTERBURY, William H. Esq. died at his residence in
    Wheeling 10 November age 52.   MORE 19 Nov 1842

ATWELL (?), T. Gordon killed at Ft. Atkinson, Iowa Ter.
    by Winnebagos.   MORE 12 Apr 1843

AUDRAIN, Col. James died unexpectedly in St. Louis --
    senator from St. Charles & Lincoln Cos.   MORE 23 Nov 1830

AUDRAIN, Samuel Wells, eldest son of the late Col. James,
    resident of St. Charles Co., died 31 Dec. age 30.   MORE 12 Jan 1841

AUGUSTIN, Michel, an old resident, died at his residence
    on Locust St. 24 May.   SWERE 25 May 1846

AULL, George died at Weston 22 December age 27. Left wife
    and children. IOOF. Ohio papers please copy.   WESJ 4 Jan 1845

AULL, James died in Chihuahua 23 June in 43rd year.
    (Long obituary from Lexington Express.)   MORE 21 Sep 1847

AULL, John of Lexington died at New Orleans 24 January.
    Returning from three years in Europe for his health.   BOLT 12 Feb 1841

AUSTIN, James B., a native of Potosi, died in New Orleans
    14 August of yellow fever in his 26th year. He
    had resided in Texas for eight years.   MORE 1 Dec 1829

AUSTIN, Elijah Phelps, native of St. Louis, died at the
    residence of his brother in Mobile 21 December
    age 28.   MORE 25 Jan 1837

AUSTIN, Horace, age 46, died in St. Louis "last Monday."
    Son of Elijah of New Haven, CT. Resident of
    Missouri for 16 years.   SLINQ 19 July '24

AUSTIN, John F. died 21 September near West Ely age
    about 56.   PWH 4 Oct 1849

AUSTIN, Moses died at the residence of Aaron Henly near
    Herculaneum.   MORE 12 June 1844

AUSTIN, William of Randolph Co. died 13 June in 31st year.   MODE 27 June 1848

AUSTIN, William J. died yesterday in St. Louis age 45.
    Funeral from St. Paul's Church.   MORE 26 Mar 1852

AYRES, Benjamin died 11 Deptember.   MORE 15 Sep 1829

AYRES, Hartsville M. died 26 September of congestive fever
    in his 48th year. Emigrated from Tennessee.   MODE 7 Oct 1846

AYRES, Thomas died in Spencer Twp. 23 September age 41.   BGRAD 30 Sep '43

BABER, George W., a printer in Jefferson City, drowned in
    Oregon.   STGAZ 1 June 1853

BACIGALUPO, John, age 41. St. Vincent's Cemetery.
    Memphis papers please copy.

BACON, Ludwell (Lydal) died in St. Louis Co. 14 July.   MORE 28 July 1835

BAGE, Robert, second son of William and Mary of Jefferson Co., died in his 29th year. New York papers please copy.   MORE 4 May 1851

BAGLEY, John F., late of St. Louis, died in Carondelet 26 August in his 36th year. Native of Vermont. Vermont and Olean, NY please copy.   MORE 28 Aug 1844

BAILEY, ___, killed in Daviess Co. 28 March while digging out a mill seat at Taylor's Ferry on the South Fork of Grand River.   BRUNS 13 Apr 1848

BAILEY, Alexander, late 1st Lieut. Co. C Mo. Battalion of Infantry died 25 February age 33.   MORE 1 Mar 1849

BAYLEY, Alonzo died at Brunswick 15 February age 28y 4m. Native of Vermont. Eastern papers please copy.   BRUNS 3 Mar 1847

BAILEY, Clifton G. died 25 July, a resident of St. Louis Co. about 15-16 years. Formerly of Kenawha Co. VA.   MORE 29 July 1844

BAILEY, David died 16 June in Troy, Lincoln Co. Age 73. Formerly of Woodstock, VT.   MORE 29 June 1826
David Albro died 1 December in Troy, Lincoln Co. In 21st year. Vermont please copy.   MORE 11 Dec 1844

BAILEY, Dudley died Tuesday evening, age 26, at the residence of Henry S. Taylor. Late of Middletown, CT.   MORE 3 Aug 1837

BAILEY, James P. died suddenly yesterday. Longtime treasurer of St. Louis & Bates Theatres. New York please copy.   MORE 25 Mar '53

BAILEY, Capt. Jonathan died 20 November in his 63rd year. Boonville MO & New York City please copy.   MORE 21 Nov 1851

BAILY, James S. died at Gravois Mills 11 February age 66 years. Formerly of Campbell Co. VA, resided in St. Louis Co. 10 years.   MORE 15 Jan 1841

BAILEY, Samuel died in Lincoln Co. 27 January in his 58th year, one of the county's first settlers. Fought against Indians and in the "last war against England." Husband, father.   MORE 1 Feb 1842

BAILEY, William -- Chariton Co. Final settlement by William Bailey.   MIN 9 Oct 1829

BAIRD, Capt. James C. died "last evening." Interred in Bonhomme Twp. (St. Louis Co.) graveyard.   MORE 21 May 1840

BAIRD, Samuel died near Louisville (Lincoln Co.) 22 Dec. age 80. Lived in Washington Co. PA, was at the Battle of Yorktown; moved to Kentucky 1792 and to Missouri 1827. Presbyterian.   SALT 23 Jan 1841

BAKER, A. Cooper, formerly of Martinsburg VA died yesterday age 30. Interred Presbyterian Cemetery.   MORE 23 June 1849

BAKER, Benjamin F. died 2 November in his 39th year. Formerly of VA.   MORE 5 Nov 1839

BAKER, James W. died 21 September at the residence of his
    brother George W. in Franklin Co., in his 20th
    year.   MORE 3 Oct 1846

BAKER, Jesse -- four negroes were executed for his murder   MORE 19 Apr 1841
    (and that of Jacob Weaver) in St. Louis. He was a   "   10 July 1841
    clerk from Worcester, ME, a nephew of Jesse Lindell.
    Age about 22. Interred Episcopal Cemetery.

BAKER, John, an old resident, native of Virginia, died at
    the age of (68? 88?) in St. Louis.   MORE 29 Apr 1851

BAKER, John of Ray Co. died of cholera 60 miles west of
    Ft. Kearney 2 June, age 29.   MORE 7 Oct 1850

BAKER, John B. died in his 24th year. Funeral from Christ
    Church, interment Bellefontaine Cemetery.
    Virginia papers please copy.   MORE 13 Jan 1853

BAKER, Martin died late in 1843, his son Dr. Thomas W.
    died in Sept. 1843. Had moved to Missouri from
    Louisa Co. VA in 1842. (see also James W. at top
    of page) Baptists. Richmond Whig please copy.   MORE 16 Apr 1844

BAKER, Martin died in Knox Co. 1 January. Born in VA on
    24 September 1773.   PWH 27 Jan 1848

BAKER, Sylvester died in Montgomery Co. 7 November. He was MORE 26 Nov 1835
    presiding Judge of the County Court.

BAKER, Timothy died in Louisiana (Pike Co.) "Friday last."
    Formerly of New York.   MORE 23 Nov 1844

BAKER, William of near Marshall committed suicide on
    14 September after having shot his daughter.
    He was about 55 or 60.   BRUNS 30 Sep 1848

BAKER, William died in Bonhomme Twp. age about 30.   MORE 2 Aug 1831

BALDWIN, Alexander O. died at Ft. Towson 29 July. He was
    a Lieut., U S Army.   MORE 22 Aug 1835

BALDWIN, J. Morris died age 33. Funeral from the residence
    of his sister, Mrs. Borden.   MORE 16 July 1851

BALDWIN, Dr. died 31 August in Franklin. He was "principal
    botanist" on a scientific expedition ascending
    the Missouri on the Western Engineer.   SLINQ 8 Sep 1819
    (MORE 15 September gives his name as William,
    place of death as Boonslick. He left a wife
    and several children.)

BALL, B. killed aboard the steamboat Banner at Cape   MORE 3 Oct 1834
    Girardeau; had come aboard from the Harry Hill.

BALL, Jesse died 1 March, "old and respected man."   BOLT 4 Mar 1843

BALL, Sheltiel died suddenly in St. Louis Co. Friday night,
    2 September, in his 57th year. Late of Fauquier Co.
    VA. Left wife, 5 sons, many friends.   MORE 8 Sep 1836

BALL, William R. -- Montgomery Co. Letters of administration
    to Enoch Ball, 9 October 1843.   MORE 9 Oct 1843
    (FS by Henry W. Owins, FULT 8 Dec 1848)

BALL, Augustin -- Montgomery Co. Final Settlement by
    Henry W. Owins.   FULT 8 Dec 1848

BALLARD, C. (or G.) found carved on the pocket knife found
    on a body pulled from the river near Hannibal.   BRUNS 7 Oct 1848

BALLEW, Rev. John died in Livingston Co. last Saturday
    age 71. Many years a traveling Methodist
    preacher in VA. "Universally respected."   BRUNS 26 Jan '48

BALMER, Gottfried died 9 September at his residence on
    Bellefontaine Rd., age 72.   SWERE 21 Sep '46

BANISTON, Rev. James, minister of the Methodist Episcopal
    Church, died "Sunday morning last."   MORE 6 Sep 1831

BANKS, Baylor died near Chariton 14 July. Left wife,
    four children. Native of Virginia.   MIN 22 July 1823

BANKS, Henry H. of Carroll Co. died 4 May, age 21, at the
    residence of his father.   BRUNS 19 May 1849

BANNING, Alexander died of apoplexy in the Boone Co. jail,
    age about 46. Of Chariton Co. Convicted of hog
    stealing. Left wife, 8 children.
    (BOLT 20 Dec 1845 gives name as Bannon, says he
    committed suicide.)   MORE 23 Dec 1845

BARADA, John died "last Tuesday."   MORE 24 May 1827

BARADA, Peter son of Sylvester died in St. Charles Co.
    25 May in his 17th year.   MORE 26 May 1852

BARBEE, Ira died in Central Twp. (St. Louis Co.), age 44,
    on 2 August. Formerly of Fayette Co. KY.   MORE 4 Aug 1846

    John son of Ira & Elizabeth died Monday in his
    18th year.   MORE 13 Dec 1838

BARBOUR, Sextus died at the residence of Dr. Thomas
    Barbour. Son of the late Judge Philip P. of
    Orange Co., VA.   MORE 21 Dec 1848

BARBOUR, Dr. Thomas . No data. Resided 9th & Locust.   MORE 19 June 1849

BARBER, Ephraim died in St. Louis 13 November in his 38th
    year. Master armorer of St. Louis Arsenal.
    "Husband, father." Buried Goshen Church.   MORE 18 Nov 1844

BARNES, James -- Chariton Co. Letters of administration
    to David Proffitt 21 Oct. 1843.   BOLT 25 Nov 1843

BARNES, William, brother of Robert A., died 26 August in
    his 41st year.   MORE 27 Aug 1851

BARNES, William died in his 73rd year, father of 11
    children and grandfather of 48.   COMB 22 Oct 1846

BARNETT, Alexander died at the residence of his mother "in
    this county" 23 April. Son of the late Alexander
    of Madison Co. KY.   LEXP 29 Apr 1845

BARNETT, Hariss (Harris) -- St. Clair Co. Final settlement
    by Hugh Barnett.   WAR 28 Apr 1849

BARNETT, Hu-rigan (Hourigan), Howard Co., died in the Santa Fe country last November. MODE 17 Feb 1847

BARNETT, James, of Ralls Co., died in the steamboat *Moselle* disaster at Cincinnati. MORE 1 May 1838

BARNHARTT, Jasper N., formerly of Huntsville, died in Kirksville 25 February, age about 23. HIM 15 Mar 1855

BARRON, Leon died in Ralls Co. 30 January. Late editor. LEXP 15 Feb 1854
BARON, Leon died at the home of his father in Ralls Co. in his 20th year. STGAZ 1 Mar 1854

BARR, Israel H. died in Louisiana (Pike Co.) Wednesday last age about 35. BGRAD 27 July 1844

BARR, John T. died in Ste. Genevieve Co. 10 March. He formerly of Baltimore. MORE 26 Mar 1841

BARR, Lewis, of Knox Co., was thrown from a wagon, run over, and killed. MORE 9 June 1845

BARRETT, S.H. -- Wright Co. Letters of administration to Prestly Askins, 23 September 1846. SPAD 31 Oct 1846

BARRET, William of Waco City TX died in his 30th year. Funeral from the residence of his mother in St. Louis, Pine between 10th & 11th Sts. MORE 15 May 1853

BARRETT, William D/ Esq. of Blaine, Thompkins & Barrett died yesterday. SWERE 9 Dec 1844
BARRET, William D. died yesterday. Resided 5th St. in Kerr's Row. MORE 6 Dec 1844

BARRY, Lt. Francis E. of the U.S. Navy died at the residence of his brother-in-law George Buchanan. SWERE 26 Aug '44

BARRY, James died 22 June. Emigrated to Missouri 1829. MORE 23 June 1847

BARTLETT, Charles F., formerly of Massachusetts, died Thursday. COMB 15 Feb 1836

BARTLETT, George, a passenger on the steamboat *Car of Commerce.* (no other data) MORE 27 May 1828

BARTLETT, Phineas died 20 May in his 68th year. New Orleans papers please copy. MORE 22 May 1854

BARTLETT, William, murdered in Pulaski Co. JEFRE 7 Nov 1840

BARTON, Joshua Esq., notice of vacancy on Board of Aldermen (St. Louis) due to his death. Obituary in MORE 3 Sept.; article in MORE 3 Dec. says he "fell in a duel." MORE 9 July 1823

BARTON, William R. died in Glasgow "Monday night last" age 36. Of K.L. Barton & Bros. HOB 6 Nov 1851

BASNETTE, Milton -- Montgomery Co. Final settlement by Elmira Basnette & John H. Hunter. FULT 29 Sep 1848

BASS, George died "a few days ago" in Montgomery Co. as a result of a tree falling on him. He lived 3 days. MORE 10 Mar 1829

BAST, Edward J., son of Mrs. Elizabeth Cox, died 10 June age 22 years 8 months. — STGAZ ? June 1852 (prob. 16 June)

BASYE, Major Alfred died in this city Wednesday evening. — JEFRE 18 May '44

BATES, Appolos D. died 10 July in Griswold City, Franklin Co., in 28th year. Attorney. Formerly of Granby, Hartford Co. CT. Recently from Ohio. Left widow. — MORE 22 July 1841

BATES, Charles E. died at the residence of his brother in St. Louis 6 January in his 19th year. Native of Brandon, VT. — MORE 9 Jan 1835

BATES, James W. age 35 died 11 February. — MORE 13 Feb 1853

BATES, John died Saturday last. — MORE 1 Sep 1819

BATES, Thomas L., native of Boston, died in Florissant. — MORE 13 Aug 1853

BATES, William died in St. Joseph 11 August in 26th year. — MORE 19 Aug 1851

BATES, William Esq. died "a few days ago" at his residence in Herculaneum. State representative from Franklin Co. — MORE 21 Aug 1822

BATTU, Henry died Friday last. — MORE 13 Sep 1820

BAUER, John, sentenced to hang on 9 June for the murder of George Thompson, Ste. Genevieve. — MORE 21 Apr 1838

BAUGH, Joseph died in Callaway Twp., St. Charles Co., age 87. A native of VA. — SLAM 13 Mar 1846

BAXTER, Charles D., formerly of Barton, VT died 8 July of smallpox. — MORE 10 July 1848

BAXTER, John died 10 November age 34. — SWERE 15 Nov 1847

BAY, Samuel Mansfield died of cholera in St. Louis. Late Attorney General. — BRUNS 12 July '49

BAYLESS, William died Friday. (MORE 15 April gives residence as 6th & Locust.) — SWERE 17 Apr 1848

BAYLOR, W. R. of Capt. Dent's Co., St. Louis, under Col. Price, died en route to Santa Fe. — MODE 13 Jan 1847

BEACH, Louis of St. Louis died in New York 14 February. — MORE 18 Feb 1851

BEAL, ___ of Linn Co. died "night before last" on his way to Brunswick. "A young man." — BRUNS 18 Nov 1848

BEAL, Benjamin died 13 August age 80. — SPAD 20 Aug 1844

BEALS, Moses H. of Liberty was killed in Nevada 12 June. Left wife and children in Missouri. — MORE 14 Aug 1851

BEARD, John murdered on Washington Ave. in St. Louis "about 2 weeks since." Clem Ryder held for murder. — MORE 24 May 1849

BEASLEY, Cornelius died 24 September in his 84th year. Born Caroline Co. VA., in VA till 1836. Private in Revolution. Minister. "Husband, father." — SALT 2 Oct 1841

BEASLEY, Hiram murdered by slaves "the 20th." — JEFRE 30 Mar 1843

BEATTIE, Alexander murdered at Far West by Samuel Bogart 11 January. — PWH 8 Feb 1840

BEATTIE, Matthew R. of Salt Pond, Saline Co. was killed by
    lightning "Wednesday week last."   MORE 10 May 1847

BEAUMONT, Dr. William died 24 April in his 67th year.
    Interred Bellefontaine.   MORE 26 Apr 1853

BECK, Abraham Esq., attorney, formerly of New York, died
    5 September.   STCHMO 12 Sep '21

BECKWITH, James M., a printer, age 37, died 2 September
    near Jefferson Barracks, of apoplexy.   MORE 12 Sep 1845

BEDFORD, William H. died near Salt Lake 4 July.   STGAZ 8 Sep 1852

BEEBE, Elijah died suddenly of bilious fever "Saturday."   MORE 28 Aug 1822

BEEBE, Levi died aboard the *General Jessup* from Vera Cruz
    to Philadelphia 29 July. Son of the late Washington
    Beebe of St. Louis.   MORE 25 Aug 1848

BEEBE, Washington died of yellow fever at Vera Cruz 16 May.   MORE 5 June 1848

BEEDING, J. S., merchant, died at Parkville 25 November
    of inflammation of the brain, age 23.   GLWT 9 Dec 1852

BEELER, Frederick died 13 December. He lived 16 miles from
    St. Louis, was born and raised in Berkeley Co. VA.
    His wife and children reside in Tennessee.   MORE 21 Mar 1812

BEEMAN, Silas M. drowned near Ste. Genevieve; son of Aaron,
    family emigrating to Pike Co. from Springfield MA.   MORE 6 June 1835

BEISLEY, Rev. Nelson R. of the Mo. Annual Conference of
    the Methodist Church died 25 Jan at his residence
    in Warren Co. age 28.   SCOMB 12 Feb 1836

BELL, F. T., mate of the *La Salle*, was killed in June 1844
    by Wm. E. Frothingham.   MORE 18 Jan 1845

BELL, E. Steel -- Washington Co. Died at Potosi 10 April,
    formerly of Franklin Co. KY.   BEA 21 Apr 1831

BELL, Henry (with wife and child) killed by lightning in
    Clay Co. 2 June.   MORE 22 June 1843

BELL, James W. died 17 April. Funeral from his residence
    opposite Central Repository, North St. Louis.   MORE 18 Apr 1842

BELL, John, formerly of Hamilton Co. OH died 23 May.
    Buried in St. Charles. "Husband, father."   MORE 24 May 1852

BELL, Nathaniel -- St. Clair Co. Final settlement by
    Elisha H. Bell, surviving son.   OSIN 18 Jan 1851

BELL, William A. -- Wright Co. Letters of administration
    to Robert N. Martin.   MORE 4 Mar 1842

BELL, *Wilson* A. -- Wright Co. Letters of adm. 1 Feb to
    J.N.B. Dodson.   JINQ 23 Feb 1843

BELL, Zephaniah died in Cooper Co. 24 March age *ca* 82.
    Died at residence of son-in-law Urlen Houx, left
    wife in her 62nd year. Children, grandchildren.
    Lived in Cooper 25 or 30 years, came from KY.
    Baptist. About to move to son in SW Missouri.   BOBS 25 Mar 1851
    " 15 Apr "

BELL, ____ of Gasconade Co. killed in the explosion of
 of the ferry at St. Charles.   MORE 9 Dec 1841

BELLAND, J.P. (or J.B.) "in his lifetime keeping the ferry
 on the Missouri opposite St. Charles." No
 other data.   MORE 29 Jan 1814

BELLES, Harrison died in Lafayette Co. "a few days ago."   LEXP 4 Oct 1854

BELLISSIME, Alexandre died Friday night last in 87th year.   MORE 27 Aug 1833

BELT, Capt. Francis T. was a victim of the explosion of the
 Saluda near Lexington 9 April. Funeral from the
 residence of Henry Belt. In 35th year. Left wife
 and 3 children.   MORE 12 Apr 1852

BELT, Thomas L. died in Howard Co. 9 September in his
 28th year. Native of Cumberland Co. VA, educated at
 Rockville, Montgomery Co. MD. A lawyer, he removed
 to Missouri in 1841.   MODE 16 Sep 1846

BELT, John A. died at the residence of Judge Walden on
 25 October, age about 22. Had come to be near
 his brother, the late Thomas L. (above).   MODE 4 Nov 1846

BELTZHOOVER, Frederick W. died yesterday in his 33rd year.
 Funeral from his residence #86 N. Main to the
 Catholic cemetery.   MORE 5 Aug 1843

BELTZHOOVER, Samuel, a pilot, died at the residence of his
 sister-in-law, age 32.   MORE 8 Apr 1851

BELTZHOOVER, Capt. Jacob died in St. Louis on 3 October,
 age 37. "Of New Orleans."   MORE 5 Oct 1846

BENCK, Christopher -- Gentry Co. Letters of administration
 to Samuel Harris, 1 June 1853.   STGAZ 29 June '53

BENNETT, James S. -- Ripley Co. Letters of administration
 to Francis Bennett, 17 August 1844.   SPAD 8 Oct 1844

BENNETT, Rev. John died 9 December at his residence in
 St. Louis Co. Methodist. Formerly resided in
 Baltimore and Kentucky.   MORE 19 Dec 1843

BENNETT, Joseph died in Callaway Co. 19 March in his
 34th year.   MORE 1 Apr 1851

BENNING, Perkins died Monday last.   PWH 3 Feb 1844

BENOIT, Mr. Francis M. died Friday morning last.   MORE 27 Oct 1819

BENSON, Henry died 4 September age 39.   MORE 7 Sep 1853

BENSON, James B., former editor of the Boonslick Times,
 died at Fayette.   NERA 25 May 1848

BENSON, sons of Edon and Celia, died in Portland (Callaway
 Co.) after returning from two years in California.
 Jefferson died 8 Dec. age 23y 8m 25d; Henson died
 12 Dec age 31y 7m 27d.   MORE 4 Mar 1852

BENSON, Dr. James H., formerly of Howard Co., died of
 cholera at Warsaw the 9th of ?.   BRUNS 21 June 1849

BENSON, James R. died at Fayette "Monday before last" leaving wife and daughter. Native of Reading PA, resident of Fayette 8 years. (BRUNS 25 May says he was 30, died of consumption, former editor of the Boones Lick Times.) — MORE 20 May 1848

BENSON, Samuel -- Grundy Co. Letters of administration to Isaac L. Henderson 16 March 1849. — BRUNS 24 Mar '49

BENSON, William died age about 35. — MORE 24 Feb 1851

BENT, Silas Esq., former judge of the Superior Court under territorial organization, died last Tuesday. At the time of his death he was clerk of the county court.

BENT, George, brother of the late Governor, died at Bent's Fort age 34. — JEM 21 Dec 1847

BENTON, E. of Dallas Co. died 5 June 6 miles east of Ft. Kearney, of cholera. Age (43?). — MORE 7 Oct 1850

BENTON, John I. died in this county 23 January, age 51. Born in Montgomery Co. MD. — LEXP 11 Feb 1845

BENTON, John Randolph only son of Col. Benton died after a brief illness, age 22 years 4 months. — MORE 18 Mar 1852

BEQUETTE, Joseph Sr. of Washington Co. died 11 April. One of its first settlers, raised a large family. In 65th year. — MORE 19 Apr 1845

BERMINGHAM, Patrick died 21 February in his 27th year. — MORE 22 Feb 1853

BERRY, Daniel died in his 75th year. Father-in-law of Robert K. Woods. — MORE 3 Sep 1851

BERRY, David Esq. died 11 January aboard the Convoy, of which he was mate, off Plumb Point. Buried Memphis. — MORE 2 Feb 1847

BERRY, David H. -- Montgomery Co. Letters of administration to Benjamin F. Berry. — FULT 13 July '49

BERRY, N.B. of Crawford Co. died 28 July after having been thrown from a horse. — MORE 16 Aug 1836

BERRY, Major Taylor of Howard Co. died at New Madrid 23 July. — SLINQ 14 Oct '24

BERRY, Thomas D. died 3 March at his residence in St. Louis Co. Formerly of Caroline Co. VA. Richmond papers please copy. — MORE 6 Mar 1845

BERRY, William died at his residence 12 miles west of St. Louis in his 86th year. Revolutionary veteran, born in VA, later of KY, in Missouri 16 years. — MORE 22 Dec 1838

BERRY, William of Liberty died 13 September in Bethany VA in his 22nd year. — MORE 11 Oct 1851

BERSINGER, Philip was found dead on the street in St. Louis -- Myrtle between Main and Second-- yesterday. Age about 40, death caused by intemperance and exposure. — MORE 28 Mar 1844

BERTHOLD, Augustus, native of St. Louis, died age 23 years 6 months. Left mother, sister, brother. — MORE 15 Aug 1837

BERTHOLD, Bartholomew died Wednesday last.	MORE 26 Apr 1831
BEST, ____, body taken from the river at Carondelet was recognized as Best, one of four men missing when Lieut. McNair was killed en route to Rock River.	MORE 29 Apr 1815
BEST, Rev. Alexander of the Methodist Episcopal Church South died in Quincy age 29.	PWH 22 Mar 1849
BESTWICK, Nathaniel, a deckhand, fell overboard from the *Herald* and drowned, below Flint Island. Pittsburgh please copy.	SWERE 1 Oct '44
BETTS, Frederick died 13 August at Bellefontaine age 23. Funeral from residence of Robert Betts, 11th between Morgan & Franklin.	MORE 14 Aug 1848
BEWLEY, Rev. Nelson R. of Warren Co. died 25 January. He was a Methodist.	MORE 9 Feb 1836
BEWLEY, Rev. George died of consumption Thursday last at his residence in Hannibal.	PWH 12 Nov 1846
BIDDLE, Thomas -- a eulogy.	BEA 8 Sep 1831
BIDSTRAP, Jesse Ludvig died in Lebanon County(?) on 4 August in 16th year. Fell from a horse.	BORE 9 Aug 1843
BIENSTEIN, William died 12 September at the residence of Israel Landis.	STGAZ 14 Sep 1853
BIGGERSTAFF, James M. age about 20 was killed by lightning near Plattsburg "Sunday last."	KCEN 9 Aug 1856
BIGGS, Rev. Davis, Baptist minister, died in Pike Co. on 1 August in his 83rd year.	PWH 13 Aug 1845
BIGGS, William died in Pike Co. 15 April of bilious colic. In his 60th year. (MODE 19 May says former member of the legislature.)	PWH 29 Apr 1847
BIGHAM, Vance -- Bates County. Final settlement by Campbell P. Hudson.	OSIN 18 Jan 1851
BILLINGSLEY, Dr. C., formerly of this place, died at the residence of his father in Morgan Co. 16 Aug.	BOLT 26 Aug 1843
BILLON, Charles died Monday.	MORE 11 Sep 1822
BINGHAM, Henry V. died 26 December in his 39th year. Left widow and children. Masonic rites.	MIN 30 Dec 1823
BIOREN, Charles B. died at Monticello, Howard Co., 14 Aug.	BOLT 19 Aug 1843
BIRCH, Major George died near Tampa Bay.	MORE 31 Oct 1837
BIRCH, J. W. died 6 February age about 32.	BORE 15 Feb 1845
BIRCH, Thomas Henry, native of Shropshire, England died last night at the residence of his brother-in-law W.J.N. Massar(?). Funeral from residence of Mr. Commons.	MORE 25 Apr 1845
BIRCHFIELD, John -- Taney Co. Letters of administration to Nathaniel Kimberling and Alexander Berry 6 Feb.	JINQ 11 Apr 1844

BIRD, Gustavus A. died in St. Louis "this morning" age 59. SWERE 12 July '47

BIRD, Thomas, a citizen of Bellevue, was shot and killed 18 January. SWERE 3 Feb 1845

BIRDWELL, Joshua -- Montgomery Co. Final settlement by Sterling Winter. FULT 22 June 1849

BIRKENBINE, Capt. John C. died at Richwoods, Washington Co., 5 October in his 35th year. Philadelphia and Reading PA please copy. MORE 11 Oct 1851

BISCH, Albert Sr. died 30 January in Ste. Genevieve in his 66th year. Native of Germany, came to U.S. in 1802, settled first in Philadelphia. Came to Missouri in 1816. Philadelphia please copy. MORE 6 Feb 1845

BISCOE, James B. died at City Hospital Thursday. SWERE 1 Nov '47

BISCON, James died of bilious fever Monday evening last in his 38th year. MORE 2 Aug 1833

BISHOP, Andrew D. died near St. Joseph 12 May in his 22nd year of consumption. Formerly of New York, on his way to the Rocky Mountains for his health. MORE 15 June '44

BISHOP, Dr. Jonathan A.D. died in New Orleans 5 December in his 28th year. Late of St. Louis Co. MORE 22 Dec 1843

BISSELL, Gen. Daniel died Sunday last. MORE 17 Dec 1833

BITTER, William, a German, died at Brunswick. BRUNS 26 July '49

BLACK, John died 8 October in his 58th year. Formerly of Tarentum, Allegheny Co. PA. MORE 13 Oct 1845

BLACK, John, a resident of Boonville, committed suicide. Cut his throat near Cincinnati. Second attempt. COLG 24 Mar 1848

BLACKBURN, Jonathan died in his 24th year, a victim of the Saluda explosion near Lexington 9 April. Buried Bellefontaine Cemetery. MORE 11 and 12 Apr 1852

BLACKBURN, William H. died Thursday last in his 48th year. MORE 8 Dec 1847

BLAIR, James died at St. Charles Sunday age 55; his father and brother had both died "within the last 5 weeks." MORE 31 Mar '46

BLAIR, Thomas, late proprietor of the Glasgow House, St. Louis and formerly of Dayton OH died 10 March. Funeral from residence of Capt. Shreve. MORE 13 Mar 1846

BLAKELY, James M., Jr. died of cholera at Warsaw. BRUNS 14 June '49

BLAKEY, William J. died of cholera at Palmyra. MORE 28 June 1833

BLANCHARD, Elisha, a merchant, died of bilious colic Thursday night last. MORE 14 Aug 1832

BLANCHARD, Jonathan died Saturday. SLINQ 2 Feb 1820

BLANKENSHIP, Jefferson hung himself in Boone Co. 30 March. PWH 13 Apr 1844

BLANKENSHIP, William died in Lexington 21 September. Formerly of VA, recently of TX, age ca 45. LEXP 24 Sep 1844

BLEDSOE, Capt. Henry died in Fayette. MIN 24 Aug 1833

BLOCK, Moses "an old and esteemed citizen" died 6 August.   MORE 15 Aug 1846

BLOUNT, Samuel of Boone Co., in Col. Price's regiment, died
    on the way to Santa Fe.   MODE 13 Jan 1847

BLOW, Peter on Saturday last in the 55th year of his age.   MORE 26 July 1831

BLUE, Christopher C., oldest son of D.G., died in Audrain Co.
    3 May as a result of injuries sustained when he fell
    on a hay fork.   MORE 10 May 1852

BOBB, Theodore died at the residence of J.A. Letcher in St.
    Louis on 24 January age 29.   MORE 25 Jan 1845

BOGGS, Ambrose K. of Pettis Co. died 14 September. Late
    representative, left wife and children.   COMB 18 Sep 1847

BOGLIOLO, Matteo, native of Italy, died age 68. Many years
    a resident of New Madrid. Served in Napoleon's
    army in Egypt. Died 24 March.   MORE 25 Mar 1849

BOLLINGER, Samuel -- Wayne Co. Letters of administration   INP summer 1823
    to Sarah Bolin and Overton Bettis.

BOLLINGER, Solomon -- Wayne Co. Letters of administration
    to George S. Bollinger.   INP Aug 1826

BOLTON, Rev. Charles died 17 November.   JEFRE 27 Nov '41

BOMPART, Edmund died yesterday in his (48th? 18th?) year.   MORE 13 Apr 1852

BOMPART, Jean Baptiste died 25 December age 50y 4m 4d at
    the residence of Lewis Bompart on Manchester
    Road, 9 miles west of St. Louis.   MORE 28 Dec 1847

BONCHNELL, Mr. J.B. of Mt. Sterling, MO, formerly of
    Berks Co. NC, died at the residence of
    J. Barclay 3 miles west of St. Louis, 30 Mar.   MORE 31 Mar 1837

BONDURANT, Capt. George D. died in Spencer Twp. (Pike Co.)
    16 July.   BGRAD 20 July '44

BONDY, _____, a young German living at Grand River City,
    died of cholera.   BRUNS 31 May 1849

BOONE, Jesse B. Esq. of Montgomery Co. died in St. Louis
    yesterday.   STCHMO 20 Dec 1820

BOONE, Daniel died at Charrette Village on 26 September.   MORE 4 Oct 1820

BOON, Hampton L. died in Fayette 25 March.   GLWT 3 Apr 1851

BOON, Col. Ratliff died in Louisiana MO 19 November age
    about 65. Emigrated from Indiana six years since,
    was a congressman in Indiana.   BGRAD 23 Nov '44

BORDIN, Worsly T.S. died last Thursday. Interred with
    military honors by St. Louis Guards.   SLINQ 22 Sep '21

BOSLEY, Dr. John died age about 69, date not shown. Born
    in Maryland, married twice, left second wife and
    young children.   PWH 6 Sep 1849

BOSSERON, Charles died 6 December.   MORE 7 Feb 1828

BOSSERON, Charles died 6 January at Havana on arrival there.   MORE 13 Feb 1837

BOSSERON, Francis, late of St. Louis, died in New Orleans on
    2 February age 26. SWERE 24 Feb 1845

BOSSIER, John B. Jr., only son of General J.B., died at
    Fredericktown on 4 April (suddenly) in 19th year. MORE 21 Apr 1840

BOSSIER, General John B. died at Fredericktown 24 October
    in his 59th year. MORE 12 Nov 1842

BOSTWICK, Oliver N, of the firm of Savage & Bostwick,
    died Friday evening last. MORE 4 Jan 1831

BOSWELL, Walter H. died at his residence in St. Charles.
    Formerly of Charles Co. MD, and for many years
    a resident of St. Louis. MORE 27 Feb 1851

BOUDEN, David: obituary notice, "to whom it may concern: MORE 1 Dec 1819
    on his way by water from Louisville to St. Louis
    with his son "a man of color" . . .left the boat
    at Cape Girardeau and died on the evening of
    8 October, being, he sayd, (71? 77?) a native
    of Geneva in Switzerland.

BOUGHEY, Benjamin died of cholera 15 July in 24th year. MORE 18 July 1851

BOUIS, Andrew died age 44 of pleurisy (wife and 4-year-old
    child died the same day). SOV 9 Mar 1833

BOUJOU, Joseph died 17 November age 76. SWERE 19 Nov '48

BOULDIN, Robert, son of Judge, died at Columbia age about 15.
    Student at University. MODE 18 Aug 1847

BOULWARE, John killed by Hardin Yates near Paris MO. PWH 16 Jan 1841

BOULWARE, Mordecai died 20 March in his 71st year. PWH 26 Mar 1845

BOUNDS, John of Lexington died at the boarding house of MORE 29 Nov 1837
    Mr. Nourse on his return from New Orleans
    "Monday last." Former sheriff of Lafayette
    Co. & one of its oldest, most respected citizens.

BOUNDS, Dr. Josiah died of cholera Saturday age 56. Inventor
    of Patent Churn. Formerly of Bourbon Co. KY BRUNS 19 July '49

BOURGOIN, ____ of Clark Co. died 21 June 4 miles west of
    Ft. Kearney. MORE 7 Oct 1850

BOWEN, Mr., killed by John Taylor at Harrison's neighborhood
    near the Merrimack, Crawford Co. MORE 4 Aug 1841

BOWEN, Capt. Samuel A. age 65 died in Hannibal 2 November. CANE 10 Nov 1853

BOWLES, __, a private in Capt. Musick's Co., killed near MORE 16 July 1814
    Capo Gray. (From estate record, James Bowles)

BOWLES, Hon. Caleb died Monday last in St. Louis age 48. He
    was a Judge of the St. Louis Co. Court. MORE 12 May 1836

BOWLES, Charles, 2nd engineer of the Oregon, died on board
    4 July. A native of New York. MORE 14 July 1829

BOWLIN, Dennis was found dying in Cherry St. between 2nd &
    Broadway (St. Louis). Intemperance and exposure. MORE 6 Oct 1848

BOWMAN, James, formerly of Bangor ME killed Tuesday night MORE 23 Apr 1840
    by a fall into a cellar excavation.

BOWYER, Godfrey, the manager, was murdered at Valle's Mines in Jefferson Co. — MORE 17 Jan 1828

BOYCE, Patrick a native of Ireland died Thursday night. — MORE 26 July 1851

BOYCE, John died in Farmington, St. Francois Co., on 30 September age 54y 4m. Formerly of Fayette Co. KY. Lexington Observer please copy. — MORE 5 Oct 1844

* BOYCE, Capt. William H. died 13 June in his 54th year. He was formerly of Bertie Co. NC and for more than 20 years a resident of St. Louis. — BRUNS 21 June '49

BOYD, Abner died in Calumet Twp (Pike Co) 15 September age about 50. — BGRAD 21 Sep 1844

BOYD, James of St. Charles Co. thrown from horse, killed. — MORE 13 Nov 1841

BOYD, Silas B. died at the residence of his father in Pike Co. 22 October age 23. — BGRAD 28 Oct 1843

BOYES, James -- Montgomery Co. Final settlement by Jemima and John B. Boyes. — FULT 15 Dec 1848

* BOYSE, William H. died in his 54th year. Formerly of Burties (sic) Co. NC, 20 years in St. Louis. Interred Methodist cemetery. — MORE 14 June 1849

BOZLAN, Thomas, a native of Co. Louth, Ireland, "yesterday." — SWERE 14 Aug '48

BRACKENRIDGE, James of St. Louis Co. died 26 June age 79. — MORE 27 June 1853

BRADBURY, ___ killed in sinking of the ferry on 16 June at Everett's Ferry near Independence. — SOV 4 July 1834

BRADFORD, Frederick died 23 March age about 55. — BRUNS 14 Apr 1849

BRADFORD, James, died at the residence of James Love. Born York District SC, resided in Pike Co. about 15 years, was "50 or older." — SALT 27 Mar 1841

BRADLEY, Daniel died of cholera at Palmyra. — MORE 23 June 1835

BRADLEY, Elias died 13 September in Caldwell Co. — LEXP 24 Sep 1844

BRADLEY, Norton, a fireman on the Car of Commerce. — MORE 27 May 1828

BRADLEY, Stephen died of cholera in Palmyra. — JEFRE 4 July 1835

BRADY, James "Wednesday last" -- "generally regretted." — MORE 14 Aug 1818

BRADY, James died in St. Louis age 23. Funeral from his residence, Morgan & 14th. — MORE 7 Mar 1846

BRADY, Patrick died Monday last. — MORE 6 Oct 1819

BRADY, Peter age 27 died yesterday at his residence on Benton St. near Broadway, North St. Louis. — SWERE 22 May 1848

BRANHAM, Hardin Moore died at the residence of John Parker in Nashville MO 24th October in his 72nd year. — COP 28 Oct 1842

BRANAN, John, born in Ireland and late of Peru IL died in St. Louis Hospital age 28. — MORE 20 June 1840

BRANNIN, Capt. Richard died 6 October in his 71st year. — MODE 20 Oct 1847

BRANNIN, Strother, assessor elect of this county, died   BOLT 11 Jan 1845
    4 January.

BRANSTETTER, Frederick died 30 January at Richmond in his   BRUNS 17 Feb 1849
    27th year.

BRANSTETTER, Frederick Augustus son of Catherine died at   BGRAD 21 Sep 1844
    Indian Creek 12 September age about 20.

BRANSTETTER, Henry died at Louisiana MO 2 June age 43. He   SALT 5 June 1841
    left a wife and 7 children.

BRANT, Peter B. -- Montgomery Co. Letters of administration   FULT 30 Mar 1849
    to John D. Anderson.

BRAWNER, Hyacinthus formerly of Wisconsin, age about 40.   MORE 22 June 1851

BRAY, Timothy died 23rd July. New York & Wisconsin,
    please copy.   MORE 25 July 1851

BRAZEAUX, Joseph, died 23 November in his 77th year.   MORE 30 Nov 1816

BRAZEAU, Louis died Friday last "of very advanced age."   MORE 9 Dec 1828

BRAZEAU, Louis Monday night "regretted by all who knew him"   MORE 6 June 1838

BRECK, Samuel died of the accidental discharge of a pistol.
    Son of Hon. Daniel of Madison Co., KY, age
    about 24. Died 24 August at St. Joseph.   STGAZ 28 Aug 1846

BREEDLOVE, Martin found dead Sunday night in the yard of Mr.
    Wilson 8 or 10 mi. north of Columbia (MO?). Both   MORE 11 Mar 1845
    had been drinking. Not known if murder or suicide.
    Left wife and four or five children.

BREEZE, William -- Chariton Co. Sale of real estate by   BRUNS 26 Jan 1848
    Public Administrator.

BREMAN, John of Davis Co. died 31 May of cholera on the Big
    Blue River. Age 25. Left wife and one child.   MORE 7 Oct 1850

BRENAN, Eugene, late of Columbia SC died 21 Aug. in 68th y.   BEA 12 Aug 1830

BRENT, Hugh J., son of the late Hugh J. of Bourbon Co. KY,
    died 20 March in his 29th year.   MORE 22 Mar 1852

BRENT, Robert Esq. died after a painful and protracted   MORE 13 Oct 1819
    illness. Late Paymaster General of the Army and
    Judge of the Washington Co. Orphan's Court. 7 Oct.

BREWER, ___, son of Charles, a cooper, died in warehouse fire. MORE 2 Sep '39

BRIDGE, Joseph died 17 April in 77th year. Funeral from
    Church of the Messiah. Interred Bellefontaine.   MORE 18 Apr 1853

BRIGGS, John C., late of Boston, died 7 September age 43.   MORE 10 Sep 1841

BRIGHT, Capt. Josiah died Wednesday evening last.   MORE 7 Aug 1822

BRINKER, Robert A., age 23, native of Washington Co., died
    near Feather River CA.   MORE 12 June 1850

BRINTON, Richard V. died 6 August in Jackson Twp.,
    Buchanan Co. Left wife, 3 children.   MORE 19 Aug 1851

BRISTOW, Dr. John of Bourbon Co. KY died at residence of Col.
    Thomas Hickman, near Franklin.   MIN 29 July 1820

BRITE, Charles H. died at the home of his father in Callaway Co. 26 October age 21.	MORE 31 Oct 1836
BRITTON, Mr. ___ fell dead on Washington Ave. (St. Louis) as a result of sun and violent exercise.	MORP 12 July 1845
BROCKWAY, Lieut. ___ of 7th Reg. U.S. Inf. died at Fort Gibson 25 September.	BEA 3 Nov 1831
BROOKMAN, Ferdinand C., master of the H.D. Bacon. Burial at Bellefontaine.	MORE 9 Sep 1853
BROOKS, ___ and ___ (two men and the wife of one) died of cholera at Harrisonville.	LEXP 2 Aug 1854
BROOKS, Caleb E. of South St. Louis, son of John of Columbus, OH died 9 Oct. Funeral from the residence of Wm. Warrance.	MORE 11 Oct 1839
BROOKS, James, formerly of Washington City, died in his 29th year at the residence of his brother.	MORE 17 June 1851
BROTHERTON, James C. Esq., sheriff of St. Louis Co., died in St. Louis 31 July. Age 27. Funeral from his residence, Spruce betw. 5th & 6th, to the Presbyterian burying ground.	MORE 1 Aug 1838
BROTHERTON, William, drowned Sunday, body found Tuesday.	MORP 29 July '45
BROWN, A. died of cholera in Chariton Co.	BRUNS 24 May 1849
BROWN, Abraham J. -- St. Clair Co. Final settlement by George W. Fain.	OSIN 28 May 1853
BROWN, Allen of Clark Co. died 11 June at Ash Hollow age 35(?). Left one child.	MORE 7 Oct 1850
BROWN, Rev. Anderson died in Monroe Co. 20 October in his 56th year. Minister of Paris Baptist Church.	PWH 6 Nov 1841
BROWNE, ___ of Petersburgh (?) died recently in St. Charles Co.	MORE 19 Jan 1836
BROWN, Alexander died in jail where he had been committed for stealing a saddle.	SWERE 26 Aug '44
BROWN, Bryant -- Montgomery Co. Letters to Philander Draper 16 May.	BGRAD 3 June 1843
" -- Samuel Crutcher resigned guardianship of heirs.	FULT 1 June 1849
BROWNE, Edward died last Tuesday.	MORE 13 Sep 1824
BROWN, Elijah -- Montgomery Co. Letters of administration to Cynthia A. Brown & Willis G. Shackleford.	MORE 2 Nov 1833
BROWN, Elisha F. son of B. G. and Jane died 14 April in his 16th year.	MORE 23 Apr 1847
BROWN, Earnest of Lawrence Co. died at the residence of James Browder 3 mi. south of Warsaw. Had been to Independence on business. Buried Warsaw.	WAR 19 May 1849
BROWN, Evan B. of Savannah died age 43y 3m 2d. Native of Harrodsburg KY. Came here 10-12 years ago. Husband and father.	SASE 9 & 20 Apr 1853

BROWN, George died at the residence of his father Francis "Friday last." — PWH 28 June 1849

BROWN, Hilliard died at the residence of John W. Hudson in Fort Osage Twp. Left widow and one child. — INJN 10 Oct 1844

BROWN, James, son of Robert of Howard Co., drowned in the Upper Platte Ferry, 110 miles beyond Ft. Laramie, 10 June on the way to California. — BRUNS 16 Aug '49

BROWN, James Perrine died Sunday in St. Louis. — MORE 6 July 1826

BROWN, James M. died in Atchison Co. 5 August, age about 24, formerly of Howard Co. — MODE 2 Sep 1846

BROWN, Major James died 4 miles NE Wednesday last, in his 53rd year; one of the first settlers. — BOLT 12 Feb 1842

BROWN, John A. of Cape Girardeau died at Natchez on or ca 3 July, wills all property to his brother James Stuttman Brown thought to be a minor. Guardian must be appointed in St. Louis. — SLINQ 7 May 1825

BROWN, John age 86 died 16 August. Resident of St. Louis for 42 years. — MORE 21 Aug 1840

BROWN, Joseph C. Jr., recently deputy sheriff, died yesterday. Interred family burying ground. — MORE 13 June 1849

BROWN, Josiah died in his 32nd year. Funeral from residence of Alpheus Smith, #95 S. Main. — MORE 8 Nov 1847

BROWN, Oscar, fireman on the Persian, killed in explosion 7 November near Napoleon. — MORE 14 Nov 1840

BROWN, Preston E., formerly of Lexington KY, died 5 Oct. Resided near General Milburn. — MORE 6 Oct 1845

BROWN, R. B. of Benton Co. died 11 June at Ash Hollow, of cholera. Age 23. — MORE 7 Oct 1850

BROWN, Robert died Friday last in his 26th year at the residence of Mr. Lewis. Native of Alexandria, Huntington Co. PA. Methodist. Interred in the Presbyterian cemetery. — PWH 12 Aug 1847

BROWN, Robert T. died in Perry Co. 14 January. Came from Tennessee 1804. Married Francois Valle's dau. — MORE 29 Jan '46

BROWNE, Robert T. died in Philadelphia 17 June in his 35th year, formerly of Potosi MO. — MORE 2 June 1834

BROWN, Samuel Sr., a Revolutionary soldier, died in Platte Co. 13 August. — BOLT 24 Aug 1844

BROWN, Stephen, son of Maj. James of this county, died age about 21. — BOLT 29 Aug 1840

BROWN, William, said to be from Mine a Breton, disappeared from the Kentuckian. Presumed dead. — MORE 24 Oct 1835

BROWNING, Elijah died of apoplexy 1 June, a highly respected citizen of this county. — BOLT 6 June 1840

BRUN, Dr. ___ died 17 March age about 90. Many years resident of St. Louis Co. — MORE 19 Mar 1839

BRUNSON, Daniel died in Herculaneum 17 September. Late of Morgan Co. IL. MORE 27 Sep 1831

BRYAN, James died 16 July in Herculaneum in his 33rd year. Left wife, four children, widowed mother-in-law. Formerly of Bucks Co. PA. MORE 24 July 1822

BRYAN, Jesse Esq. died in Ste. Genevieve in his 86th year on 18 January. Born in Rowan Co. NC. MORE 7 Feb 1843

BRYAN, John of Warren Co. died 8 February, left wife and children. MORE 18 Feb 1836

BRYAN, John P. died at the residence of John C. Bryan on 11 April. SPAD 13 Apr 1847

BRYAN, William died in St. Louis Co. 1 June in his 48th year. Native of KY, resided in MO 20 years. STEGPD 18 June 1853

BRYAN, William Sr. died 18 June age 50. Funeral from his residence, Bates & Lewis near the Shot Tower. MORE 19 June 1849

BUCHANAN, J.W.L. died in Fayette 8 March in his 34th year. Recently returned from California. GLWT 13 Mar 1851

BUCHANAN, John H., constable of St. Louis Twp., killed when thrown from a horse. Left large family. MORE 7 Oct 1848

BUCHHOLTZ, Henry died 30 September age 22. Recently from Germany. JEFRE 3 Oct 1840

BUCCHOLTZ, William died 23 July age about 40. JEFRE 24 July '41

BUCKLEY, James M. died at Ft. William on the Arkansas R. in December. Formerly St. Louis merchant. MORE 22 Apr 1844

BUCKNAM, William -- "a man calling himself" this name came to the house of David Diggs in Lincoln Co. on 26 September, peddling oilcloths and died there. Native of Bedford Co. ME. Formerly engaged by firm Sampson & Pottle. MORE 15 Oct 1839

BUCKNER, ____ murdered by wife and stepdaughter in Bollinger Co. HIM 15 Feb 1855

BUCKNER, Alexander and his wife died a few hours apart of cholera. Had been a state senator and was originally from Indiana. (This was from the Jackson Eagle.) MORE 25 June 1833

BUCKNER, Alfred T., M.D., died at the residence of Stanton Buckner age 24. SALT 1 Aug 1840

BUDDE, Casper died 16 May. MORE 17 May 1853

BULCHER, Joshua, Co. L., Capt. Price's Reg., died 29 Oct. in or on the way to Santa Fe. MODE 13 Jan 1847

BULFINCH, Samuel, eldest brother of B.S. Bulfinch, at present in St. Louis, died at Philadelphia in 31st year. MORE 14 Dec 1816

BULLARD, William, overseer at the penitentiary, Jefferson City, was killed by a group of convicts, all of whom escaped. MORE 18 June 1841

BULLITT, William died at New Orleans 12 May.   MORE 30 May 1835

BULLOCK, Robert Morton died near Far West 19 December.   MORE 7 Jan 1846

BULLOCK, Wirkfield died in Wellsburg MO 23 February. Formerly of Woodford Co. KY.   MORE 2 Mar 1853

BUNCH, James, formerly of KY, died 25 March.   SPAD 30 Mar 1847

BUNCH, David -- Montgomery Co. Final settlement by Elizabeth Bunch & Williamson Kelly.   FULT 4 Aug 1848

BURBRIDGE, Benjamin died at Louisiana (Pike Co.) Of the firm of Burbridge & McCune. Left young family.   MORE 5 Jan 1838

BURBRIDGE, Rowland, died near Louisiana age 100. Veteran of the Revolution, born near Fredericksburg VA campaigned against Indians in 1774. Once a spy. Removed to KY after the Revolution, came to MO about 14 years ago.   MORE 3 Mar 1842

BURCH, Robert N. -- St. Clair Co. Notice by order of the court to sell real estate.   OSIN 16 Apr 1853

BURCH, Thomas C. died 5 October in Keytesville, Judge of the 11th Judicial District.   MORE 30 Oct 1839

BURCH, Washington C. -- Chariton Co. Final settlement by J. T. Burch.   BRUNS 10 Feb 1849

BURCHARD, R. of Osage Co. died 19 June 170 miles west of Ft. Kearney, age 21.   MORE 7 Oct 1850

BURCKHARTT, George Tompkins died in Fayette 26 August in his 27th year.   BRUNS 2 Sep 1848

BURCKHARTT, Joshua -- Texas Co. Letters of administration to James M. Burckhartt, 19 January.   MORE 24 Feb 1853

BURCKHARTT, Col. Nicholas died 13 June in Howard Co.   MIN 21 June 1834

BURGIN, Charles died at the residence of Mrs. Birge on 4 December in his 79th year.   MODE 15 Dec 1847

BURGIN, John died in Audrain Co. ; in 57th year; of Sullivan Co.   SEE BELOW   BRUNS 20 Apr 1848

BURGIN, James of Sullivan Co. died 10th April at the residence of Curtis Gentry, in his 57th year.   MODE 18 Apr 1848

BURKS, Isham died at the residence of his son-in-law George Sexton in Boone Co. 21 August, age about 90. Born VA, served in Revolution. Removed early to Cumberland Co. KY, then Alabama, then to MO. Methodist.   WEM 5 Sep 1839

BURKES, James R. of Johnson Co. died in Mexico.   COMB 16 Dec 1847

BOURKE, Martin died at the home of Jordan O'Bryan. He was about 27, native of Ireland, raised near Limerick. Died 26 September 1838.   WEM 14 Feb 1839

BURNETT, Isaac died in Carondelet 6 October, formerly a merchant. (SWERE 12 Oct gives age as 30)   MORE 7 Oct 1846

BURNS, George, formerly of Capt. David Musick's Co., killed in a canoe.   MORE 27 May 1815

BURNS, John D. committed suicide at Union (Franklin Co.) age about 23. Left father, two brothers, and two sisters.   MORE 19 Apr 1839

BURNS, John -- Grundy Co. Letters of administration 26 June to Jacob T. Tindall.   BRUNS 12 July '49

BURNS, John drowned in the Mississippi between Clarksville and Louisiana (Pike Co.) 3 August.   MORE 11 Aug 1845

BURNS, P. Jr., merchant, died Tuesday last in his 29th year of inflammation of the bowels.   MORE 3 July 1845

BURNS, Peter B. died at Sacramento age 37.   MORE 4 May 1850

BURR, William, mate of the *Banner*, killed. (No data.)   MORE 3 Oct 1834

BURROUGHS, Jacob died near Pisgah, one of the oldest and most respected citizens.   COMB 13 Jan 1848

BURT, Andrew died at his residence in Potosi on 29 April in his 63rd year. Native of Scotland, and formerly of Baltimore.   MORE 7 May 1839

BURTON, Strother died of cholera, age 48, on 5 June.   MORE 6 June 1851

BUSBY, Mr., killed by Indians at the upper settlements of St. Charles Co. "a few days ago."   MORE 25 Mar 1815

BUSHEY, Lewis K. died 22 October in his 24th year. Funeral from residence of his father on Green St. Interred Methodist cemetery.   MORE 23 Oct 1840

BUSHEYHEAD, Isaac murdered (place not stated, possibly in Iowa Ter. or Wisc. Ter.) His brother John offered $1250 reward for the killers.   MORE 7 Sep 1843

BUSTER, Judge William died Monday last, an old and highly esteemed citizen.   MODE 30 Jan 1849

BUSTON, David of Norfolk VA died at the residence of his brother-in-law William Richards in St. Louis.   MORE 3 Dec 1845

BUTLER, Benjamin F. died at the residence of Richard Sampson Esq. in Boone Co. 27 February in his 28th year.   MORE 9 Mar 1846

BUTLER, Frederick A. drowned in the Mississippi near the mouth of the Ohio; had been in St. Louis as a trader recently. "New London CT papers please copy."   MORE 30 Sep 1815

BUTLER, George M. of Lafayette Co., Adjutant, died at Santa Fe in November. Mason, IOOF.   MODE 3 Mar 1847

BUTLER, John of Franklin Co. died of cholera at Ash Hollow 8 June age 39. Left wife, six children.   MORE 7 Oct 1850

BUTTERFIELD, Sgt. Benjamin died at Ft. George, Upper Canada.   MORE 20 Nov 1813

BUTTERWORTH, Pleasant died in Petersburg of hydrophobia.   MORE 15 Oct 1838

BYNUM, Tompkins died at the residence of his father near Fayette Tuesday last age 16y 8m.   MODE 23 Sep 1846

BYRARE, Edward, no known kin, died in Pike Co.(?) or in   STCHMO 22 June 1822
       St. Louis, in the fall of 1820. Born in Kildare,
       Ireland. (Estate settlement in Pike Co.)

BYRD, John Esq. died Thursday morning last at his residence
       near Caledonia, Washington Co. In 85th year.   MORE 6 Mar 1818

BYRD, John, murdered by his son in Cape Girardeau Co.   JEFRE 22 Oct 1841

BYRNE, John, a policeman, died suddenly Monday (5 June).   MORE 7 June 1848

BYRNE, Luke of New Madrid murdered by Samuel Houk 10 April. STEGPD 30 Apr 1853

BYRNE, Martin died 29th inst in his 76th year.   MORP 30 Dec 1845

BYRNE, Michael died in St. Louis.   MORE 29 Mar 1831

CABANNE, Augustus E., second son of John P., died "last   MORE 24 Jan 1825
       Saturday. (Obituary in issue of 14 Feb.)

CABANNE, John P., a resident for 40 or 50 years, died   MORE 27 June 1841
       "advanced in life."

CABEEN, William of Old Chariton died 27 Feb. age 65 years.   MODE 18 Mar 1846

CABELL, Richard R. died at the residence of his brother
       Edward B. in Chariton Co. 7 October age 21y 3m.   BOLT 14 Oct 1843

CABELL, Edward D., of Keytesville, died in Brunswick   MORE 5 Sep 1850
       age 62.

CAGLE, Jacob -- Barry Co. Letters of administration to   JEFRE 13 Aug 1836
       Wm. Southward & Geo. Damron.

CAGLE, James -- Barry Co. Final settlement, Wm. Southward.   JEFRE 7 Sep 1839

CALDWELL, Bolivar S., age about 19, died 21 August at the   COMB 27 Aug 1846
       residence of F.M. Caldwell. Recently from
       Greenbriar Co. VA.

CALDWELL, Dr. James D. died in Ralls Co. 7 June in 36th y.   PWH 19 June 1841

COLHOUN, Andrew "of this place" died at Chambersburg PA   WEM 11 Apr 1839
       22 March. Left wife & 2 daughters.

CALAWAY, Bottswood H. of Boone Co. died 7 July.   MORE 14 July 1829

CALLAWAY, Capt. James killed by Indians near Loutre Island. MORE 11 Mar 1815

CALLIGAN, Martin, deckhand on the Fayaway, drowned 19 Nov.   MORE 23 Nov 1848

CALLIHAN, Dr. O.W.S. died at New Franklin 10 Aug.   JEFRE 7 Sep 1839

CALLISON, A. -- Dallas Co. Letters of administration to   SPAD 1 June 1847
       Cinthia Callison 5 May 1847.

CALVERT, James Milton age 26 died in St. Louis 10 April.   SWERE 13 Apr 1846

CALVERT, John died at the residence of his father in   PWH 19 Mar 1846
       Warren Twp. Sunday last.

CAMDEN, Marshall died in St. Louis in his 34th year.   MORE 21 Aug 1840
       Funeral from residence of Peter G. Camden,
       3rd & Green.

CAMERON, Mr. ____, died Tuesday last, 4 miles up the
       Missouri River.   BRUNS 19 July 1849

CAMPBELL, Dudley C. died at Cave Spring on Manchester Rd., age about 33. — MORE 29 June 1839

CAMPBELL, George W. -- Dallas Co. Final settlement by Rebecca Campbell. — SPAD 30 May 1846

CAMPBELL, Isaac -- Chariton Co. Final settlement by Thomas Fristoe & Alex. Campbell. — BOLT 20 Feb 1841

CAMPBELL, James killed in the sinking of the ferry at Everett's Ferry near Independence 16 June. — SOV 4 July 1834

CAMPBELL, Joel age about 40 died in Louisiana, Pike Co. 3 March, "highly respected and worthy." (PWH 11 Mar. says died 1 March age 48) — BGRAD 11 Mar 1843

CAMPBELL, John died 21 Feb. at the residence of John Sappington Jr. Formerly of Monroe Co. VA. — MORE 27 Mar 1844

CAMPBELL, John R. died near Hillsboro in his 75th year. — MORE 1 Sep 1845

CAMPBELL, Matthew died 10 December age 35 years, a native of Pittsfield MA. — MORE 12 Dec 1834

CAMPBELL, ____ hit by bottle in fracas at eating house under Globe Tavern. Not expected to live. — MORE 23 June 1841

CAMPBELL, David died at Brunswick 15 October in his 56th year. Formerly of Knoxville, E. TN. — MORE 24 Oct 1844

CAMPBELL, Sutton F. of Co. E., Doniphan's Reg., died in Santa Fe between Nov. 1 and Nov. 15. — MODE 11 Jan 1847

CAMPBELL, T. drowned from the *Banner* en route to Burlington IA where he had a daughter and son-in-law. — MORE 28 Oct 1845

CAMPBELL, Thomas died of cholera near Boonsboro 16 Aug. — GLWT 21 Aug 1851

CANOLE, Charles died 6 Feb. "Had he survived until the 14th would have attained his 60th year." A native of TN, served in the legislature 12 years. A Mason. — MODE 12 Feb 1848

CANTER, Emanuel died Tuesday in his 35th year, many years a resident of St. Louis. "Affectionate husband and parent." (MORE 11 Dec. says resided #70 4th St., interred Methodist cemetery.) — SWERE 16 Dec 1844

CANTLEBERRY, George died 31 January. — CAMP 2 Feb 1849

CARBERRY, John Esq. died at Ste. Genevieve 23 Feb. age 45. By profession a teacher, lived in Beauvais Twp. "Too addicted to drink." Left wife and family in Osage Valley. "Comparatively a stranger in the area, although a J.P." — MORE 4 Mar 1845

CARDINAL, Charles missing and presumed dead after a battle between Indians and Capt. Craig's Co. near Ft. Howard on the lower Cuivre Ferry. — MORE 27 May 1815

CARMAN, Charles B. Esq. died at Co. Farm House Sunday 22nd inst. Formerly of Trenton NJ. — MORE 26 Jan 1843

CARNES, Thomas died Thursday morning.   MORE 21 July 1837

CARR, Alfred W. died in Lincoln Co. Wednesday last, formerly of Lexington, KY.   MORE 20 Sep 1831

CARRE, ____ of Doniphan's Reg., from Saline Co., died in Santa Fe.   MODE 13 Jan 1847

CARR, Anthony U., Indian sub-agent, died at the Osage agency.   MORE 4 Jan '31

CARR, Dabney Esq. died Tuesday.   MORE 7 Aug 1822

CARR, Francis died at the residence of his aunt Mrs. Sarah Drummond in his 29th year.   LEXP 28 June 1854

CARR, Francis Esq., attorney and counsellor, died 14 Sep. (SWERE 19 Sep says died 15th, age 26.)   MORE 19 Sep 1821

CARR, John A., a respectable merchant of Florida, Monroe Co. died in the calaboose Wednesday night last. He had d.t.s, threatened Mr. Lewis keeper of the coffee house next door, who hit him with a stick. Later died from effects of drink. Was of "respectable fortune and high standing," a judge of the Monroe Co. Court, in the Santa Fe trade. Interred Methodist cemetery.   MORE 10 June 1841

CARR, J. W. died yesterday, formerly of Maine. Funeral Green Tree Tavern.   MORE 8 June 1844

CARR, William died of erysipelas in his 69th year.   MORE 1 Apr 1851

CARROLL, Henry murdered by Richard Gentry in Howard Co. some time before January 1820 when Gentry was indicted for his murder.   MIN 29 Jan 1820

CARROLL, Charles of Bellevue (Howard Co.) died at Williamsburg NY. Formerly Register of the Land Office at Franklin.   MIN 6 Jan 1824

CARROLL, John age about 24 died in Peno Twp., Pike Co. 31 September.   BGRAD 5 Oct 1844

CARROLL, Lawrence died in St. Louis, a native of Ireland.   MORE 8 Mar 1824

CARSON, Alexander -- Shannon Co. Letters of administration to John N. Clark, 9 March 1843.   JINQ 13 Apr 1843

CARSON, David died in Jackson, MS 14 October, a highly respected citizen of Lexington, MO. Left a large family.   MORE 11 Nov 1836

CARSON, Nehemiah died 13 July, one of the Howard Co. volunteers to Mexico. Buried at Pawnee Rock.   MODE 12 Aug 1846

CARTER, Benjamin -- Wayne Co. Letters of administration to David Carter 17 Oct. 1823.   INP 1 Nov 1823

CARTER, Charles E. died in Hannibal 4 March in 60th year.   PWH 22 Mar 1849

CARTER, Dr. James Augustus died Friday night last at the residence of C. Rhodes. Late of New York.   MORE 18 Nov 1834

CARTER, Josiah -- Ripley Co. Letters of administration to Jane Carter, 1 April.   SPAD 2 May 1846

CARTER, Robert of Osage Co. died in the explosion of the Big   STGAZ 15 Aug '45
    Hatchee at Hermann on 23 July.

CARTHRAE, Lewis died in Saline Co., late of Rockingham Co. VA.
    In MO since 1833. Staunton Spectator and
    Rockingham Register please copy.   MORE 6 Sep 1844

CARTMILL, Thomas age 33 died Tuesday.   MORE 14 Apr 1819

CARTMILL, Col. William W. died at his residence in Lafayette
    Co. in his 47th year. Native of Botetourt Co. VA
    and for a short time resident of Bedford Co. TN.   LEXP 22 Apr '45
    Left widow and children.

CARTNEY, Nicholas late of Lisnabuntry, Mullaugh Parish,   MORE 19 July 1851
    Co. Cavan died in his 35th year.

CARTY, Joseph died of smallpox 20 Jan. A long-time resident   PWH 22 Jan 1846
    of North River, Warren Twp. (Marion Co.)

CARWIN, Michael drowned from the Redwing. A deckhand, Irish,   MORE 22 July 1847
    "of industrious and sober habits."

CARY, Jefferson killed in the sinking of the ferry at   SOV 4 July 1834
    Everett's Ferry, near Independence, 16 June.

CASE, William died 7 January age 57y 6m. Utica NY
    please copy.   SWERE 10 Jan 1848

CASEY, George died in Washington Co. in his 71st year.   MORE 20 May 1853
    Native of Cork, Ireland.

CASEY, Matthew died 13 December age 55y 4m 2f. Funeral   MORE 15 Dec 1842
    from his residence between 9th & 10th Sts.

CASH, Capt. John died near Frankford, this county,   SALT 29 Aug 1840
    Thursday 27th last.

CASH, Thomas killed in Williamson Co. TX by Samuel and   MORE 24 Mar 1829
    John Caperton. Reward of $200 offered by Thos. W. Cash.

CASSELL, James killed Saturday 11 July when a bank of earth
    fell on him on Market St. Native of Ireland.   MORE 13 July 1846
    Left wife, 2 children.

CASSILLY, Philip Esq. died Saturday evening last.   MORE 20 Feb 1837

CASTEEL, Joseph -- DeKalb Co. Final settlement by Thos. J. Hudson.   STGAZ 13 Apr 1853

CASTLEMAN, Lewis died in Washington Co. 21 October,   MORE 2 Nov 1847
    formerly of KY.

CATRON, Mr. C. died of cholera in Palmyra.   MORE 28 June 1833

CATRON, Thomas C. of Wayne Co. died 15 June at Ft. Kearney
    age 36. Left wife, 2 children.   MORE 7 Oct 1850

CAYOU, Joseph died 22 September age 32. Interred   MORE 23 Sep 1848
    Catholic cemetery.

CELLINI, Very Rev. Francis, Vicar-general of this   SWERE 8 Jan 1849
    diocese, died 6 January.

CENTEL, Charles died in Carondelet Twp. 1 October age   MORE 16 Oct 1843
    about 22.

CERRE, Pascal L. died 9 March age 77. — SWERE 14 May 1849

CHAMBERLAIN, Hector died at St. Charles. Late of Vermont, was preparing for the ministry. — MORE 10 June 1840

CHAMBERLAIN, Edward T., formerly of Westfield, Medina Co. OH died 13 Dec. age 20y 8m. (Issue of 24 Jan says he was brother of F. B. of St. Louis.) — SWERE 20 Dec 1847

CHAMBERLAIN, Jason drowned 1 August while crossing the river near Davidsonville, Ark. Territory. Left wife and family. — MOH 5 Aug 1820

CHAMBERLAIN, Joseph died in St. Louis yesterday, late captain of the Dolphin. — MORE 20 June 1821

CHAMBERS, Ludlow died in Saline Co. 4 September at the residence of his br-in-law John Pulliam, ae 34. — MORE 11 Sep 1853

CHAMBERS, William died 21 September age 78, a resident of Cooper Co. Born NC, fought near the end of the Revolution, a spy at 15. Later a mounted ranger. One of Cooper Co.'s oldest settlers. — BORE 1 Oct 1844

CHAMBERS, Col. William died yesterday at an advanced age. — MORE 3 May 1848

CHAMBLIN, William N. age 19 died of cholera at the residence of his uncle, N. Chamblin, 8 June. — MORE 9 June 1851

CHAMNESS, Alfred died in Andrew Co. of "winter fever" on 3 December. — SASE 6 Dec 1851

CHANDLER, Richard "a responsible citizen of this county" died 17 September. — FAR 22 Sep 1836

CHANDLER, Richard W., a Palmyra merchant, died of cholera. — JEFRE 28 June '33

CHAPIN, Erastus S., son of Erastus of St. Louis, died in Springfield MA 1 May age 21. — MORE 1 June 1840

CHAPMAN, Daniel H., many years a resident, died 23 July. Funeral from his farm on St. Charles Rd., 7 mi. west of St. Louis. — MORE 25 July 1842

CHAPMAN, Edmund S., formerly of Huntsville, killed mining in CA. Had two brothers there' went in 1849. — HIM 16 Nov 1854

CHAPMAN, Peyton -- Chariton Co. Notice to Creed Chapman and other heirs of petition to sell slave by Preston Gaines, adm. — BRUNS 25 Nov '48

CHAPMAN, Col. Thomas S. of St. Louis died in Legtown CA 1 February age 38. — MORE 24 Feb 1851

CHARLES, Alexander died Sunday last. — MORE 27 Aug 1833

CHARLES, R. M. age 60 died 28 February. Belleville IL & Louisville KY please copy. — SWERE 5 Mar 1849

CHARLESS, Edward died 22 June age 50. — SWERE 26 June 1848

CHARLEVILLE, Joseph died at his residence on River des Peres 10 September in his 73rd year. — MORE 12 Sep 1843

CHARLTON, Levi -- Montgomery Co. Final settlement by Wm. W. Charlton.   FULT 30 Mar 1849

CHARTRES, George died Saturday last.   SWERE 9 Sep 1844

CHAUNCEY, John, many years a resident of Missouri, died 9 Feb. in Illinois. Native of Hartford Co. MD, buried in Clay Co. MO.   MORE 22 Feb 1849

CHAUVIN, Jacques, age 83, died at the residence of his son LaFreniere near St. Charles last Saturday.   MORE 18 May 1826

CHAUVIN, Joseph died in his 38th year at the home of his mother.   MORE 12 Jan 1851

CHAUVIN, LaFreniere age 55 died 11 April in St. Charles. Interred Catholic cemetery there.   MORE 13 Apr 1846

CHAVIS, ___ Santa Fe trader, murdered near the Little Arkansas some time ago. (His murderers were to be executed.)   MORE 15 Aug 1844

CHEETHAM, George of Saline Co. died 8 June at Plum Creek age 27.   MORE 7 Oct 1850

CHEILEY, Joseph died 2 November age about 26.   STCHRO 9 Nov 1850

CHENIE, Antoine "an old and highly respectable Frenchman" died yesterday of apoplexy. Born in Montreal 14 Apr 1768, resident of St. Louis "rising 40 years."   MORE 3 Feb 1840

CHEWNING, John age 58 died 16 November in St. Louis Co. Native of Virginia.   MORE 19 Nov 1840

CHIBEAUX, Rev. John Francis, late of the Ursuline Convent of New Orleans died St. Louis.   MORE 8 Sep 1840

CHICK, George O. died 22 July at his residence 12 miles north of St. Louis in his 26th year. Little Rock, Louisville, Natchitoches please copy.   MORE 27 July 1840

CHICK, Col. William M. died at Kansas, MO two weeks since, "a respectable citizen."   MORE 26 Apr 1847

CHILDS, Nathaniel Sr. died in his 74th year.   MORE 9 Oct 1851

CHILES, Lieut. ___, MO Vol., killed at Camp Gentry FL accidentally 11 November last.   SMAD 2 Jan 1838

CHILES, Capt. William died 23 Jan. at Union, Franklin Co., in his 69th year.   MORE 9 Feb 1846

CHILTON, Charles, postmaster at Boonville, died Wednesday last age about 29. Virginia papers please copy.   COMB 19 Nov 1847

CHILTON, Thomas, constable of Boons Lick Twp, died Friday 23 January.   BOLT 31 Jan 1846

CHISHAM, William died 28 December age 24 (21?).   MIN 1 Jan 1821

CHISON, William A. died 2 October in his 33rd year.   MORE 3 Oct 1846

CHOUTEAU, Auguste "Patriarch of St. Louis" died this morning age 80 years. Funeral tomorrow.   MORE 24 Feb 1829

CHOUTEAU, Lewis son of Maj. Peter died May 28 at　　　　MORE 5 July 1831
　　　　Cantonment Gibson, Ark. Terr., in 27th year.

CHOUTEAU, Paul L. died yesterday.　　　　SWERE 24 Apr '48

CHRISMAN, Alb. G. age 26 died at the residence of his　　　　LEXP 15 Mar 1854
　　　　father 28 April.

CHRIESMAN, Franklin, son of George, died "in this town"　　　　MIN 15 Apr 1823
　　　　11 April age 24.

CHRIESMAN, Daniel, apprentice to Mr. Rice, drowned　　　　MIN 5 Feb 1824
　　　　near Boonville.

CHRISMAN, Henry a citizen of Fayette died at Linnaeus　　　　BOLT 29 Jan 1842
　　　　17 January while visiting.

CHRISTMAN, James died Sunday regretted by all who knew him.　　　　MORE 28 Aug 1822

CHRISTMAN, Peter, brother of the late Jonas, died Tues.　　　　MORE 11 Sep 1822
　　　　(from probate, Jonas is correct)

CHRISTY, William Jr. died at St. Charles 15 April,　　　　MORE 19 Apr 1839
　　　　age about 70.

CHRISTY, Edmund Taylor, eldest son of Maj. William, died　　　　MORE 22 Nov 1839
　　　　age 29 years. Funeral from residence of his
　　　　mother in north St. Louis.

CHRISTY, Major William died "this morning" at his residence　　　　MORE 4 Apr 1837
　　　　near St. Louis, one of the oldest American
　　　　settlers in Missouri. Buried North
　　　　　　　　St. Louis cemetery.

CHRYSTIE, Col. John died at Ft. George in Upper Canada　　　　MORE 25 Sep 1813
　　　　after an illness of 3 days. Third son of
　　　　the late Maj. James of New York.

CHURCH, Col. Francis died yesterday at the Virginia Hotel,
　　　　a resident of Clark Co.　　　　MORE 19 Aug 1841

CHURCH, Leander eldest son of Jonathan of Monroe Co. IL　　　　MORE 21 Feb 1846
　　　　died in Ste. Genevieve Co. in his 17th year.

CHURCHILL, Ezekiel died in Atchison Co. 25 July, age　　　　STGAZ 9 Oct 1846
　　　　about 45, supposedly born New York State,
　　　　no known heirs.

CLACK, Rev. Spencer died of cholera in Palmyra.　　　　MORE 28 June 1833

CLAMORGAN, Jacques died "last week."　　　　MORE 19 Nov 1814

CLANTON, Drury died in St. Louis 19 September.　　　　MORE 27 Sep 1827

CLARK, B.O. Esq.
CLARK, George W. died of cholera in Palmyra.　　　　MORE 28 June 1833

CLARK, Capt. Christopher of Lincoln Co. died Friday 7 Sep.　　　　MORE 24 Sep 1841
　　　　age about 75. Born NC, later of KY, fought
　　　　in the Indian wars.

CLARK, David died 18 Nov.,"aged & respectable citizen."　　　　PWH 30 Nov 1848

CLARK, David -- Chariton Co. Public Administrator took　　　　BRUNS 26 Jan 1848
　　　　over his estate.

32

CLARK, Daniel -- Montgomery Co. Petition to foreclose mortgage held by deceased. Richard Relf & Beverly Chew, administrators.	SLINQ 6 May 1820
CLARK, Edwin Downer, son of E.D. & J. of St. Louis, died in New Orleans 27 May. Native of Westfield NJ.	MORE 3 June 1846
CLARK, Edward W. died Saturday 12 August, formerly of Newburyport MA.	MORE 15 Aug 1837
CLARK, George formerly of Lexington KY and for 8 years a resident of St. Louis died at his residence near the city.	MORE 1 Jan 1846
CLARK, George W. -- Miller Co. Letters of administration to William Clark 1 Nov. 1841.	JINQ 2 Dec 1841
CLARK, Henry -- Montgomery Co. Final settlement by William Knox.	FULT 30 Mar 1849
CLARK, Isaac -- Montgomery Co. Letters of administration to Henry Clark, 6 August.	JEFRE 17 Sep 1831
CLARK, Major J.B. Funeral notice. From Christ Church to the Episcopal Cemetery.	MORE 14 Apr 1848
CLARK, James a marble cutter died in his 42nd year on 14 June. New York papers please copy.	MORE 16 June 1849
CLARK, James died in Holt Co. in February in his 80th year. Methodist. Mason.	STGAZ 3 Mar 1852
CLARK, James died at Ste. Genevieve age (?37?).	MORE 10 Apr 1832
CLARK, John died in Callaway Co. 24 December. "Husband and father."	BEA 27 Jan 1831
CLARK, John G. died yesterday age 33.	BEA 7 July 1831
CLARK, Bennet of Howard Co. died 29 October. "Husband and father."	MIN 2 July 1822
CLARK, Martin a passenger for Weston on the *Jane* fell overboard; body believed his found on Cat Island about 9 June.	MORE 8 May 1843
CLARK, Robert -- Chariton Co. Letters of administration to Public Administrator 23 September.	BRUNS 28 Oct 1847
CLARK, Capt. Robert died in his 52nd year.	BOLT 21 Aug 1841
CLARK, Samuel resident of St. Charles Co. 21 years, son of Capt. Norman of Princeton, MA died 3 August. Left wife, four children.	MORE 19 Aug 1840
CLARK, William died at his residence in Polk Co. 20 Aug.	SPAD 23 Aug 1845
CLARK, Gov. William died Saturday night at the residence of his son Meriwether Lewis.	MORE 3 Sep 1838
CLARK, William Preston son of the late Gen. William died Saturday age 29.	MORE 7 Jan 1839
CLARK, William C. late of Lincoln Co. died on the waters of Green River in July age 34.	MORE 8 Jan 1851

CLARKSON, George died 14 March at Columbia in a pistol affray, age 15 years some months.   BOBS 25 Mar 1851

CLAY, Abraham or Abram -- Montgomery Co. Lawsuit naming his heirs.   MORE 25 Sep 1832
SALT 23 Aug 1840

CLAY, William, a printer, died in St. Louis 20 August.   MORE 23 Aug 1843

CLAYTON, Thomas, native of England, principal of Farrington School for 30 years. No death date. He was 57 years old.   MORE 18 June 1849

CLAYTON, William, formerly of the Grand Turk. Funeral from Boatmen's Church.   MORE 13 Aug 1853

CLEEVER, Jeremiah died 3 March.   MORE 5 Mar 1845

CLEAVER, Stephen of Ralls Co. died 31 May, one of the oldest settlers in the Salt River country.   MORE 10 June 1846

CLEMENS, John M. Esq. died in Hannibal 24 March in his 49th year.   PWH 1 Apr 1847

CLEMENT, Benjamin S. died Saturday 7 September in his 46th year. Resided at 29 Spruce St.   MORE 6 Sep 1845

CLEMENTS, Thomas H. died at LaGrange 2 December.   CAMP 5 Jan 1849

CLENDENNEN, William, aged 70, died 20 January. He was married 47 years and raised 10 children, 9 of whom lived in Cole Co.   JEFRE 10 Feb 1844

CLIFFORD, John D., partner in the firm of James Clemens Jr. & Co., died -- no date shown.   MORE 31 May 1820

CLIFTON, Mr. A. W., formerly of Florence, AL, died Friday last.   MORE 24 Jan 1832

CLIFTON, Joseph died in Buffalo Twp. (Pike Co.) Wednesday age about 40.   BGRAD 17 Aug 1844

CLINE, John, native of Germany, died Monday morning last in his 75th year.   SLDU 7 Nov 1846

CLINKSCALES, Levi died near Carrollton 29 January age about 58.   BRUNS 17 Feb 1849

CLINTON, Charles D. died in St. Louis last Saturday.   MORE 11 Mar 1828

CLUFF, Alfred formerly of Wisconsin died Sunday morning last at the home of Mr. Todd, age ca 40.   STGAZ 19 Jan 1853

CLUFF, James, youngest son of Jonathan, died in his 26th year.   PWH 29 July 1843

COALTER, Dr. Beverly T. of Pike Co. died at the residence of his brother Gen. John D. in St. Louis on 10 Oct. in 43rd year. Wife, 3 children.   MORE 3 Oct 1851

COATES, Jackson, legal notice to his mother; he had been killed in the Mexican War. (He was from Carroll Co.)   STGAZ 13 Jan 1848

COATS, John of Fulton died from the effects of being thrown from a buggy 5 or 6 weeks ago.   BRUNS 30 Sep 1848

COBB, Shelton T. -- Montgomery Co. Final settlement by Public Administrator.	FULT 7 Dec 1849
COCHRAN, John age 32 died 25 May. Iowa papers pls copy.	SWERE 28 May 1849
COCHRAN, John, a native of western OH, died 27 March in Washington Co.	MORE 8 May 1843
COCHRAN, Calvin E., son of Rev. & Mrs. W.P., died 9 July age about 20.	PWH 19 July 1849
COCKE, Richard died of typhus at his farm near Keytesville. Formerly of Campbell Co. VA.	MORE 4 Oct 1833
COCKRILL, F.G. died at Weston 19 July age 37.	BRUNS 2 Aug 1849
COCKRILL, Joseph -- Chariton Co. Letters of administration to Fielding Cockrill 18 October.	MIN 9 Nov 1826
COCKSTILL, _____ of Callaway Co., of Doniphan's Regiment, died at Santa Fe.	MODE 13 Jan 1847
COFFEE, Henry died in his 34th year. Funeral from residence of Mr. Cuniffe, 6th & Wash.	MORE 6 Mar 1848
COFFEY, Thomas died 11 March. Formerly of Mercer, PA. Funeral from residence of Thomas Weston.	MORE 13 Mar 1846
COGLAND, _____ "executed Saturday last."	MORE 29 Sep 1829
COGSWELL, Maj. John B., age 26, died 29 August at the residence of his father, Col. James M., in Jackson Co. Formerly of Bourbon Co. KY.	INJN 12 Sep 1844
COLBURN, Jesse died at Carondelet on Saturday last.	MORE 19 Aug 1834
COLBURN, ____ of St. Louis, a Santa Fe trader, found shot in the head.	MODE 12 May 1847
COLBURN, Benjamin, age 42, formerly of Canton (Lewis Co.) died in California 17 January.	CANE 22 Mar 1855
COLE, Amos, son of Richard, a well-known tavern keeper 10 miles from St. Louis, stabbed to death over a fight in a "Will" case in the Ct. of Appeals.	MORE 31 May 1827
COLE, Henry, age about 22, a passenger on the *Envoy*, fell overboard near Cape Girardeau Saturday night. Inf. wtd. by W.H. Cole, St. Louis.	MORE 25 Aug 1853
COLE, Jesse -- Gentry Co. Letters of administration to William A. Childers 8 November.	STGAZ 24 Nov 1852
COLERICK, Lt. Charles died at Jefferson Barracks 8 Jan.	MORE 7 Feb 1828
COLLET, Robert Esq. died in his 64th year. Funeral from Christ Church.	MORE 12 Sep 1846
COLLIER, John died in St. Louis and was buried at St. Charles.	SLINQ 26 May 1821
COLLIER, Mortimer F. died 23 April at Georgetown, Pettis Co., in 28th year. Wife and infant.	WEM 2 May 1839
COLLINS, Augustus, a merchant, died Friday.	MORE 19 Feb 1828

COLLINS, James N., formerly of Granby, CT, died 11 December age 23, at residence of James Newberry. MORE 13 Dec 1851

COLLINS, John, a carpenter, died in the Car of Commerce disaster. MORE 27 May 1828

COLLINS, John died in Oregon, Holt Co.-- many years Clerk of the Circuit Ct. SASE 20 Aug 1853

COLLINS, James -- Chariton Co. Letters of administration to John Collins, Executor. MIN 26 May 1826

COLLINS, William B., notice, missing. Resided in Barry Co. when last heard from. Father Mordecai Collins left inheritance. Native of Orange Co. VA. MORE 17 Dec 1844

COLTON, Wells Esq. died age 38. Funeral from residence of O. West, Washington between 4th & 5th. MORE 26 May 1849

COMMINS, Capt. William H. of Lewis Co. reported lost in the sinking of the Eliza. COP 11 Nov 1842

COMPTON, Joseph died at the residence of his father near St. Joseph 15 Sept. in his 20th year. MORE 25 Sep 1851

COMSTOCK, Lee, father of Dr. T.G. of St. Louis, died in LeRoy NY age 62 on 3 January. MORE 10 Jan 1853

CONANT, Lieut. Rowell of St. Louis, formerly of Windsor VT and late of the 1st U.S. Rifle Regiment died 16 February age 23. MORE 21 Feb 1821

CONDON, Richard died 27 June age 51y 4m. Superintendent of the Workhouse. Baptist. MORE 28 June 1847

CONE, E.B., formerly of Huntsville, died recently in CA. GLWT 30 Jan 1851

CONNAUL, Joseph died in his (52nd?) year on 31 October. Albany & Schenectady please copy. SLDU 3 Nov 1846

CONNELL, Michael, native of Burr, Kings Co., Ireland died in Florissant 17 July. BEA 4 Aug 1831

CONNELLY, Thomas age 31 died near Kansas City 22 June of lung fever. Native of Galway. KCEN 5 July 1856

CONNER, Abel M. died in his 22nd year leaving wife and two children. Native of MO, four years resident of St. Louis; moved to New London in 1832 and resided there until a few weeks ago. Methodist. MORE 22 May 1834

CONNER, Henry died 3 January age 66. SWERE 10 Jan 1847

CONNER, James, a native of Jessamine Co. KY, died Saturday night last, "a worthy young man." STGAZ 14 Sep 1853

CONNETT, Anderson, youngest son of Wm. C. and Matilda, died 30 Jan. ae 17y 8m 24d, near Sparta. Formerly of Fayette Co. KY. STGAZ 9 Feb 1853

CONRAD, Henry C. "this morning" age about 25. JEFRE 19 Aug 1843

CONSAUL (CONSAUD) Col. Joseph 31 Oct. in his 52nd year. Schenectady and Albany please copy. MORE 4 Nov 1846

CONVERSE, Joel died 3 July of consumption, age 28. Late of Cleveland OH, formerly of Tolland CT.   MORE 5 July 1839

CONVERSE, Seth of Illinois Town, St. Louis Co., died near Belleville Tuesday last. Thrown from his horse and run over by speeders.   MORE 17 Nov 1840

CONWAY, Joseph died at his late residence in Bonhomme Twp. in his 69th year. Native of VA, came to MO in 1793.   MORE 18 Jan 1831

CONWAY, Samuel, a Revolutionary patriot, died in Marion Co. 17 September age 74.   MIN 16 Oct 1830

CONWAY, Judge Thomas died in Fayette 2 Sept. age 65.   MIN 12 Sep 1835

CONWAY, Walter -- Montgomery Co. Sale of realestate by Samuel Conway. (MORE 24 Feb 1829 shows final settlement also by Samuel and gives date of letters as 30 July 1823)   SLINQ 10 May 1824

COOK, Dewey B. died 21 May. An attorney, formerly of Otsego Co. NY.   MOAR 24 May 1839

COOK, Harlow late of New Hartford CT died at the home of his aunt Mrs. T. Spencer in 18th year.   MORE 1 Apr 1851

COOK, Dr. James H. died of cholera Wednesday last. (from Weston Journal)   BRUNS 19 July 1849

COOK, Judge John D. died in Cape Girardeau; he was Dist. Atty for US in Missouri Dist.   HANJ 11 Nov 1852

COOK, John of Fulton died near Clarksville, Cumberland River, TN, on 28 March, of cholera. In his 50th year. Absent several months on business.   FULT 13 Apr 1849

COOK, Dr. J.H. died at St. Joseph 11 July, son-in-law of Capt. Thos. Caldwell of Callaway Co. Brought up in KY, resided St. Louis 5 years, served in the Florida War. Names wife, no children.   FULT 24 Aug 1849

COOK, James of St. Louis died Wednesday 6 January.   MORE 9 Jan 1841

COOK, Oliver died Friday.   MORE 7 Aug 1822

COOK, Samuel, native of Wilmington DE died yesterday at the hospital in his 26th year.   MORE 25 Jan 1842

COOLEY, Joseph of Howard Co. died 3 April.   MIN 14 Apr 1826

COOLY, Mark (Mack?) -- Chariton Co. Letters of administration by Pub. Adm. 23 Sep.   BRUNS 28 Oct 1847

COOLEY, William D. died at Independence 15 December.   JEM 21 Dec 1847

COOLIDGE, Dr. ____ sentenced to hang for murder of Mr. Matthews at Augusta MO.   MORE 7 Apr 1848

COONS, David died Saturday last, several years a resident.   MORE 3 Jan 1842

COONS, Nicholas, in Dardenne Twp., injured and died after fall from a horse on 1 September.   STCHMO 5 Sep '21

COOPER, Benjamin Sr., at Cooper's Bottom, age 59.   BRUNS 19 May 1849

COOPER, Braxton killed by Indians "a few days since" in the Boone's Lick area.	MORE 29 Oct 1814
COOPER, Dulaney F. of Howard Co. died at Mobile recently of cholera.	BRUNS 21 Apr 1849
COOPER, John of Howard Co. died Wednesday last in his 63rd year.	MODE 12 Aug 1846
COOPER, John R., mate of the Champlain, died of paralysis at the hospital, age about 31. Formerly of Marietta OH.	MORE 5 Jan 1844
COOPER, William Esq. died at Sulphur Springs in Jefferson Co. 18 August in his 57th year.	SLDU 22 Aug 1846
COOTE, George Thomas died 17 August at the residence of James Barry in 26th year. Formerly of Washington City.	MORE 21 Aug 1847
COPENHAVER, Martin -- St. Clair Co. Final settlement by Thos. Copenhaver.	OSIN 8 Jan 1853
CORCORAN, John died 16 Sept. at his residence near the US Arsenal. An old resident.	MORE 21 Sep 1848
CORDELL, Presley T. died at St. Louis 3 Aug. in 23rd year. Attorney at Jefferson City.	BRUNS 16 Aug 1849
CORLEY, Joseph, native of Bordeaux, France died 14 April age 57. Funeral from "North Star" on Broadway.	MORE 15 Apr 1853
CORN, Joseph H., sugar manufacturer at Hannibal, found dead there. Coroner's verdict, intemperance.	BOLT 6 Sep 1845
CORNELIUS, Abner died at the home of his son-in-law, Lewis Collier, near Huntsville. Age 77.	BRUNS 21 Oct 1847
CORNFORTH, William P. died in St. Charles 14 June age 24y 11m 9d. Formerly of St. Louis.	SWERE 26 June 1848
CORNWELL, George, of the firm of Tunis & Cornwall, died Thursday last.	MORE 16 Oct 1832
CORR, Charles D. of Johnson Co. died 24 January in his 47th year.	MORE 27 Feb 1851
CORREL, Burdine died in Bowling Green Saturday last.	BGBD 17 May 1845
CORUM, Herod died 26 October at Franklin.	MIN 11 Nov 1820
CORUM, James died 19 Sept. at the residence of his father age 21y 8m 20d.	WEM 26 Sep 1839
CORWIN, George died suddenly Friday 10 August.	MORE 13 Aug 1838
COSBY, William D. died in Santa Fe about 25 April, in his 24th year. Volunteer from Ste. Genevieve Co.	MORE 24 June 1847
COSNER, Peter (of St. Louis?) believed to have been a native of NC or SC, died in the Rocky Mountains.	MORE 30 Sep 1834
COSSIT, Ephraditus S. died in Shelbyville 7 November in his 22nd year. Methodist.	PWH 20 Nov 1841

COTTER, William age 36. Funeral from residence of J.T. McClelland. In 36th year, native of New York. Interred Bellefontaine.	MORE 22 Apr 1851
COTTERAL, John M. died Tuesday.	MORE 4 Sep 1822
COTTON, Henry F. died 20 May age about 20.	OSIN 28 May 1853
COULTE, J. D. died 22 September, of the *Oregon* and late of Cincinnati.	BEA 23 Sep 1829
COUPLAND, William cut his throat Saturday last near Camp Springs. A bookkeeper, Stettinius & January.	MORE 28 Apr 1840
COUPLAND, William J. of St. Louis died at the residence of his uncle Col. Manly Dixon in Upper Canada. Accidental discharge of gun. Age 21.	MORE 6 May 1841
COURET, Jean Bertrand, died in July, native of the north of France, baker by trade.	MORE 22 Aug 1825
COURSALLE, F., with three others, killed by Indians at Cote sans Dessein.	MORE 29 Apr 1815
COUSIN, Bartholomew Esq. died, lately of Cape Girardeau, an old and respected inhabitant of this state.	MORE 23 Feb 1824
COUTTS, Charles died in St. Louis 13 November. Native of Scotland, master stonecutter. Resided on Almond St. Interred Catholic cemetery.	MORE 14 Nov 1840
COWAN, Campbell G. died in Lawrence Co. 2 March, aged and respected.	SPAD 7 Mar 1846
COWAN, George R. -- St. Clair Co. Administrator's sale by Publ. Adm.	OSIN 21 May 1853
COWAN, Lieut. Stephen late of the US Army died 11 May.	MORE 13 May 1828
COWHERD, Charles A.) Montgomery Co. Final settlements William R.) by John Baker.	FULT 30 Mar 1849
COWIE, William of St. Louis died 13 December.	MORE 20 Dec 1827
COX, Charles of Lafayette Co. died of cholera 25 June at Ft. Laramie, age 19.	MORE 7 Oct 1850
COX, Jackson of Cape Girardeau Co. died at Scott's Bluff 28 June age 29.	MORE 7 Oct 1850
COX, George B. -- Wright Co. Letters of administration to Samuel H. Barnett, 26 August.	SPAD 3 Sep 1844
COX, Horatio -- Montgomery Co. Final settlement by William S. Cox.	MORE 11 Aug 1837
COX, Isaac (with wife and four children) drowned in a terrible storm that covered parts of Johnson, Van Buren and Jackson Cos. "Saturday the 6th"	LEXP May 1844
COX, James Sr. died in Clinton 7 Aug. age about 60.	PWH 27 Aug 1846
COX, Moses died in Fredericktown 6 June in his 50th year. Left wife and daughter.	MORE 18 June 1833

COX, Thomas drowned off the St. Louis Oak. English.   COMB 16 Dec 1847
    A deckhand.

COX, Thomas W. -- Montgomery Co. Letters of administration   BGRAD 15 Apr 1843
    to Ann & W.E. Cox, 8 March.

COX, Col. William M., merchant of Osceola, died 12 July   COMB 2 Aug 1847
    age about 44.

COYLE, Benjamin -- John & Jeff Gibson sought for his murder.   JINQ 17 Nov 1841

COZENS, Horatio Esq. died in St. Louis last Friday.   MORE 20 July 1826

CRADDOCK, Major John C. died at the residence of his   MORE 23 Sep 1843
    father in Madison Co. 10 Sept. age 29.

CRAIG, Capt. _____ killed by Indians at the lower   MORE 27 May 1815
    Cuivre Ferry, near Fort Howard.

CRANE, Col. Aaron T., late postmaster, died 26 September.   MORE 29 Sep 1819
    Buried with Masonic honors.

CRANE, Tarlton L. died 5 June leaving a large family.   PWH 14 June 1849
    Born in VA 1781, emigrated to MO 13 years ago.

CRAVENS, _____ son of Dr., struck by lightning and killed   BRUNS 8 June 1848
    "Sunday week."

CRAVENS, Charles, Co. M, Col. Price's Reg., died 3 Nov.   MODE 13 Jan 1847
    at Santa Fe.

CRAWFORD, John W. died at Portage des Sioux 20 April.   MORE 29 Apr 1841
    Formerly of KY. Louisville please copy.

CRAWFORD, Redford died at Major Delaunay's boarding   MORE 13 June 1811
    house Tuesday. Indian trader from Canada.

CRAWLEY, James died in the hospital age 35. In St. Louis   MORE 20 June 1840
    5 years, before that in Boston. Irish.

CREASY, L.V. died at the Virginia Hotel, lately of   MORE 29 Jan 1842
    Louisville KY. Lynchburg VA please copy.

CREAL, Burton, age 15, died 20 April in St. Joseph.   STGAZ 14 May 1847

CRENSHAW, William "aged and highly esteemed" died 25 Sept.   SPAD 27 Sep 1845

CREWS, Andrew died 30 October.   MODE 11 Nov 1846

CREWS, Milton died Sunday in his 41st year. Formerly of   BOLT 23 Aug 1845
    Madison Co. KY.

CRIGLER, Richard died in Chariton Twp, Howard Co., 27 Aug.   MIN 30 Aug 1827

CRISSWELL,___(Robert?) "formerly residing at the mouth of   MORE 22 Nov 1817
    the Missouri, drowned during the late gales."

CRITTENDEN, John died in St. Louis 10 Oct. Formerly of KY.   MORE 6 Oct 1840

CROCKER, James P., formerly of New York, died 16 Sept.   MORE 18 Sep 1837
    in St. Louis.

CROCKER, John died "lately of St. Louis."   MORE 14 Apr 1829

CROCKER, Seth, oldest son of Deacon Josiah, died 23 Oct.   MORE 26 Oct 1826
    in Lebanon IL age 30. Fell from a horse.

CROMWELL, John a native of Maryland died 28 August at White Haven Farm on the Gravois near St. L.	SLINQ 1 Sep 1821
CRONK, Andrew found dead in bed 14 Sept. Cause believed to be apoplexy.	MORE 16 Sep 1844
CROSS, William B., eldest son of Anderson, died 24 Feb. of typhoid age 21y 6m 17d.	HIM 8 Mar 1855
CROSS, Horatio N. of St. Louis died Sunday.	MORE 19 Apr 1836
CROSSLAND, A.V. died 2 March at the home of Joel Atkinson. A tailor. Parents believed in Indiana.	PWH 12 Aug 1843
CROSTHWAITE, Thomas "aged and respectable" died in the vicinity of Columbia 9 Sept.	MIN 18 Sep 1830
CROUSE, Daniel died, formerly of Baltimore.	MORE 23 June 1851
CROW, Thomas, engineer of the <u>Oceana</u>; funeral from Franklin House to Methodist cemetery.	MORE 8 Sep 1843
CROWL, Alexander died Saturday evening last age 39.	MORE 11 Dec 1838
CROWTHER, James B., "a young man of respectable connections in this community" died in Sacramento 16 Nov.	BOBS 18 Mar 1851
CROXTON, Ely killed in St. Louis 23 June when a cart ran over him.	MORP 27 June 1845
CRUFT, Edward, late member of the Bar; Circuit Court adjourned in his honor.	MORE 24 Apr 1846
CRUMPACKER, John of Missouri killed in Roanoke Co. VA by fall from horse.	GLWT 7 Apr 1853
CRUTGENTON, George W. of Dallas Co. died 10 June 6 mi. west of Ft. Kearney, age 30.	MORE 7 Oct 1850
CRUXTON, __, a young man, fell between wagon and horses while loading wood. (See CROXTON, Ely)	MORE 27 June 1845
CUBBERLY, Thomas W. died Wednesday in his 32nd year. Trenton NJ please copy.	MORE 7 Oct 1842
CULBERTSON, Andrew M. drowned at Osceola.	STGAZ 15 Dec 1852
CULBERTSON, James died when a cart upset Monday. "Aged."	SALT 11 July 1840
CULP, Price -- Gentry Co. Final settlement by Martha Culp exr.	STGAZ 27 Jan 1854
CULTON, Hugh W. died in Barry Co. August 20. Athens TN please copy.	SPAD 30 Aug 1845
CULVER, Dr. H. of Washington Co. died in New Orleans 16 Mar.	MORE 26 Mar 1849
CUMMINS, Benjamin -- Chariton Co. Publ. administrator took over 2 Nov. 1847.	BRUNS 26 Jan 1848
CUMMINS, Charles Kavanagh, son of Maj. Richard, died at West Port, Jackson Co. 25 May age 28y 6m 27d. Widow and 5 children.	MORE 4 June 1849
CUMMINS, James formerly of KY died in his 70th year. Father-in-law of Henry Maxwell. Louisville <u>Journal</u> please copy.	MORE 17 May 1849

CUMMINS, James A. Jr. died 20 July age 23. Funeral from   MORE 21 July 1845
    residence of his father, #28 S. 8th St.
    Interment Methodist cemetery.

CUMMINGS, Luther died 28 July. Formerly of Augusta GA, in   MORE 9 Aug 1841
    his 52nd year.

CUNIFFE, James Joseph, resident of St. Louis, died in New   MORE 25 Nov 1844
    Orleans 26 October of yellow fever, age 21.

CUNIFFE, Jerome O'Connel, native of Ireland, died 28 May   MORE 29 May 1848
    at the residence of his mother, 6th & Wash.

CUNNINGHAM, ____, a one-armed man, froze to death two   BRUNS 24 Feb 1849
    weeks ago while intoxicated.

CUNNINGHAM, James A. died in St. Louis 4 August age   MORE 5 Aug 1848
    about 18. Parents reside in Lebanon IL.

CUNNINGHAM, Thomas age 52y 11m 20d died in Pike Co. 19 Mar.   BGDB 19 Apr 1845

CUPP, Silas -- Chariton Co. Final settlement by Thos. Alford. BRUNS 30 Aug '49

CURD, Dr. Isaac, formerly of Fulton, died at St. Joseph   MORE 24 June 1850
    in his 67th year.

CURLE, Richmond I. died yesterday, age 50.   SWERE 30 Apr 1849

CURRAN, Thomas Esq., clerk of the Circuit Court of   MORE 6 Apr 1826
    Independence Co., Ark. Terr., died 31 Mar.

CURRY, Henry died in St. Louis 25 Jan. age 35. Formerly   MORE 27 Jan 1842
    of Orange Co. NY. NY papers please copy.

CURTIS, Cyrus of Liberty, Clay Co., died 8 June. Resident   MORE 22 June 1844
    of MO for 32 years.

CURTIS, Edmund D. died of congestive fever 5 September.   PWH 11 Sep 1841

CURTIS, John A., youngest son of Mrs. Maria, died 31 Aug.   MORE 3 Sep 1853
    age 19y 5m.

CURTIS, William H. of Moniteau Co. died in St. Joseph   STGAZ - Sep 1847
    "yesterday."

CUSHING, Albert died last evening at the residence of   MORE 20 July 1838
    John Torode in 23rd year. Formerly of
    Sciutate, MA.

CUTBERTH, ____, a teamster died in the Santa Fe country.   MODE 13 Jan 1847

CUTLER, William, engineer on the Rowena, died 16 May.   SWERE 17 May 1847

CUTTING, Edward of St. Louis died in Jefferson City 4 Feb.   MORE 13 Feb 1845

DALE, George W., printer at Rocheport, Boone Co., died in   BOLT 29 Mar 1845
    New Orleans 6 March.

DALY, Lawrence J. died in Fayette 4 March in his 84th   BOLT 9 Mar 1844
    year. Citizen many years, a Mason.

DAILY, Maurice died Monday last.   MORE 15 Sep 1819

DAILEY, Michael drowned, deckhand on the Clermont No. 2.   MORE 21 Dec 1846

DALE, Col. Jesse B., formerly of Rocheport, died on the   BRUNS 18 Nov 1847
    Arkansas River on the way to Santa Fe.

DALES, John, late cashier of the Bank of Missouri, died on Sunday last.	MORE 22 Sep 1819
DALE, Thomas, a native of England, drowned 5 June age 36.	MORE 6 June 1853
DALLAM, J. Middlemore died in Baltimore 19 October in his 62nd year.	MORE 23 Oct 1846
DALLAS, Alexander James died at Philadelphia.	MORE 13 Feb 1817
DAMERON, Benjamin died 25 March in Randolph Co. in his 50th year.	BOLT 1 Apr 1843
DAMERON, George B. died in Randolph Co. 20 November in his 78th year.	MODE 4 Dec 1848
DAMERON, John Sr. of Huntsville died in CA in August.	GLWT 9 Oct 1851
DAMERON, Joseph C., P.M., at Huntsville of fever, age about 45.	MODE 7 Oct 1845
DANGEN, Antoine died in St. Louis 11 April, "an old and respectable inhabitant."	MORE 12 Apr 1827
DANGEN, John Joseph, son of John P., died in St. Louis County a few days ago.	SLINQ 18 Aug 1821
DANIELS, Col. Samuel died 13th April age 38. Many years a resident.	MORP 24 Apr 1845
DANLEY, Caleb -- Wayne Co. Letters of administration to Catharine Danley 11 March.	INP Mar 1826
DARLINGTON, Thomas died yesterday.	MORE 28 Jan 1853
DARNEAL, Dr. W. S. died in Weston 21 Dec. age about 36.	KCEN 3 Jan 1857
DA ROCHER, Auguste died age 70. Resided Green betw 6-7.	MORE 8 Nov 1847
DARST, John died yesterday after a short illness. Funeral from his residence on Walnut St.	MORE 12 Dec 1835
DAUGHERTY, Patrick died 13 May, age 63, native of Ireland.	SOV 18 May 1833
DAVAULT, Henry -- Montgomery Co. Letters of administration to Peter Davault 25 April.	FULT 1 June 1849
DAVID, H.F. of Ray Co. died near Chimney Rock on 17 June. Left wife, 2 children.	MORE 7 Oct 1850
DAVIDSON, Jesse died a few days ago at the residence of of his brother in Montgomery Co.	SWERE 19 Fb 1849
DAVIS, Andrew J. killed by W.P. Darnes in an "affray."	MORE 8 June 1840
DAVIS, Benjamin of Howard Co. died Monday last.	BOLT 8 Feb 1845
DAVIS, D.R. died of cholera at Galena Wednesday last.	MORE 10 May 1833
DAVIS, Edward died in Howard Co. 5 April in his 70th year. One of the earliest settlers. "Left a large circle of friends and acquaintances."	BOLT 13 Apr 1844
DAVIS, Elijah murdered in Green Co. John Shanks accused of the crime, escaped jail. (MORE 21 April says he was from Smith Co. TN and was murdered near Springfield MO.)	JINQ 8 July 1841

DAVIS, Rev. Ephraim died in Lincoln Co. 10 October in his (60th?) year. Formerly of Shelby Co. KY, a Calvinistic Baptist minister for 42 years.   MORE 21 Oct 1851

DAVIS, Maj. James died 30 January age 77y 4m 15d. Native of Virginia.   BGRAD 26 Mar 1842

DAVIS, James H. died 9 January in his 39th year -- husband, father. Lost 3 brothers in past 18 months.   BGRAD 20 Jan 1844

DAVIS, James H. of Randolph Co. died in the Santa Fe area 23 Nov. 1846.   MODE 17 Feb 1846

DAVIS, John, Member of the St. Louis Bar, died 20 Sept. at Northborough MA in his 30th year.   SWERE 14 Oct 1844

DAVIS, Joshua -- Dallas Co. Letters of administration to Milton Davis, 6 May.   SPAD 12 July 1845

DAVIS, Major, funeral to be preached by Elder T.P. Green of the Baptist Church on 4th Sunday in Nov.   INP 8 Nov 1826

DAVIS, Robert M., son of Col. Peter I., formerly of Carroll Co., died near Far West on 4 May. Family en route to CA.   BRUNS 25 May 1848

DAVIS, Albis Barty, eldest son of Col. Samuel, died near Troy, age about 21.   BGRAD 7 Dec 1844

DAVIS, Samuel W. died at Campbell's Mill on the Sac River in Polk Co. Son of Jesse of Saline Co.   WEM 18 Apr 1839

DAVIS, Silas -- Montgomery Co. Final settlement by C. A. (?) Davis   FULT 6 July 1849

DAVIS, Thomas A. of Howard Co. died 21 Nov. in his (28th or 26th) year.   BOLT 25 Nov 1843

DAVIS, Thomas, formerly of Amherst Co. VA, died at Valle's Mines, Jefferson Co., 17 October.   MORE 13 Nov 1832

DAVIS, Thomas J. died near Canton 9th August.   PWH 10 Aug 1848

DAVIS, Tyree -- Chariton Co. John W. Frame administrator.   BRUNS 27 Sep 1849

DAVIS, Thompson H. -- Montgomery Co. Final settlement by Dickerson Davis.   FULT 22 Sep 1848

DAVIS, W. Barton died in Canton 1 July.   CANE 12 July 1855

DAVIS, William H. -- Chariton Co. Letters of administration to John M. Duncan d.b.n. 1 March.   BRUNS 30 Mar '48

DAVIS, William Henry esq., attorney (probably same as above) died 20 June in Keytesville. Formerly of Nelson Co. KY. Came to Howard Co. at age of 8, to Keytesville at age 24.   MORE 4 July 1845

DAVIS, Wilson -- Chariton Co. Final settlement by James D. Fowler.   WEM 15 Mar 1836

DAWSON, Robert died near New Madrid 6 April in his 52nd year. Formerly of Montgomery Co. MD. Came to MO in 1812.   MORE 5 May 1843

DAWSON, William S., medical student, died 16 July.   JINQ 15 July '41

DAY, Charles died 24 January age 65. Native of Strasburg,   MORE 25 Jan 1852
     interred St. Vincent's cemetery.

DAY, Frederick M. of St. Louis, formerly of Hartford CT,   MORE 27 July 1839
     died at the Lightner & Bemis Mills in Illinois
     17 July. Interred Cape Girardeau. Pittsburg
     and Hartford, please copy.

DAY, William committed suicide in Wayne Co. Left wife and   STEGPD 8 Oct 1853
     two children.

DEAN, James died Friday 4 January, late Capt. US Infantry,   MORE 7 Jan 1839
     veteran of War of 1812.

DEAN, Robert "an old and respected citizen" died last   PWH 18 Feb 1843
     night. Methodist.

DEASON (DEASHAN), John, killed by Indians.   MORE 18 Mar 1815

DEATHERAGE, Amos, old and respected citizen, died yesterday. BOLT 26 Sep 1840

DEAVER, George E., age 27, formerly of Virginia, died   MORE 13 Oct 1847
     10 October. Charleston & Martinsburgh pls copy.

DEAVER, Larkin died in Baltimore 21 March of hemorrhage   MORE 22 Mar 1851
     of the lungs. Age 56.

DeBOIS, C., St. Louis merchant, died in New York 25 Feb.   MORE 26 Feb 1852

DEEGAN, Daniel died 2 Sept. of bilious fever in 42nd year.   MORE 5 Sep 1853

DEEGAN, Martin died 30 June in his 28th year.   MORE 1 July 1851

DEJARNETT, Joseph died in Audrain Co. three weeks after   MORE 1 Apr 1851
     his return from CA. Age 35.

DELANEY, Dr. D. of St. Louis died 28 May at Havre, France   MORE 12 Aug 1845
     age 37.

DELAURIERE, Charles Fremon died 8 October age 72.   MORE 9 Oct 1846

DELAURIERE, Auguste Fremon died 16 November age 43.   MORE 17 Nov 1851

DELLINGER, Dr. ___ shot by Edward H. Horrell, Waynesville,   SWERE 19 Aug 1848
     for slander, some weeks ago.

DELONGE, Elias, many years a pilot, died yesterday.   MORE 13 Nov 1843
     Interred Methodist cemetery.

DELVILLE, Pierre killed near Florissant by a runaway   MORE 11 Oct 1848
     horse and wagon.

DE MUN, Julius Esq., clerk of the Co. Court, died 15 Aug.   MORE 17 Aug 1843
     Funeral from residence of son-in-law Edw. Walsh.

DENNIS, William Sr. -- Taney Co. Letters of administration   SPAD 15 Oct 1844
     to Wm. Dennis Jr., exr, 14 September.

DENNISON, James age 25 died 26 May.   MORE 27 May 1852

DENNEY, Alexander died at his residence in Polk Co. 17 Aug. SPAD 23 Aug 1845

DENNY, George son of Samuel & Elizabeth died 1 May   MORE 2 May 1853
     age 23y 5m.

DENNY, Charles of St. Charles Co. died "Friday last." His   MORE 11 Jan 1844
     wife had died a few weeks previously.

45

DEPESTRE, Col. died at Ste. Genevieve "a few days ago." MORE 19 Oct 1816
DE GUIRE, Michael died 22 February at Fredericktown. MORE 13 Mar 1839
DERBY, Horatio N., son of Edward & Mary (Powers) died MORE 4 Aug 1840
    2 August age 19.
DeROSSE, Augustine died age 54. Buried Rock Springs. MORE 20 June 1852
DESHAZER, John -- DeKalb Co. Letters of administration STGAZ 17 Aug 1853
    to John Deshazer Jr. 1 August.
DETAILLE, Peter died 8 May age 31y 6m 15d. MORE 9 May 1853
DETCHEMENDY, Clement Jules son of Maj. C.C. died in MORP 28 Aug 1845
    Ste. Genevieve 25 August.
DETCHEMENDY, Pascal S. died near Old Mines, Washington Co. MORE 13 Sep 1844
    on 4 Sept. in his 82nd year.
DEVERS, Merit -- Gentry Co. Final settlement by STGAZ 25 Aug 1852
    John P. Devers.
DEVOL, Hiram died in Crawford Co. 28 March in his 37th MORE 7 June 1849
    year. Formerly of Morgan Co. OH.
DEWARD, Charles died 26 October of typhus. MORE 28 Oct 1841
DHRO, Casper E., died 27 July age 46; native of France. COMB 30 July 1846
    "Husband and father."
DICKEY, Jamison -- Bates Co. Petition to divide real est. OSIN 18 Jan 1851
    Names heirs.
DICKINSON, Maj. Obadiah died 31 August. PWH 25 Dec 1845
DICKINSON, David -- Montgomery Co. Final settlement by FULT 28 Sep 1849
    David J. Talbot.
DIEZ, William died in St. Louis last Friday from testing BRUNS 10 Feb 1848
    oil of bitter almond (Prussia acid) for
    its strength by tasting it.
DILL, Solomon of St. Joseph died 20 June en route to CA. MORE 5 Sep 1850
DILLON, Col. Patrick M. died 20 January age 67. MORE 21 Jan 1851
DILLON, Robert -- Montgomery Co. Letters of administration JEFRE 2 May 1835
    to Jacob Groom 2 May 1835.
DINN, Walter, of Dinn & Grubb, died yesterday. MORE 23 Oct 1843
DINNING, John D. -- Taney Co. Letters of administration SPAD 25 Oct 1845
    to James Stallcup 27 September.
DISMUKE, Maj. Joseph, age 71, died at Bowling Green, Pike MORE 6 Sep 1844
DISMUKES   Co. Emigrated about 12 years ago from
    Mercer Co. KY.
DIXON, Thomas B. of Cole Co. died Saturday. JINQ 5 Oct 1843
DIXON, William, a stonemason, died 23 April age about 45. SWERE 30 Apr 1849
DOANE, Harvey died in Potosi 6 May age (40?)y 8m 25d. MORE 19 May 1852
DOBYNS, J. Milton son of Maj. E. and Anna died age 25. MORE 26 Feb 1851
DODD, Richard, a city policeman, died Saturday. SWERE 30 Aug 1847

DODGE, Jacob -- Putnam Co. Letters of administration to Thomas Hargrave.	CANE 16 Nov 1854
DOLAN, Hugh died 24 September age 27.	MORE 25 Sep 1851
DONALDSON, James died of consumption Wednesday last. Interred with Masonic honors.	MIN 1 Oct 1822
DONALDSON, Thomas Lyon died at the residence of his brother Dr. A.C., 5th between Wash & Carr. Age 25.	MORE 30 Nov 1848
DONIPHAN, __ son of Col. A.W. of Clay Co. took a dose of corrosive sublimate by mistake and died.	SASE 21 May 1853
DONNELL, Rev. James died at his residence one mile west of Rush Tower, Jefferson Co. 6 March. Twin brother to Thomas, decd. Presbyterian minister, Washington Co. Nashville please copy.	MORE 18 Mar 1845
DONNELL, Rev. Thomas died 8 February in Washington Co. in his 57th year. Born NC, later in Tennessee. Presbyterian.	MORE 16 Feb 1843
DONELLAN, Patrick died in Mobile 27 January, will be returned to St. Louis for burial.	MORE 31 Jan 1851
DONOHUE, Alonzo H. died at Moro, Santa Fe, in January.	MODE 31 Mar 1847
DONOHOE, Thomas, son of Stephen of Howard Co., died in Sacramento 11 August.	MORE 9 Oct 1851
DONNALLY, Charles of Co. Tyrone died 1 December in his 32nd year. Lived at 92 Mulberry St. Interred Presbyterian cemetery.	MORE 2 Dec 1844
DONOVAN, Alfred, age 29, died of pleurisy 29 March.	STGAZ 2 Apr 1847
DOOLY, Aaron died 8 December at the house of Benjamin Rugels in Washington Co. (Old Mines) Said to have relatives in NJ, either Essex or Sussex Co.	MORE 15 Jan 1838
DOREY, John died yesterday in his 72nd year. Buried Shilo IL.	MORE 5 Sep '48
DORMAN, C.H. of Boonville died on the road near New Franklin, effects of heat and drinking cold water.	MORE 12 Aug 1846
DORR, Joseph died at Belle Fontaine on the Missouri.	MORE 21 Dec 1808
DORSEY, ____ shot by McMillan in an affray in Saline Co. about 6 miles north of Marshall.	BRUNS 24 Feb 1848
DOUBERMAN, John C. died in St. Louis Saturday last.	MORE 5 May 1835
DOUGHERTY, Alfred died 26 May, resident of St. Louis Co. and formerly of Mason Co. KY.	MORE 6 Apr 1848
DOUGHERTY, Daniel -- Montgomery Co. Final settlement by Jacob Groom.	JEFF 19 May 1827
DOUGHERTY, James, a useful citizen, died Saturday last.	MORE 9 Oct 1818
DOUGHERTY, Judge Thomas M. murdered by unknown assailant on road between St. Louis and Carondelet.	MORE 16 July 1838
DOUGHTY, Nathan B. Esq. died 20 March. Funeral from Paul House to Presbyterian cemetery.	MORE 21 Mar 1843

DOUGHTY, James W. age 35 died 18 March in New Orleans.   MORE 20 Mar 1851

DOUGLASS, Francis N. of Howard Co. died in Santa Fe 7 Apr.   MODE 13 June 1848

DOUGLASS, James Sr. died 1 January in his 83rd year.   BOLT 11 Jan 1845

DOUGLAS, William died 27 Dec. 1851 age 63.   STCDE 10 Jan 1852

DOW, David Coffin died yesterday age 21. Formerly of NH, came to St. Louis 6 years ago. Funeral from L.B. Shaw home, corner Walnut & 4th.   MORE 22 Oct 1838

DOWLING, Patrick died yesterday.   BEA 1 Mar 1832

DOWNING, James died in Lincoln Co. 2 August in his 56th year. Left wife and large family.   BGRAD 5 Aug 1843

DOXEY, John of Bowling Green Prairie, Chariton Co., died Saturday last. Age more than 60 and one of the first settlers.   MODE 1 Dec 1847

DOYER, Henry died age 27y 9m. New York please copy.   MORE 11 Aug 1853

DOYLE, William age about 40 died 22 February. Resided 10th and Market.   MORE 23 Feb 1853

DOYLE, James died yesterday age 20. Funeral from residence of Mr. Layton, Elm between 2nd and 3rd.   MORE 27 Feb 1843

DRAKE, Robert, a Frenchman, died at the home of Joseph Christenson in Waynesville, Pulaski Co., on 26 July. Before his death he stated that he had children in St. Louis.   MORE 19 Aug 1837

DRAPER, Henry C. died in Ashley 5 March. (MORE 11 March says he died of "black tongue" -- apparently an epidemic -- and was about 42)   BGRAD 9 Mar 1844

DROWN, Charles, engineer of the Chicago, was shot in Peoria by J.C. Smith, a runner for a hotel, and subsequently died.   MORE 18 Sep 1844

DROWN, Capt. Philip, for 15 years engineer and commander of steamboats on the Missouri, Mississippi, and southern rivers, age 37. Cincinnati please copy.   MORE 23 Sep 1843

DRUMMOND, Horatio N. died at the residence of Mrs. Sarah Drummond 8 June in his 25th year.   LEXP 28 June 1854

DRUMMOND, Rev. Thomas of the M.E. Church died yesterday of cholera.   MORE 16 June 1835

DRURY, Lawson -- Montgomery Co. Letters of administration to Charles J. Drury.   MORE 30 Sep 1836

DUBAY, Mr. ___ died "Tuesday morning last" in a melancholy accident, not described; the ferryman and two assistants, taken from the wreck, died on shore.   MORE 16 Nov 1816

DUBKINS, Jacob said to have been murdered by Robert Turk on 7 March 1843.   JINQ 15 May 1845

DuBREUIL, Charles B. died 7 January in his 26th year. Funeral from residence of his brother Lewis, Spruce & 2nd. Catholic cemetery.   MORE 8 Jan 1844

Du BRESSE, ___ killed at Warrenton 17th March by _ Keating.	MORE 10 Apr 1844
DUCATE, Baptiste killed 25 December 1842 by his father-in-law, an IowaIndian named Burnt Kettle.	MORE 19 Apr 1843
DUCHOQUETTE, Baptiste died Wednesday 10 July(?)	MORE 9 July 1833
DUCHOQUETTE, Henry died at the residence of L. Bompart yesterday age 78y 4m 19d.	MORE 22 May 1837
DUDLEY, L.A. -- Montgomery Co. Letters of administration to Lewis Castleman, 14 November.	BEA 24 Nov 1831
DUDLEY, Parker died in Palmyra 15 September. Native of Fayette Co. KY. Left wife, 4 children.	MORE 19 Sep 1853
DUDLEY, Dr. Simeon A. -- Montgomery Co. Letters of Administration to Alfred W. Carr.	MORE 25 Nov 1828
DUDMAN, Thomas died 26 February.	SWERE 1 Mar 1847
DUFF, John M., a soldier of Capt. David Musick's Co. of US Rangers, died at Fort Madison of wounds received in a skirmish with Winnebagoes. Buried in St. Louis on 10 July.	MORE 24 July 1813
DUFF, Alexander died at the residence of Kenneth McKenzie Saturday, age about 35. Native of Aberdeenshire, Scotland.	SWERE 15 July 1844
DULANEY, William G. died in Monroe Co. 14 May, age about 36. Left a large family.	BOLT 30 May 1846
DUMME, DUMEY, Isaac died of cholera.	BRUNS 24 May 1849
DuMONT, Charles, funeral to be held from St. Francis Xavier Church.	MORE 2 Dec 1843
DUNCAN, Robert, brother of Coleman, died in St. Louis 11 February after falling from a horse. Age 54.	MORE 19 Feb 1842
DUNCAN, John executed at St. Michaels, Madison Co., for the murder of J.B. Stephens, wife and two children on 13 December 1820. He was born in Albemarle Co. VA, and left a father in Sumner Co., TN.	MIN 4 June 1821
DUNCAN, Mason died of cholera in Palmyra.	MORE 28 June 1833
DUNCAN, Thomas C. (G?) Esq. died yesterday age 47. Formerly of Philadelphia. Resided on St. Charles St. between 4th-5th. Interred Methodist cemetery.	SWERE 14 May 1849
DUNCAN, Elder William died 9 October. Minister of Baptist Church at Huntsville, a minister nearly 50 years, left widow Sally and family.	MODE 21 Oct 1846 " 9 Dec 1846
DUNCAN, William, father of John M., recently of the Brunswicker office, died on Mussel Fork Tuesday.	BRUNS 24 June 1848
DUNCAN, William F., attorney, died in St. Louis Thursday.	MORE 30 July 1833
DUNDRIGAN, Michael, an Irishman, was kicked overboard the Ellen Douglas 19 October (about 20 mi. above the mouth of the Ohio) and was killed.	MORE 12 Nov 1838

49

DUNHAM, Harris B., late of St. Louis and formerly of MA, died 22 September in Yuba, CA.   MORE 26 Nov 1851

DUNKEL, ___ died in a fire at Patrick McDonald's residence which was used as a grocery store. He had been a physician from Baltimore. Drunk and deranged.   MORE 17 Mar 1834

DUNKLIN, Daniel, former governor, died in Jefferson Co.   SWERE 29 July 1845

DUNLAP, David, died 29 June at Portland, of cholera.   FULT 6 July 1849

DUNLAVY, Richard died Saturday.   MORE 16 July 1833

DUNLAP, Robert, died at the home of his daughter Mrs. Craghead on 26 September. Born Ireland 26 Feb. 1763, emigrated with father in 1772, came to Callaway Co. in 1818.   FULT 6 Oct 1848

DUNN, Robinson died 30 July in his 38th year. Formerly of Baltimore.   MORE 1 Aug 1851

DUNNICA, Granville T. died in Glasgow 1 Sept. age 26.   JEFRE 5 Sep 1840

DUNNICA, Col. William H. died 28 April at Cote sans Dessein leaving widow & 5 infant children.   STCHMO 23 May 1822

DURINGERS, ___ deck passenger on the *Princess* drowned near Prophet's Island.   MORE 21 June 1847

DUSKINS, ___ of Grundy Co. died of cholera 23 June at Fort Laramie age 35.   MORE 7 Oct 1850

DUTZCHKY, Charles C., a tribute to him (at his death) by the Masonic Lodge.   STGAZ 19 Apr 1854

DUVAL, William died 17 October at the house of Mr. Biggs. Resident of Paynesville, age about 35.   BGRAD 21 Oct 1843

DYE, David, formerly of New York, died age 40.   MORE 4 June 1851

DYER, Jefferson died 6 July at his residence in St. Charles Co. "an old citizen of that county."   MORE 15 July 1848

EADS, Hon. William H. of Brookville, IN died in St. Louis yesterday morning.   MORE 7 Nov 1835

EAGERS, Josiah was killed in a street fight. Joseph Rolof acquitted.   MORE 21 Feb 1849

EARICKSON, Judge James died 10 June at his residence in Howard Co. "old and respected" etc.   BOLT 15 June 1844

EARL, George died in St. Louis 27 September.   MORE 4 Oct 1827

EARVAN, James, native of Ireland, drowned Monday. Employed at Dock Saw Mill. Had resided in Philadelphia and Pittsburgh.   MORE 9 Nov 1839

EAST, James J. of Boonville died in Mexico.   COMB 16 Dec 1847

EASTMAN, Edward E. died 26 September age 20.   MORE 28 Sep 1839

EASTON, Joseph died of fever in St. Louis 31 July, lately from New York, age 50, brother of Col. Rufus.   MORE 2 Aug 1817

EASTON, Col. Rufus died of cholera Saturday evening at St. Charles, several years delegate to Congress.   MORE 7 July 1834

EASTWOOD, Elijah, was murdered at the headwaters of the Gasconade; three Osage charged.	MORE 28 May 1814
EBERLEIN, Theodore S. of St. Louis died 25 March at Steubenville OH.	SWERE 2 Apr 1849
EBERTS, Richard died after a short illness age 20.	MORE 3 Feb 1853
ECHOLS, Joseph, about 16, drowned in the Missouri River at Providence.	BRUNS 12 July 1849
ECKERT, William died in St. Charles Thursday last in his 49th year. Born and raised in KY, 25 years in St. Charles Co. Husband, father.	MORE 4 Apr 1846
ECKSTEIN, ___, merchant tailor, formerly of Philadelphia died 14 Sept. (From probate, Jacob.)	MORE 19 Sep 1821
EDDICOTT, Montague formerly of Lexington died in Nevada 18 March age 92 (?).	MORE 3 May 1853
EDDINS, Thomas of Howard Co died 24 January, age nearly 70. From Orange Co. VA in 1831.	BRUNS 3 Feb 1848
EDMISTON, Andrew J. -- Daviess Co. Letters of administration to James Rhea, Jonathan Jordan 4 Nov.	LEXP 12 Nov 1844
EDMONDS, John, fireman on the Car of Commerce.	MORE 27 May 1828
EDRINGTON, William H., a printer, late of St. Louis, died at Troy MO 19 May age 22.	MORE 24 May 1836
EDWARDS, James G. of St. Charles Co. committed suicide age 35. (Probably insanity.)	MORE 6 Apr 1847
EDWARDS, John died 18 June near Jefferson City, age ca 60.	JEFRE 27 June 1835
EDWARDS, Oliver -- Dallas Co. Letters of administration to William B. Edwards 15 December.	SPAD 27 Dec 1845
EDWARDS, William S. died in Saline Co. 21 May in his 34th year leaving wife and infant son.	MIN 27 May 1823
ELAM, Chesterfield S. died Friday last.	MORE 15 July 1834
ELKINS, Thomas -- St. Clair Co. Letters of administration to Elizabeth Elkins 28 March.	OSIN 16 Apr 1853
ELLETT, Hon. W. R. died 17 March in Franklin Co., late senator from Franklin District. 10 children. (MORE 22 March says Elletle, Gen. Wm. R.)	JEFRE 16 Mar 1844
ELLINGTON, John died in St. Louis Co. 10 November age 63.	MORE 11 Nov 1844
ELLIOTT, Dr. Aaron died at Ste. Genevieve 5 August age 53. Formerly of Connecticut.	MORE 8 Aug 1811
Charles, son of above, died "about 3 weeks ago"	MORE 28 Feb 1811
ELLIOTT, Archibald -- Chariton Co. Final settlement by Mary Elliott.	BOLT 29 Jan 1842
ELLIOTT, Jack executed at Lexington for the murder of a man in Cass Co.	STGAZ 6 Oct 1852
ELLIOTT, James -- Chariton Co. Letters of administration to Martha Elliott.	MIN 17 Oct 1835

ELLIOTT, Reginald H. died age 20y 26d. Son of William P.   MORE 18 Apr 1853
    of Lewistown PA.

ELLIS, Elisha died at Herculaneum 27 March. One of the   MORE 31 Mar 1838
    oldest and most respected citizens of the state.

ELLIS, Jesse, printer late of Canton IL, died 15 August.   MORE 16 Aug 1851

ELLIS, Dr. Samuel, surgeon-dentist, died at New Orleans.   MORE 22 Sep 1829

ELLIS, Robert B. died 11 Sept., native of Tennessee.   PWH 21 Sep 1848

ELLIS, William died at Fredericktown 27 May.   MORE 1 June 1848

ELLISON, Cinatus an orphan age 8 accidentally hung himself. COMB 12 Aug 1847
    He was a son of John Ellison decd. and lived
    with a relative, Green Ellison.

ELLSLEY, _____ murdered at his woodyard near the mouth of   MORE 29 May 1841
    the Missouri, found partly buried. Murdered
    possibly by his partner, not named. Mother
    lives in Alton.

ELY, Joseph died Sunday.   MORE 30 July 1833

EMBREY, D. of Pettis Co. died 16 June 15 mi. east of   MORE 7 Oct 1850
    Ft. Kearney age 27. Cholera. Wife, 2 children.

EMERINE, _____ died of cholera. (From Columbia   BRUNS 24 May 1849
    Statesman.)

EMERSON, John died at Davenport, Iowa Ter., 29 December.   MORE 15 Jan 1844
    Assistant surgeon, US Army.

EMERSON, Francis D. died yesterday, formerly of Vermont.   MORE 28 Aug 1848
    Peoria and Pekin IL please copy.

ENGELKEN, _____ died 11 July, one of the proprietors of   MORP 15 July 1845
    Washington Brewery and Garden.

ENGLE, P. Hill, late Judge of the St. Louis Court of   MORE 19 Feb 1844
    Common Pleas, died Saturday.

ENGLISH, David, disappeared from a steamboat and believed   MORE 27 Feb 1846
    drowned. Thought to have brother John in Detroit.

ENGLISH, John died 29 August, age 68, one of the first   JEFRE 5 Sep 1844
    settlers, Representative many years.
    Emigrated from TN about 1816, served in the   JINQ 26 Sep 1844
    legislature from St. Charles.

EPPERSON, Joel, E. C., and Hiram, all of Boonville, on   COMB 16 Dec 1847
    list of deaths occurring in Mexico.

ESSEX, Thomas, a bookseller in St. Louis, died yesterday.   MORE 13 Dec 1827

ESTES, Coleman died 21 Feb. age 65. Formerly of Albemarle   BGRAD 9 Mar 1844
    Co. VA, in Lincoln Co. 7 or 8 years.

ESTES, Dr. James R. died at his residence in St. Charles Co. MORE 31 Mar 1819
    on 16 March of a pulmonary complaint, left
    widow and two infant children. Age 27.

ESTES, Thomas, of Gay & Estes, died 8 July.   MORE 13 July 1830

ESTES, Samuel died near Louisville, Lincoln Co. 19 Aug.   BGRAD 23 Nov 1844
    "in prime of life." Left family.

ESTES, Spencer-- St. Clair Co. Letters of administration   OSIN 9 July 1853
       to Joseph Montgomery and John Bedell.

ESTILL, ____, son of Col., near Weston, accidentally shot.   BRUNS 1 June 1848
       Third child the family has lost this year.

EUBANK, Achilles, Revolutionary soldier, died at his home   BORE 20 Aug 1844
       south of Boonville on 16 August in his 91st year.
       Born Bedford Co. VA 13 July 1754. After the
       Revolution he moved to KY, then to MO about 1829.

EUBANK, Roger died at the residence of his brother-in-law   MORE 24 June 1847
       Mr. Shurlds in 37th year. Formerly Gloster Co. VA.

EUSTACE, Rev. Thomas died of cholera in his 48th year.   MORE 26 June 1848
       Interred Presbyterian cemetery.

EVANS, Benjamin died Saturday morning last. A Mason.   JINQ 13 Mar 1845

EVANS, Joseph M. recently of Boonville died age 21.   MORE 2 July 1851
       Formerly of Brown Co. OH.

EVINS, Joseph -- DeKalb Co. Letters of administration   PLAR 7 Apr 1848
EVANS   to Samuel S. Halfain
       Final settlement by Samuel Halpain   STGAZ 24 Mar 1852

EVANS, Nathaniel, oldest son of Henry, died last evening   MORE 24 Apr 1840
       age 16.

EVANS, William died on the Big River in St. Francois Co.   MORE 28 Aug 1851
       31 July in his 60th year. Born in Claiborne
       Co. TN. Methodist.

EVERETT, William killed in the sinking of the ferry at   SOV 4 July 1834
       Everett's Ferry near Independence, 16 June.

EVERSOLE, Jacob B. died last evening, many years a   MORE 18 Dec 1845
       resident. Funeral from the residence of his
       son, Morgan between 13th & 14th.

EWIN, Watts D. Esq. died in the Fayette vicinity 3 July.   MODE 15 July 1846

EWING, Capt. Baxter M, son of Rev. Finis of Cooper Co.,   MIN 3 Sep 1822
       died age 19.

EWING, Bertheir B.M. died at the residence of his mother   BRUNS 26 July 1849
       near Keytesville. Student at Georgetown Military,
       Kentucky. Age 18 or 19.

EWING, Rev. Finis died in Lafayette Co. in his 79th year.   BOLT 24 July 1841

EWING, Nathaniel W. died near Keytesville 6 April. Mason.   BRUNS 13 Apr 1848

EWING, Judge Young died 25 Oct. near Lexington, native   LEXP 5 Nov 1844
       of Bedford Co. VA, from early life a resident
       of KY.

FACKLER, Dr. Henry of Union, Franklin Co. died 22 Sept.   MORE 1 Oct 1840
       age 54y 2m.

FAIRFOWL, Stephen died 26 May at Mt. Pleasant, youngest   MORE 30 May 1837
       son of Capt. James and Hannah, formerly
       of Philadelphia.

53

FALKER (FALQUER), _____ a teamster died in the Santa Fe country.   MODE 13 Jan 1847

FALLS, Henry A. died 12 June in his 23rd year. Funeral from residence of his father on Centre St.   MORE 13 June 1849

FANT, George B. died in Femme Osage in his 53rd year.   BGRAD 11 Nov 1843

FARMER, Robert of Marion Co. accidentally shot on way to Santa Fe. In Col. Willock's command.   MODE 13 Jan 1847

FARNHAM, Russell died Tuesday night "of the prevailing illness" (cholera).   MORE 30 Oct 1832

FARR, Bethel S. was killed by Lee D. Walker on 10 Jan. He was 25. Interred Episcopal cemetery.   MORE 11 Jan 1843

FARRAR, Dr. Bernard died in St. Louis 1 July age 65.   BRUNS 12 July 1849

FARRER, R.S. of Franklin Co. died 28 June at Ash Hollow age 35. Left wife and family.   MORE 7 Oct 1850

FARRELL, Thomas of Clinton Co. died at Jefferson Barracks 25 February.   MOAR 27 Feb 1838

FARRELL, Will died in the Car of Commerce disaster.   MORE 27 May 1828

FARIS, Aaron Jr. died 7 June of pleurisy in his 22nd yr. Son of Capt Aaron, late of KY.   MORE 23 June 1819

FARRIS, Col. Robert P. died in St. Louis 27 December.   MORE 4 Jan 1831

FERRIS, Dr. Jabez died at Fenton 18 Dec. age 54.   MORE 23 Feb 1848

FAULKNER, B., a merchant of Savannah MO died in St. Louis 11 April. Buried Savannah. Wife, 1 child.   MORE 14 Apr 1846

FAULKS, Christopher died Thursday age 75.   SWERE 7 Sep 1846

FAWCETT, Joseph, a postman, died in St. Charles 11 Sept. age 76. (MORE 14 Sept. says postmaster)   BGRAD 21 Sep 1844

FAWKS, William C. -- Chariton Co. Final settlement by Alfred W. Fawks   HIM 29 Mar 1855

FAY, Albert died 26 Feb. in Jefferson City age 30.   JEFRE 7 Mar 1835

FAY, Nahum died Monday night last of congestive fever age 41. Native of Southborough MA. In St. Louis 8 years. Left wife, numerous children.   SWERE 16 Sep 1844

FEAGEN, William B. died Saturday last of apoplexy. Left wife and young children.   PWH 30 Apr 1846

FEMISTER, Edmund, bookkeeper with St. Louis Reveille, died 10 Apr. Formerly Baltimore. Left widow, no children. (MORE says Episcopal cemetery.)   SWERE 13 Apr 1846

FERGUSON, Dugal -- Montgomery Co. Final settlement by James Ellis.   SALT 24 Oct 1840

FERGUSON, Jefferson died Sunday. Resided Bonhomme Twp.   MORE 22 Mar 1842

FERGUSON, Montgomery died yesterday in his 30th year. Funeral from residence of John H. Gay, 4th St.   MORE 23 Mar 1843

FERGUSON, Fergus Esq. of St. Louis died yesterday morning.   MORE 13 Feb 1836

FERGUSON, Joshua died Wednesday week in Callaway Co. age 84.   JEFRE 7 Jan 1837

FERGUSON, Peter Esq. a citizen of Franklin died last Wednesday age 45.   MIN 18 Feb 1820

FERGUSON, Robert Bolen died yesterday in his 27th year. Formerly of Goochland Co. VA. Funeral from residence of John Staff, 11 S. 4th.   MORE 3 Dec 1840

FERGUSON, W.D.H., address not given, working his passage and killed in explosion of the Big Hatchee at Hermann 23 July.   STGAZ 15 Aug 1845

FERRALE, John Jr. died 13 September age 37.   MORE 15 Sep 1853

FERRALL, William Louis died in St. Louis yesterday age 30. Funeral from residence of his father, 180 S. 4th, to Catholic cemetery.   MORE 16 Aug 1845

FERRELL, _____ "a man of no family" living in Henry Co. was murdered and his home set on fire on the 10th, about 5 miles south of Clinton on Grand River. Believed done by a Nichels, who absconded. Ferrell supposedly had money.   OSIN 21 May 1853

FERRILL, Jackson M. age 20 died at the residence of his brother, Judge of Osage, leaving mother & "connections."   JINQ 7 Nov 1843

FERRY, John formerly of St. Charles Co. died last April near Alexandria, Lincoln Co., age 70.   MIN 22 May 1829

FICKLIN, Thompson H. died of cholera in New Orleans, formerly of Washington Co., late of Ark. Terr.   MORE 19 May 1835

FIELDING, William M. died 9 June age about 45.   MODE 17 June 1846

FIELD, John W., formerly of Lamington NJ died 15 Nov. in his 23rd year. New Brunswick, please copy.   MORE 16 Nov 1837

FIELD, Jasper age about 55 died 21 April. Native of Warren MA.   MORE 25 Apr 1853

FIELD, Matthew late editor of the St. Louis Reveille died at sea on the voyage from New York to New Orleans. (SWERE says brother of Editor Joseph Field)   MORE 16 Dec 1844

FIELDS, James killed in Scotland Co. 25 November by Abner McPherson. (From Paris Mercury)   BRUNS 30 Dec 1848

FIFE, Beverly, late of Virginia, died Thursday last.   MORE 26 Nov 1836

FIFE, Samuel, age 38, a native of Elizabethtown, Hardin Co. KY died 26 May.   MORE 27 May 1849

FINAN, Thomas age 45 died 21 May. Buried Rock Springs.   MORE 24 May 1852

FINCH, Gen. Aaron died at Bolivar, Polk Co. in his 53rd year. Formerly of Washington Co. TN.   SPAD 16 May 1846

FINDLAY, Major Jonathan S. died near Lexington 21 Sept. in his 55th year. Native of Franklin Co. PA. Left wife and children.   MORE 30 Oct 1832

FINDLEY, Dr. John died Sunday night in Herculaneum, age about 65. Formerly of Charleston SC.   MORE 30 Nov 1830

FINDLEY, Rev. Samuel died 8 November at his residence in Lincoln Co. in his 79th year. Formerly of Lincoln Co. KY. — BGRAD 12 Nov 1842

FINNELL, Morgan -- Chariton Co. Final settlement by Abner Finnell. — BRUNS 30 Mar 1848

FINNERTY, Patrick shot and killed 12 August in Tarry Co. (should be Taney) near Yocum's Mill. Murderer escaped. (from Springfield Advertiser) — BOLT 30 Aug 1845

FINNIE, John, native of Aberdeen, died 19 June age ca 45. — MORE 21 June 1849

FINNEY, James died yesterday. Funeral from residence of his brother Bernard, on Spruce betw. 13-14. — MORE 19 July 1844

FINNY, Mr. _____ died Sunday. — MORE 4 Sep 1822

FISHBACK, William died 10 January near Jackson (MO?) Many years resident of St. Louis Co. Age 46. — MORE 10 Feb 1835

FISHER, Archibald died yesterday age 44, resident of St. Louis the past few years. Of Wheeling, VA. — SWERE 3 Jan 1848

FISHER, Governor S. killed in Grundy Co. by Andrew Spencer "lately." Fisher drunk and abusive. — BRUNS 19 May 1849

FISHER, John accidentally shot himself en route to CA. — BRUNS 5 July 1849

FISHER, Solomon died 28 May at Frankford in his 68th year. — SALT 5 June 1841

FISK, Asa -- Putnam Co. Letters of administration to Thomas Hargrave. — CANE 16 Nov 1854

FISKE, Lyman, late of Sturbridge MA died on 13 August of bilious fever. — MORE 21 Aug 1832

FISSER, John Henry, a carpenter, German by birth, died leaving wife and 3 children. — MORE 13 July 1839

FITHIAN, Lott died at the residence of Charles Barnard in St. Louis on 4 October. — MORE 6 Oct 1841

FITZPATRICK, Michael died at the residence of his father in his 28th year. Native of Hagerstown MD. Buried Rock Spring. Resided Broadway & Wash. — MORE 17 Mar 1853

FIX, Jacob fell off the ferry opposite Market St. on 13 March and is presumed dead. — MORE 19 Mar 1846

FIZER, _____ a cabinet maker committed suicide in Saline Co. — BOLT 22 Oct 1842

FLANAGAN, Dr. C.W. died in Paris, Monroe Co. on 8 February in his 39th year. — BGDB 22 Feb 1845

FLANAGAN, William died of apoplexy near Manchester 21 June. Baltimore and Nashville please copy. — MORE 23 June 1852

FLEISCHMAN, Capt. B.F. died in St. Louis Tuesday night. — MORE 28 Apr 1835

FLETCHER, Alvin died in St. Louis Thursday of consumption age about 28. Native of MA. — MORE 21 May 1833

FLOOD, Bernard formerly of St. Louis died in Mobile 3 Feb. age 25. — MORE 26 Feb 1849

FLORENCE, Thomas and William murdered in Lincoln Co. Fanny & Elleck, slaves of C. Prewitt, tried. — MORE 3 Dec 1839

FLORR, Jacob died December last at the cliffs of Selma MO.   MORE 6 Apr 1830
    Came from Louisville but is believed to have
    " connections" in Indiana.

FLOYD, Major Gabriel J., a resident from Florida, was   MORE 29 Aug 1842
    attacked with guns, bludgeons, and knives when
    his house was entered. He lived about 4 miles
    from St. Louis. Interred Episcopal cemetery.
    (James McLean convicted and sentenced to die.)

FONTANA, Felix died 27 Feb. at his residence, 3rd & Green.   MORE 28 Feb 1840
    Interred Catholic cemetery.

FOOT, Simon H. of Carondelet disappeared from the   MORE 27 Jan 1829
FOOTE   Missouri on passage from St. Louis to New
    Orleans. Had been ill 14 days, believed to
    have fallen overboard.

FORBES, Duncan, a woolcarder born in Aberdeen, late of   MORE 25 Nov 1834
    Milberry or Southbridge MA.

FORBES, Samuel T. died in New Orleans a few days ago, to   COMB 11 Feb 1847
    be buried at Boonville with friends and
                              relatives.

FORD, James died 29 July on his way from Ste. Genevieve   MORE 23 Nov 1811
    to Mine a Breton. Supposed about 50 years old.
    Originally from Great Britain, lately from
    Vernon, Oneida Co. NY.

FORD, Nathaniel of Fayette died recently in New Orleans.   MORE 10 July 1832

FORD, Oliver died at Machinac on his way east, age 41.   MORE 15 July 1853

FORD, P.H., former editor of the Inquirer, died Saturday.   MORE 25 Jan 1827

FORDER, Peter, native of Baltimore Co. MD, died age 55.   MORE 13 Feb 1852

FORRESTER, Grandison F. died 12 March in his 36th year.   MORE 14 Mar 1853
    Brother-in-law of Daniel McGill.

FORRESTER, Henry died 28 September age 33. Left widow   SWERE 7 Oct 1844
                     and orphans.

FORRESTER, Richard son of Stephen, formerly of TN,   MORE 6 Sep 1831
                     died 27 August.

FORRESTER, Stephen died yesterday. He lived near Chouteau's
    Pond and was killed in an argument with men   MORE 15 June 1841
    who took his skiff without permission. The
    murderer Garret Alberger, a butcher, fled.

FORSYTH, Major Thomas, late Indian agent of the U.S.,   MORE 1 Nov 1833
    died Tuesday last.

FORT, Elias, age about 45, died in Franklin yesterday.   WEM 1 Dec 1835
    Wife and large family. Many years resident of
    Randolph Co., was moving south.

FOSTER, John died 13 September.   PWH 7 Sep 1845

FOSTER, John died of cholera in Palmyra.   MORE 28 June 1833

FOSTER, John died last evening. Resided Laurel St.   MORE 7 May 1841
    Interred Presbyterian cemetery.

FOSTER, William killed at Roanoke by Mr. Chitman, a tavern- GLWT 9 Dec 1852
    keeper. Foster, inebriated, was ejected from tavern
    but returned and was struck by a poker. Inquest.

FOULX, F. of St. Louis died 2 July.   MORE 7 July 1829

FOUNTAIN, Absolem of Boone Co. died 20 March.   MORE 10 Apr 1852

FRAME, John W. age about 28 died in Saline Co. 5 August.   BRUNS 16 Aug 1849

FRANCIS, Edwin died of cholera in St. Louis 22 June in   MORE 25 June 1833
    his 26th year. Left brothers & sisters.

FRANCIS, Henry, formerly of Boston, died 17 October in   SLDU 19 Oct 1846
    his 46th year.

FRANEY, FREANEY, Matthew died in St. Louis Tuesday.   MORE 7 Dec 1830

FRANEY, William died 24 October age 22.   SWERE 1 Nov 1847

FRANKLIN, Henry drowned near Rees Settlement, IL. Had   STCHMO 22 June 1822
    escaped jail in St. Louis. Parents in
    Campbell Co. VA.

FRAY, James S. died at his residence in Boone Co. in   BOLT 7 June 1845
    his 37th year, 26 April. Wife, 3 small children.
    A Methodist for 17 years.

FRAZER, Henry of Ray Co. died 22 June at Chimney Rock   MORE 7 Oct 1850
    age 21.

FRAZIER, James, silversmith and watchmaker, 30 August.   INP 31 Aug 1822

FRAZER, Lieut. William died at Lancaster PA 27 June in   MORE 22 July 1844
    his 29th year. 3rd Reg. US Artillery.

FRAZER, William D., clerk of the <u>Hannibal</u>, fell over-   MORE 19 Nov 1844
    board and drowned near Chester IL Sunday.
    (SWERE 25 Nov. says son of Capt. Frazer and
    gives name as William N.)

FREAM, Lewis F. died 13 January at the residence of   SPAD 24 Jan 1846
    Dr. Perkins. "Highly esteemed."

FREDERICK, a sailor, died in the <u>Car of Commerce</u> tragedy.   MORE 27 May 1828

FREDERICK, Simeon died in Lexington 31 October.   LEXP 1 Nov 1854

FREE, John, pilot of the <u>Highlander</u>, killed by the fall   MORE 24 Sep 1846
    of a tree across the boat.

FREELAND, Robert S. of St. Louis died in New Orleans   MORE 18 Dec 1846
    on 8 December.

FREELAND, William killed Wednesday in the explosion of   MORE 17 Oct 1845
    a flour mill "in prime of life." Left
    wife and 2 children.

FREEMAN, ____ killed by lightning at the home of   MORE 23 Aug 1845
    Dr. Thompson in St. Charles.

FREEMAN, David B. formerly of St. Louis died 14 Jan.   MORE 10 Feb 1849
    in Stillwater IA.

FREEMAN, William died 26 June age about 80. "His son had   FULT 6 July 1849
    recently been in St. Louis." (Cholera?)

FRELIGH, J. H. found in a slough of the Missouri River near Wellington with a rope around his neck, shot in the head. A Spaniard named Joseph Ralph Saville was apprehended.   MORE 29 July 1841

FRENCH, Thomas H. died in St. Charles Co. 28 August age 23. Formerly of Powhattan Co. VA. Resident of St. Charles only a few months.   MORE 5 Sep 1843

FRIEHOFFER, John Frederick murdered 11 March. Frederick Rolache tried but found not guilty.   MORE 7 June 1848

FRIEDLORDER, Solomon died in Stockton 4 December age 33.
FRIEDLANDER   Formerly of St. Louis. Jewish rites.   MORE 9 Dec 1851

FRISTOE, Richard, a justice of the county court, died in Jackson County.   MORE 8 Dec 1845

FRIZEL, Joseph died Wednesday in his 29th year. Merchant, left widow, small children, mother. Native of MA, emigrated as a youth.   INP 6 Sep 1823

FROST, J. W. of Boone Co. died 5 June near Ft. Kearney, of cholera, age 35. Wife, one child.   MORE 7 Oct 1850

FROST, Wealthy died 16 June. Funeral from residence of his son-in-law W.H. White, 174 Market St.   MORE 17 June 1845

FRUITS, William Henry believed killed. He had been apprehended for horse and negro stealing, had escaped from Fayette jail recently, was shot at Yellow Creek by Constable Gaines and Frederick Hamilton, who were acquitted.   BRUNS 30 Sep 1848

FRY, Jacob committed suicide. (Possibly should be FREY)   MORE 9 Aug 1824

FRY, Dr. Jacob "an old and respected citizen" died Wednesday night last.   PWH 4 Nov 1843

FRY, James died 13 December in his 36th year.   PWH 26 Dec 1840

FUGATE, William C. of St. Ferdinand Twp. died 9 Oct. at his residence near the mouth of the Missouri.   MORE 21 Oct 1828

FUGEY, Thomas died about 10 September at the Fort of Bent and St. Vrain at the headwaters of the Arkansas. Formerly of Pittsburgh, several years in St. Louis.   MORE 11 Oct 1839

FULBRIGHT, William died at Walnut Hill near Springfield on 22 Sept. Born in Lincoln Co. NC on 8 Jan. 1785, emigrated ca 13 years ago.   JINQ 2 Nov 1843

FULKERSON, Capt. Isaac died at his residence in St. Charles Co. 19 April in his 61st year. Citizen of the county 32 years.   MORE 26 Apr 1836

FULKERSON, William N., postmaster at St. Charles, died 24 April.   MORE 27 Apr 1846

FULLER, J. W., formerly of Jefferson Co., died in CA last July.   MORE 30 Oct 1851

FULLERTON, Rufus, former state legislator, died 27 Feb. at Hickory Grove, Warren Co. Age ca 45.   MORE 12 Mar 1842

FULTON, Thomas died in the fall of 1817; " from Ireland many MORE 24 Apr 1818
    years ago," lately of Washington Co.

FUQUA, Nathaniel died in Hannibal 10 April. PWH 19 Apr 1849

FUQUA, Elder William died at Hannibal 6 September. PWH 24 Sep 1846

FURBER, Joel B. died at Leechburg, PA; for several years MORE 25 July 1843
    a resident of St. Louis.

FYKE, _____ "a young man wounded at the door of a house MORE 19 Dec 1812
    of ill fame" died the next morning, victim
    of intemperance and evil company. (In the
    next issue the editor says objection had been
    made to the account of Fyke's death but that he
    had intended only to point out the evils of that
    type of living. The murderer was Alex Morin.

GABRIEL, Edward accidentally shot by David Lee in St. MORE 29 May 1834
    Charles Co. Lately from Tennessee, left a
    wife and family. (Salt River Journal)

GAGE, Thomas P. -- Chariton Co. Letters of administration MIN 20 May 1823
    to Isaac Campbell.

GAINES, _____ died in the Big Hatchee explosion at STGAZ 15 Aug 1845
    Hermann, 23 July.

GALE, _____ dropped dead, a young man employed at the MORE 16 Jan 1846
    Planter's House Hotel.

GALAHER, Rev. James died at Brunswick 18 October, in his STGAZ 2 Nov 1853
    61st year. Presbyterian.

GALLAGHER, James, insane, hanged himself in Shelby Co. HANT 27 July 1852
    but was a resident of Ralls.

GALLAHER, Michael -- Franklin Co. Letters of administration
    (Nov.)to Patrick Gallaher & Alexander Geiser SLDU 4 Jan 1847

GALLOWAY, Jesse -- Taney Co. Letters of administration SPAD 18 Feb 1845
    to Zachariah Henson 3 February.

GAMBLE, Joseph Esq., clerk of the US Circuit Court, died MORE 10 Jan 1848
    Sunday in St. Louis.

GANNON, Timothy died 4 October age 54. MORP 7 Oct 1845

GANTT, Levi fell at Chapultepec. Brother of T.T., Esq. MORE 1 Mar 1848
    Funeral from Christ Church.

GANTT, Maj. Stoughton died on Sunday, 25 April and was MORE 28 Apr 1819
    interred with military and Masonic honors.

GARAUX, Ulis and William were killed in a fall from a MORE 25 Feb 1847
    roof. They were brothers, originally from
    Pittsburgh. Ulis lived at Morgan near 15th and
    left a widow and 2 or 3 children. William was
    about 19.

GARDNER, George, formerly of New York, murdered on the MORE 27 Mar 1839
    riverfront by Thomas Berry (believed insane)
    Monday night. Left 2 children, mother, 2 sisters.

GARDNER, John died at the residence of his father, William, MORE 18 Sep 1839
    in St. Louis Co. 15 September, age 23.

GARESCHE, Vital age 61, late of St. Louis, died in Havana.   MORE 22 Apr 1844

GARNER, William of Ray Co. died at Jefferson Barracks 26 Feb.   MOAR 27 Feb '38

GARNER, William died of cholera at Palmyra.   MORE 28 June 1833

GARRARD, Jephtha D. died 28 January, late of Cincinnati.   MORE 16 Feb 1836

GARRITY, John age 53 died 6 October.   MORE 7 Oct 1851

GARY, Gideon, shot Sunday, died Tuesday. Husband, parent.   MIN 14 Oct 1823
    Wm. O. Short, charged with the killing, escaped.   " 11 Nov   "

GASH, Joseph (Major) died Friday week, an old citizen.   PWH 5 July 1849

GATES, Mr. _____ of Macon Co. died on the way west.   BRUNS 14 June 1849

GATES, Elijah, E.H., or H.F. -- body found one mile above   MORE 30 Apr 1844
    Hannibal in the Missouri River had papers
    showing these names. Thought to have been a
    victim of the <u>Shepherdess</u> disaster.

GATES, Hezekiah, editor of the <u>Valley Farmer</u>, died in   BRUNS 5 July 1849
    St. Louis 21 June age 51.

GATES, Thomas J. died at his residence 6 April.   SPAD 13 Apr 1847

GATHER, John died at his residence on the Mississippi   JASO 15 Sep 1838
    River 8 September.

GATY, William -- his death in 1825 cited in a suit by   MORE 9 Aug 1835
    Timothy Phelps, Perry Co. Charity Gaty was
    administrator and sold the land.

GAW, John died in Franklin 11 September. Merchant, and   MIN 17 Sep 1822
    "a worthy man."

GAY, Stephen "a respectable mechanic of this town"   MORE 22 Dec 1819
    died last week.

GEIER, Lieut. James of the 5th Reg. US Inf. died at   MORE 26 Aug 1828
    Jefferson Barracks 22 August.

GENNER, H.M., late of Lafayette IN, died 29 December.   BEA 5 Jan 1832

GENTRY, John W. died 8 October in his 37th year in   MORE 20 Oct 1851
    Georgetown, Pettis Co.

GEORGE, John -- Ripley Co. Petition to sell real estate   SPAD 20 Sep 1845
    by James B. George & James Snider.

GEORGE, Orr, late of Wheeling VA died 5 February at his   MORE 8 Feb 1841
    residence on Spruce St. age 27.

GEORGE, Robert died in Chariton Co. 21 March.   GLWT 3 Apr 1851

GERARD, John B. died 14 May. Resided on 5th St. between   MORE 15 May 1849
    Morgan and Franklin.

GIBBONER, Frederick, a stonemason from St. Louis, drowned   MORE 31 Dec 1845
    in the Arkansas River. He was employed at
    Fort Smith, and had a family.

GIBBONY, Alexander, killed by Indians on the lower Cuivre   MORE 27 May 1815
    ferry near Ft. Howard; Capt. Craig's Company.

GIBBS, Hiram, an "upright and industrious citizen" died   PWH 19 Nov 1846
    Friday age about 45.

GIBSON, Henry H. formerly of Pittsburgh died in St. Louis   MORE 30 Aug 1843
    yesterday. Resident 10 years. Funeral from
        Virginia Hotel.

GIBSON, Jordan W. murdered by Reuben Jackson alias Reuben   MORE 7 Mar 1843
    Smith near New Hope, Auburn, MO. Reward
        offered by Goin Gibson.

GIBSON, Pleasant -- Wright Co. Letters of administration   JINQ 18 Apr 1844
    to Wm. Bohannon 5 February.

GIBSON, William B. died 10 April in his 46th year at his   MODE 29 Apr 1846
    residence in Boonslick Twp. (Howard Co.)

GIBSON, William R. died aboard the *Little Red* on 14 Sept.   MORE 1 Oct 1838
    Formerly of Cincinnati, lately rafting between
        Arkansas and New Orleans.

GIBSON, Capt. Woolman died at the Washington Hotel. He   MORE 27 Oct 1835
    commander of the *John Watchman*.

GIDDINGS, Dr. Lloyd B. died in Fayette 24 March.   MIN 4 Apr 1835

GIDDINGS, REV. Salmon died in St. Louis last Friday.   MORE 7 Feb 1828

GIGON, Faustian, native of Canada, died 21 September.   MORE 3 Oct 1811

GILBERT, Archibald died in Georgetown about 25 years   BORE 9 Aug 1843
    old on 24 April. Residence unknown.

GILBERT, William L. died in Jackson Co. on 22 October.   MORE 30 Oct 1832

GILDEA, William Brown MD, dental surgeon late of St.   SWERE 17 Aug 1846
    Louis, died at Ft. Helvetia CA age 26.

GILDERSLEEVE, Noah died in St. Louis Sunday morning.   MORE 25 Oct 1836

GILHULY, Bernard died 21 May age 32, a merchant. Native   MORE 23 May 1825
    of Co. Leitrim. Left wife, one child.

GILLAM, Joshua of Henry Co. died 13 June 13 miles west   MORE 7 Oct 1850
    of Ft. Kearney age 21. Inflammation of brain.

GILLARD, George recently of Philadelphia died 1 November.   MORE 3 Nov 1846

GILLILAND, John son of John died in Lincoln Co. 29 Jan.   MORE 20 Feb 1852
    age (59?) Formerly of Simpson Co. KY.
        Baptist.

GILLESPIE, Arthur Thomas, late of Bloomington IL, died   SWERE 5 Nov 1848
    6 October age 22y 4m 17d.

GILLESPIE, Charles died in Shelby Co. 16 September. Left   PWH 25 Sep 1841
    wife and young children.

GILMAN, James died 29 July 1835, estate notice by   JEFRE 16 July 1836
    Wm. J. Gilman. Born Hanover Co. VA 1779. No
        known heirs.

GIVENS, James died in Fayette 29 July age about 25.   BOLT 2 Aug 1845

GIVENS, R.B. died 13 February in his 23rd year at the   BOLT 17 Feb 1844
    residence of Nicholas Dysart, Randolph Co.

GIVENS, Thomas J., attorny, died at Potosi; formerly of KY.　MORE 15 Sep 1835

GLASBY, John M. died at the home of his brother-in-law　MORE 1 Oct 1842
　　　　John S. McCune, Collins St. Late of Chester Co. PA

GLASCOCK, Asa died in Ralls Co. 27 Jan. in his 58th year.　BGRAD 10 Feb 1844

GLASCOCK, Col. Charles died 28 September at his residence　MORE 9 Oct 1839
　　　　in Ralls Co. Settled in Missouri in 1838.

GLENN, Hugh died in Cincinnati. (Estate in Callaway Co.)　MORE 7 June 1833

GLENN, Robert S. -- DeKalb Co. Final settlement by　STGAZ 3 May 1854
　　　　Major A. Glenn.

GLOVER, D. Perron son of P.G. died Thursday in 28th yr.　JINQ 8 Feb 1845

GLOVER, James L., youngest son of Col. John of Knox Co.,　PWH 7 Dec 1848
　　　　died 27 November age 19.

GODFREY, Francis, age about 19, formerly of Rochester NY.　MORE 15 July 1851

GODFREY, Capt. Hosea died 10 January in his 62nd year.　MORE 12 Jan 1853
　　　　Massachusetts and Rhode Island please copy.

GODWIN, ____, a soldier, drowned crossing the Mississippi　MORE 22 Nov 1817
　　　　in a small boat.

GOGE, Levi, formerly of Ohio, died at the St. Louis　MORE 16 Oct 1844
　　　　Hospital. Parents in Akron OH.

GOLL, George Henry, son of B.G. and Harriet, died　SWERE 31 Jan 1848
　　　　22 January age 16.

GOOCH, Benjamin
　　　　James　both died of cholera in Palmyra.　MORE 28 Jan 1833

GOOCH, John J. formerly of Washington City died 17 Jan.　MORE 18 Jan 1853
　　　　age 22.

GOODE, Thomas, formerly of Amelia Co. VA died 19 Feb.　JEFRE 19 Feb 1842
　　　　age 57. Resided near Jefferson City. Lost
　　　　son 8 months ago. Wife, children.

GOODE, William died 28 December in his 70th year. Once　PWH 11 Jan 1849
　　　　member of the KY legislature. Methodist.

GOODE, R. Seth died 11 July at the residence of his　JEFRE 12 July 1841
　　　　father, Thomas, of measles. Age 24.

GOODFELLOW, John son of Peter B. and Anna died 13 Nov.　HIM 16 Nov 1854
　　　　age 32y 4m.

GOODING, Capt. George, late of the US Army, Saturday.　MORE 23 March 1830

GOODRICH, D.W., first clerk and part owner of the Columbus.
　　　　Funeral from residence of his sister-in-law　MORE 16 Sep 1853
　　　　Mrs. Rowe, 6th-O'Fallon. Burial Bellefontaine.

GORDON, David died at his residence near Columbia　MODE 30 Jan 1849
　　　　7 January age 70y 9d.

GORDON, Charles, a young man long engaged at the Post　MORE 2 Sep 1839
　　　　Office, died at the residence of Wilson P. Hunt.
　　　　Formerly of Geneva NY.

GORDON, Francis P. son of Capt. John C. died Tuesday　JEFRE 26 Sep 1835
　　　　in his 17th year.

GORDON, James Esq. funeral notice; service at Fee Fee Church.   MORE 26 Feb '52
GORDON, John died 9 August in his 76th year.   JEFRE 13 Aug 1836
GORE, Stephen died yesterday in his 56th year. Resided   MORE 17 Sep 1845
    8th near Olive.
GORMAN, Thomas died yesterday age 35. Funeral from home   MORE 9 Sep 1843
    of his brother Patrick, Greene betw. 4th-5th.
GOTT, William age 19 died 5 March.   SPAD 9 Mar 1847
GRAGG, Jesse-- Chariton Co. Final settlement by   BRUNS 8 July 1848
    Lewis Garrett.
GRAHAM, James G. died Saturday in his 49th year.   MORE 28 Nov 1848
    Norfolk VA please copy.
GRAHAM, Richard Ewing died in Lexington 31 October.   LEXP 1 Nov 1854
GRAHAM, Richard Jr. died 29 April at the home of his father   MORE 6 May 1828
    Maj. Richard, of a pulmonary affection. A
    native of Kentucky.
GRAHAM, Lieut. John, son of Maj. Richard, died 27 June   MORE 7 July 1846
    while visiting his grandmother in Maysville
    KY. In his 42nd year.
GRANDVER, John, a German waiter at the US Hotel, fell   MORE 24 Apr 1844
    from the roof and was killed while dusting carpets.
GRANE, Zenas P. died in New Madrid Co. 10 March in his   MORE 5 Apr 1836
    23rd year. Only son of widowed mother.
GRANT, A. Sydney, a clerk in the QM Dept. of the Army,   MORE 31 May 1827
    died at Jefferson Barracks 18 May.
GRANT, Asa Nelson A.M. (?) died at Paris, Monroe Co.   CANE 3 May 1855
    23 April age 29y 3m 16d.
GRANT, Capt. David died 26 March age 47. Formerly of   SWERE 3 Apr 1848
    Philadelphia and Maysville KY, a resident of
    St. Louis for a number of years past.
GRANT, James of Boone Co. committed suicide. Left wife   STGAZ 26 Apr 1854
    and several children.
GRANT, Capt. William died 15 Sept. in his 53rd year. Born   FULT 21 Sep 1849
    Fayette Co. KY, in MO about 29 years. Left
    wife and children. Presbyterian.
GRAPEVINE, William, a pilot, died 12 April in St. Louis.   SWERE 13 Apr 1846
GRATE, William N. age 62 died in St. Louis Co. 8 Feb.   MORE 10 Feb 1852
    Born in York Co. PA.
GRATIOT, Charles Sr. died 20 April. A Swiss immigrant.   MORE 3 May 1817
    Left a numerous family.
GRATIOT, Henry, formerly of St. Louis Co., died in Baltimore.   MORE 10 May '36
GRAVES, Levi died of cholera.   MORE 6 Nov 1832
GRAVES, Richard died 13 Sept. in his 79th year. Resident   MODE 29 Sep 1847
    of Howard Co. 23 years.

GRAVES, William -- Montgomery Co. Letters of administration BGRAD 20 Nov 1841
    to David Graves 29 October.

GRAY, Alexander Esq. died in St. Louis 2 Aug. age 35.   MIN 26 Aug 1823

GRAY, William C. died 3 July at the residence of William   COMB 11 July 1846
    after a long and painful illness. /Harley

GREELY, _.S., died 24 June 13 miles east of Ft. Laramie   MORE 7 Oct 1850
    (of Lafayette Co.) age 31.

GREEN, David, 1st Engineer of the *Persian*, killed in an   MORE 14 Nov 1840
    explosion at Napoleon.

GREEN, James Y., printer, died at his father's home in   MORE 19 Sep 1834
    Cape Girardeau 7 September. Nearly 21.

GREENE, Dr. J.B. of Huntsville, Randolph Co., died in his   BOLT 16 Aug 1845
    31st year. Emigrated from KY some years ago.
    Left wife.

GREENE, Rev. Jesse, presiding elder of the M.E. Church   MODE 5 May 1847
    South, died at the residence of H.Y.Elbert Esq
    in Benton Co., 18 April. Minister more than 30
    years in Missouri and Arkansas.

GREEN, Jesse Soule, youngest son of Mrs. Mary and the late   LEXP 9 Aug 1854
    Rev. Jesse, died of cholera Thursday.

GREEN, Dr. Joel H. died Saturday last in his 54th year.   BOLT 9 Nov 1844

GREEN, Capt. John died at the home of his son D.D. on   MORE 10 Feb 1853
    7 Feb. age 67. Formerly of Washington Co. OH.

GREEN, John, from Virginia, died Wednesday last age 22.   MORE 22 Sep 1819

GREEN, N., died in the *Car of Commerce* disaster.   MORE 27 May 1828

GREEN, Lieut. P.R. died at Jefferson Barracks 30 June.   MORE 15 July 1828
    5th Reg. US Infantry.

GREEN, Reuben died 9 Jan. on the *Emily* near San Francisco.   MORE 16 Apr 1852
    Of Cass Co.

GREEN, Sion R. died 9 Jan. at Vandalia, eldest son of   BOLT 19 Mar 1842
    Rev. T.P. Formerly of Cape Girardeau.

GREEN, Elder Thomas P. died at his residence in Cape   BOLT 5 Aug 1843
    Girardeau 11 July in his 54th year. Born in   " 26 Aug "
    Chatham Co. NC 3 June 1790. Moved in 1807 to
    Maury Co. TN. Converted in 1812; came to Cape
    Girardeau in 1817.

GREEN, William of Howard Co. died 25 October age 64.   BRUNS 11 Nov 1848

GREENHAIGH, Thomas son of Rev. J. died 23 May age 24.   MIN 2 June 1832

GREENWELL, Ignatius age 96 died 23 Jan. in Ralls Co.   PWH 4 Feb 1847
    A Revolutionary veteran.

GREER, Nathan, notice of dissolution of partnership of   MORE 2 Oct 1822
    Edwards and Greer due to his death.

GREFFET, Joseph Auguste died at his residence of 3½ mi.   MORE 2 Nov 1848
    west of St. Louis age 46.

GREGG, James -- DeKalb Co. Final settlement by John Dice.   STGAZ 16 June 1848

GREGG, John, formerly of Rochester NY, died 28 May. Funeral   MORE 29 May 1845
   from residence of N.N. Burchard, #62 2nd St.

GREGG, William, late of Washington Co. PA, died yesterday   MORE 21 Jan 1846
   age 23. Funeral from Alfred Vinton home, 28 Vine St.

GREGOIRE, Cyril died at Perry Mills, Ray Co. age 74, on   MORE 27 Nov 1832
   16 November. Native of Valence, France.

GREGORY, William Sulden died in Amherst Co. VA after an   MORE 13 Oct 1836
   illness of 20 days, age 24y 10m.

GRIDER, John of Polk Co. died on the way to Santa Fe.   MODE 13 Jan 1847
   In Lieut. Col. Willock's command.

GRIEWSKI, Anthony Bonezye died 17 August of yellow fever   MORE 24 Aug 1839
   aboard the _Empress_ from New Orleans to St.
   Louis. Formerly Lieut. of Inf. Knight of the
   Golden Military Cross of Poland.

GRIFFEY, John stabbed at Troy, Lincoln Co. by Byrd Milsap.   MIN 10 Apr 1824
   Little hope for his recovery.

GRIFFIN, Brev. Capt. George died 8 October in Florida.   MORE 5 Nov 1839

GRIFFIN, G., engineer of the _Banner_, died at Kaskaskia.   MORE 3 Jan 1832

GRIFFIN, Lieut. H.J. drowned in the Mississippi near   MORE 11 Mar 1828
   Ft. Armstrong on 20 February.

GRIFFIN, John a stonemason stabbed by William Ray   MORE 23 June 1829
   Saturday evening; Bray committed.

GRIFFIN, William B. died of cholera Thursday last near   GLWT 21 Aug 1851
   Jefferson City.

GRIFFITH, Hayden died 27 October age 22y 26d.   PWH 11 Nov 1847

GRIFFITH, Isaac H. "a respectable mechanic" died Thursday.   MORE 3 Nov 1819

GRIFFITH, Joel Sr. of Buffalo Twp., Pike Co., died 5 Nov.   BGRAD 14 Dec 1844
   Oldest citizen of the county.

GRIFFITH, Joseph died at the residence of his father in   MORE 27 Jan 1851
   Ste. Genevieve Co. in his 15th year.

GRIFFITH, Caleb son of Daniel Esq. died 26 August in   MORE 6 Sep 1843
   his 21st year.

GRIFFITH, Samuel died near Portage des Sioux.   MORE 26 Aug 1815

GRIFFITHS, Thomas Grant Esq. murdered by his son Abel who   MORE 8 Oct 1823
   then committed suicide, at the home of
   Mrs. Wynn, Maddox St. near Bond.

GRISHAM, William -- Montgomery Co. Final settlement by   FULT 14 Oct 1849
   Green B. Bush.

GRISWOLD, Rev. Whitting W., Rector of St. John's Church   BRUNS 2 Aug 1849
   in St. Louis, died. (No date.)

GROENEMAN, John age 38 died 7 July at his residence   MORP 8 July 1845
   opposite the post office.

GROOM, Aaron -- Montgomery Co. Final settlement by Jane Groom.	FULT 29 Sep 1848
GROOM, James -- Montgomery Co. Estate taken over by Publ. Adm. Joseph P. Wiseman.	FULT 26 Jan 1849
GROOM, Richard W., overseer for Mr. Moore, died of cholera "this last week."	BRUNS 19 July 1849
GROOMER, _____ killed in Daviess Co. when digging out a mill seat at Taylor's Ferry, South Fork of the Grand River.	BRUNS 13 Apr 1848
GROSE, Mr., a German died of cholera this last week.	BRUNS 19 July 1849
GROVE, GROCE David -- Chariton Co. Letters of administration to David Proffitt 29 October.	BOLT 25 Nov 1843
GROVES, Frederick A., late of Philadelphia, died Tuesday.	MORE 14 July 1829
GRUBB, Charles T. died yesterday of bilious fever in his 32nd year. Formerly of Wilmington DE.	MORE 22 Aug 1837
GRUBB, John of Dinn & Grubb died 19 March in St. Louis.	SWERE 23 Mar 1846
GRUBBS, William -- Chariton Co. Final settlement by John Grubbs.	BRUNS 30 Sep 1848
GRUNDY, Armstead S. Esq. died in Franklin Friday last age 23.	MIN 18 Feb 1823
GUERNSEY, Aaron died near Hannibal 11 April, an old and respectable citizen formerly of St. Louis Co.	MORE 21 Apr 1845
GUILMARTIN, William died 19 January in Weston, an honor graduate of St. Louis U. "a few years ago." In 22nd year.	MORE 12 July 1844
(He was reburied in St. Louis in 1847.)	MORE 21 Apr 1847
GUIN, Hubert died yesterday at Jefferson Barracks.	MORE 24 May 1833
GUNSOLLES, Capt. James an old and respected pilot died 13 June. Resided at Plum and 2nd.	MORE 14 June 1851
GUNSALLIS, Richard -- Gasconade Co. Petition to sell real estate by William Bumpass. (Gunsallis is elsewhere said to have been murdered.)	JEFRE 19 Dec 1840
GUSEMAN, Amaziah formerly of Virginia died yesterday. Funeral from home of C. Faulks. Interred in Methodist cemetery.	MORE 14 Mar 1846
GUTHRIDGE, Elijah died 23 January age 19y 5m 23d at the home of his mother Mrs. Elizabeth Guthridge in Darst Bottom.	MORE 5 Feb 1848
GUTHRIE, Robert -- Chariton Co. Final settlement by A. W. Guthrie.	BRUNS 1 July 1848
GUYLER, William -- Montgomery Co. Final settlement by Green B. Bush.	FULT 4 Aug 1848

HACKAWAY, Fields B., a trunk-maker, committed suicide 17 Dec.   MORE 18 Dec 1846
    Formerly of Edwardsville IL. Wife, 3 children.

HACKLEY, Lott, age about 65, died 31 Dec. Originally from   MODE 10 Nov 1847
    Culpeper Co. VA, from there to Franklin Co. KY
    and then to Missouri. Old citizen. Baptist.

HACKMAN, Frederick William died Monday age 37y 4m 15d.   MORE 13 Apr 1852
    Columbia MO please copy.

HACKNEY, Aaron died "today." Friends of James S. Thomas   MORE 14 Oct 1841
    invited to funeral.

HAGER, ____, a German, murdered in Jasper Co. by Wm. McClure.   MORE 26 Apr 1847

HAGER, Jonas Geyer died 6th Sept. in his 28th year. Native   MORE 8 Sep 1853
    of Hagerstown MD.

HAGERTY, H. of St. Louis died 8 July.   MORP 10 July 1845

HAGESS, Peter died aboard the *Washington* en route to   MORE 31 May 1836
    Hannibal 21 May. Resident of Accomack Co. VA.

HAINES, Joseph, formerly of Philadelphia, died 19 May.   SWERE 28 May 1849

HALBERT, A.G. age 33 died 29 April. Funeral from residence   SWERE 30 Apr 1849
    of William Graves.

HALE, Aquila, formerly of Baltimore Co. MD, died in   MORE 15 Oct 1835
    St. Louis 12 October.

HALE, Titus, died in Baltimore 2 April; had removed to St.   MORE 13 Apr 1844
    Louis 10 years ago; left widow and two children
    by his first wife.

HALEY, Philip age about 60 died in Lewis Co. 25 May.   MORE 5 June 1853

HALL, Bartlett drowned near Boonville. He was an apprentice   MIN 5 Feb 1824
    of Mr. Rice.

HALL, Alexander S. -- Saline Co. Letters of administration   LEXP 1 Nov 1854
    to Publ. Adm. Late of Augusta Co. VA.

HALL, Edward, funeral preached by Rev. Jesse Green.   INP 7 May 1825

HALL, George, a German dray driver, drowned.   MORP 29 Aug 1845

HALL, George W. died 8 May in his 28th year. Funeral from   MORE 9 May 1849
    residence of his father, Capt. John, #32 Collins.

HALL, John D. died Sunday morning at his home in Soulard's   MORE 11 Feb 1839
    Addition to St. Louis. Methodist cemetery.

HALL, Marcus L. -- DeKalb Co. Letters of administration   PLAR 7 Feb 1848
    to Harriet Hall 7 Feb. 1848.

HALL, William died at DeWitt Wednesday last, age about 45.   BRUNS 3 Feb 1849

HALL, Silas B. died 6 Jan. in his 22nd year. Removed from   BOLT 1 Apr 1843
    Virginia with his family last summer (probably
    to Glasgow). "Brother, son."

HALL, Warner of St. Louis died at Keokuk 11 Feb.   MORE 21 Feb 1853
    Formerly of Frederick Co. MD.

HALLEY, M.C. of Chariton Co. died 25 June age 41 at the   MORE 7 Oct 1850
    crossing of the South Fork of the Platte. Left
    wife and family.

HALIGAN, John, native of Dublin, died in St. Louis Co.   MORE 11 July 1835
    Left 3 children.

HAMER, Louis -- DeKalb Co. Letters of administration to   STGAZ 20 Oct 1852
    Susanna Hamer exr. 4 October.

HAMILTON, Major Thomas died Tuesday morning last   MORE 2 Aug 1833

HAMILTON, James A. died in Lincoln Co. 7 Oct. in his 61st   MORE 20 Oct 1851
    year. Formerly of Rockingham Co. VA.

HAMILTON, Robert, a merchant on Market St. (St. Louis)   MORE 30 Sep 1844
    between Main & 2nd, apparently committed   " 24 Sep "
    suicide. Found with 4 shots in his head.

HAMMOND, Dr. A.D. of St. Louis died in Memphis 9 Feb.   MORE 21 Feb 1853
    in his 53rd year.

HAMMOND, Alden died 30 August near Herculaneum, a resident MORE 12 Sep 1835
    of Jefferson Co.

HAMMOND, George Esq., late deputy sheriff, stabbed to death SCOMB 29 Apr 1836
    while trying to quell a fight. Funeral from
    residence on Market St. Methodist cemetery.

HAMMOND, William, late of Jefferson Co., died 5 Dec.   MORE 12 Dec 1834

HAMMOND, William died 20 August, no age given. Funeral   MORE 21 Aug 1847
    from his residence, Bank of Missouri.

HAMPTON, Abel died near Cambridge, Saline Co., 17 May.   GLWT 22 May 1851
    Member Oddfellows.

HAMPTON, S.H. -- Montgomery Co. Notice of intent to   FULT 16 Dec 1849
    divide his slaves (to John M. and Madison J.
    Hampton by George W. Blair, adm.).

HAMPTON, William died in Howard Co. 14 Oct., son of John BORE 24 Oct 1843
    of Frankfort KY.

HANDY, J.H. killed at Potosi in a duel with Samuel Perry MIN 30 Dec 1823
    on 8 December.

HANEY, Tarlton -- St. Clair Co. Letters of administration BORE 24 Oct 1843
    to John Haynie 6 September.

HANLEY, Thomas died last Saturday.   MORE 22 Jan 1823

HARLAN, James M. age 13 died in Canton 20 July.   CANE 3 Aug 1854

HARBISON, George C.C., attorney, died at Cape Girardeau   MORE 19 Sep 1811
    1 Sept. age 31y 5m 18d.

HARBISON, John C., Methodist minister, died 27 March.   INP ?7 Apr 1826

HARDEMAN, John of Howard Co. died of yellow fever in   BEA 23 Sep 1829
    New Orleans.

HARDESTY, Samuel T. died at Bethany, Harrison Co., on   WEPT 11 Oct 1851
    29 September. A Mason.

HARDIN, ___, son of Joseph, accidentally killed by the   BOLT 16 Jan 1841
    discharge of a shotgun Monday last.

HARDIN, Charles, lately and for many years Postmaster in MIN 11 Sep 1830
    Columbia, died 20 August.

HARDIN, Capt. Joseph died in Washington MO 7 Jan., late   MORE 12 Jan 1851
    of the steamboat Lake of the Woods.

HARDY, Joseph died at the residence of his brother C.C. in   MORE 28 Feb 1845
    St. Louis 26 Feb. in his 25th year. Native of
    Lunenberg Co. VA.

HARLEN, Eli J. died Sunday last at the residence of Eli   SPAD 27 Aug 1844
    Jessup. Formerly of Hendrick Co. IN.

HARPENDING, Stephen son of A. Harpending of Caldwell Co. KY   MORE 26 June 1834
    died in St. Louis 17 June.

HARPER, Matthew -- Dallas Co. Letters of administration   SPAD 27 Dec 1845
    to Richard H. Fowler 29 November.

HARPER, Robert reported dead after being severely wounded   MORE 5 Aug 1846
    by James Keeler after an election argument. He
    was the younger brother of Andrew, of St. Ferdinand
    Twp. (But whether he died is not clear.)

HARR, Philip M., native of Movil, Co. Donegal, died 6 Feb.   BEA 13 Feb 1830

HARRINGTON, Dennis, died at City Hospital yesterday age 25.   SWERE 29 Nov 1847
    A printer. Interred Catholic cemetery.

HARRINGTON, Capt. George F. Funeral notice: Church of   MORE 23 June 1853
    the Messiah.

HARRINGTON, Henry died in St. Joseph 15 Aug. in 35th year.   MORE 19 Aug 1851

HARRINGTON, Jeremiah died Sunday in St. Louis. Old resident. MORE 17 Oct 1838

HARRINGTON, Lewis P., member of Rockwell & Co. Circus   SWERE 20 Dec 1847
    Corps, died in St. Louis 14 Dec.

HARRIS, Hezekiah murdered in Cooper Co. by Luke, a   MIN 17 Aug 1826
    black man (who was hanged 7 September).

HARRIS, James W. died in his 36th year.   GLWT 23 Oct 1851

HARRIS, John, formerly of Pennfield NY, died yesterday   MORE 20 Aug 1838
    age about 29.

HARRIS, Robert W. died at the home of his mother in Cape   MORE 20 Aug 1839
    Girardeau age 49.

HARRIS, Rev. Tyree C., pastor of First Baptist Church,   LEXP 11 Oct 1854
    died of typhoid Wednesday age about 28.

HARRISON, John -- Chariton Co. Letters of administration   MIN 1 Mar 1827
    to Samuel C. Davis 12 November.

HARSHAW, William H. formerly of St. Louis died 28 June   MORE 24 Aug 1850
    near South Pass OR. Left wife, family.

HART, Armstrong died 24 Dec. in Franklin Co., formerly   MORE 25 May 1830
    of Geneva NY. Husband, father.

HART, E.S., funeral notice. Resided 7th & Chestnut.   MORE 4 May 1853

HART, Henry M., recently returned from Mexico, died age 18.   MORE 10 Aug 1848
    Funeral from father's residence, Morgan between
    11th and 12th. Interred Methodist cemetery.

HART, Jesse Esq. died in Columbia last night.   MIN 22 Aug 1835

HART, John, late of Lexington KY, died in St. Louis 2 Sep.   SLINQ 6 Sep 1820

HART, John A. son of Capt. Samuel of Cole Co. died in CA   JEM 27 Jan 1852
    26 Oct. age 26. (or 36)

HART, Thomas C. died in Fulton 28 Nov., son of S.L. of   JEFRE 2 Dec 1843
    Jefferson City, age 24. Buried Jefferson City.

HARTINGIER, John of Ralls Co. died 16 May near St. Joseph   MORE 7 Oct 1850
    age 39. Left wife, 5 children.

HARTMAN, Will, a sailor, died in the Car of Commerce disaster. MORE 27 May '28

HARTSHORN, Lewis Augustus died Thursday in his 24th year.   MORE 4 Aug 1843
    Funeral from St. John's Church.

HARVEY, John R. died 12 Sept. in his 22nd year at the   BOLT 20 Sep 1845
    residence of his father.

HARVEY, William, "one of the early settlers" died age   MODE 4 Apr 1848
    78y 3d Saturday last.

HARVEY, William Henry of Boonville died 29 November age   COMB 9 Dec 1847
    21y 1m 9d. Richmond VA Enquirer please copy.

HARWOOD, Dr. Samuel M. died in Florissant in his 26th year.   MORE 18 Sep 1838
    Left 3 single sisters.

HATTON, Ben of Moniteau Co. died 18 June 100 mi. west of   MORE 7 Oct 1850
    Ft. Kearney age 40. Left wife, 6 children.
    John of Moniteau Co. died 50 mi. west of the
    South Fork of the Platte, age 20.

HAVEN, Joseph died 22 Dec. age 50. Resided Poplar betw.   MORE 23 Dec 1848
    3rd & 4th. New Orleans & eastern papers pls copy.

HAWKEN, Jacob Sr. died in his 63rd year. Funeral from   MORE 9 May 1849
    residence of his brother Samuel, 156 6th St.

HAWKES, Thomas M. age 11 drowned in the Missouri River   BRUNS 12 Aug 1848
    opposite Liberty Landing in Clay Co.

HAWKINS, John and wife died of cholera at Harrisonville.   LEXP 2 Aug 1854

HAWKINS, Moses died in Ralls Co. 29 Dec. age 55y 11m.   LEXP 18 Jan 1854
    Born in Boone Co. KY.

HAWKINS, Sandford A. died near New London at the residence   SALT 9 Oct 1841
    of his brother on 25 September.

HAWLEY, Francis, native of NY, died at Jefferson Barracks.   MORE 13 Aug 1833

HAWLEY, John -- Caldwell Co. Letters of administration to   STGAZ 4 Feb 1852
    to George Smith ? January.

HAWLEY, William S. late of NY died at Mr. Musick's on   MORE 5 Sep 1825
    Tuesday last.

HAWTHORN, Samuel D., son of Rev. James of Princeton KY,   MORE 12 June 1851
    died age 26.

HAYDEN, Enoch Sr. died 16 July in his 89th year. Native   PWH 22 July 1843
    of NJ.

HAYDEN, James son of Elisha killed in warehouse fire.   MORE 2 Sep 1839

HAYDEN, Thomas J. died 18 August age 20. Alexandria VA please copy. MORE 20 Aug 1851

HAYER, L. of St. Louis died in the <u>Big Hatchee</u> disaster at Hermann, 23 July. STGAZ 15 Aug 1845

HAYES, C. died at his home on Manchester Road 24 June. MORE 27 June 1852

HAYS, J. B. of Chariton, a student at Centre College, Danville died 18 January. MORE 31 Jan 1852

HAYS, Maj. John of Liberty, Clay Co. was killed Sunday morning last by a young man named Turnham. BOLT 22 Oct 1842

HAYS, Washington died in St. Joseph 9 Aug. in his 35th yr. MORE 19 Aug 1851

HAYES, William died in Saline Co. 18 March in his 77th year. BRUNS 23 Mar 1848

HAZZARD, John died in Boone Co. 25 February age 21. MIN 3 July 1830

HEAD, Thomas, just off the <u>West Newton</u> from Nashville, died 7 Feb., a patternmaker at Broadway Foundry. MORE 8 Feb 1852

HEAD, Dr. Waller of Huntsville, Randolph Co. died 9 August. Left wife and children. MORE 16 Aug 1845

HEALD, Jonas, native of NH, died 23 January. Resided 16th & Chestnut. MORE 24 Jan 1848

HEALD, Maj. Nathaniel (or Nathan) died 27 April at his farm in St. Charles Co. in his 57th year. Resident of the county 14 years. Wife, one child, one brother. MORE 1 May 1832

HEATH, Charles condemned to die 9 March for the murder of Hugh Jones at Ste. Genevieve. MORE 29 Feb 1812

HEATH, Judge John G., one of the pioneers of the state, died 26 March. COMB 1 Apr 1847

HEATH, Robert A. died 28 March in his 60th year. Native of PA but long a resident of MO. MORE 19 Apr 1843

HEATHER, David R. shot himself. Age about 24, lived with Mr. Husky in Marion Co. JEM 19 Dec 1848

HEATON, Townsend, of Loudon Co. VA, died 25 November at the residence of N. E. Janney. MORE 26 Nov 1841

HEFFORT, J. committed suicide in Weston. PLAR 27 Oct 1848

HEININGER, Frederick died of cholera. BRUNS 24 May 1849

HEIGENSTEIN, Nick, died of cholera in Brunswick. BRUNS 21 June 1849

HELLER, John, formerly of Charleston VA, died at the home of his son-in-law D. Edwards in his 85th year. Interred Episcopal cemetery. MORE 21 July 1851

HELM, Riley, wife and son aged about 18 all died within 15 days of typhoid. LEXP 1 Feb 1854

HELM, Robert died in Lincoln Co. 20 April in his 72nd year. Baltimore please copy. MORE 24 Apr 1852

HEMMERMAN, Jacob of St. Charles died 11 June 120 miles below Fort Laramie, age 23. MORE 7 Oct 1850

HEMPSTEAD, Dr. Benjamin, native of CT, died 13 May last   MORE 28 June 1831
          in Cape Girardeau Co. age about 47.

HEMPSTEAD, Joseph of St. Louis Co. died Sunday Last.   MORE 27 Sep 1831
          Native of CT.

HEMPSTEAD, Edward Esq. died Saturday night after a short   MORE 16 Aug 1817
          illness at the plantation of his father, Stephen.

HEMPSTEAD, Stephen Sr. died at his residence in the county.   MORE 4 Oct 1831

HENDERSON, ___ murdered on Big Creek in Lincoln Co. by a   MORE 23 Aug 1837
          man named Foster.

HENDERSON, John died in Pike Co. Friday age about 40.   BGRAD 11 Nov 1843

HENDERSON, John R. died in Cape Girardeau 19 Mar. age 46.   MORE 1 Apr 1851

HENDERSON, Joseph of Middle Grove Twp., Monroe Co. died   BOLT 18 Oct 1845
          25 Sept. age about 25, left "many friends."

HENDERSON, Robert H. (M?) died a few miles from Jackson   SMAD 2 Jan 1838
          last Saturday.

HENDREN, Isaac died at the residence of James M. Preston   PWH 19 Apg 1849
          17 April age 30y 7m.

HENDRIX, Edmund, a young man, died 16 May.   SALT 22 May 1841

HENDRICK, Harrison died in Pike Co. 15 April age 65y 12d.   MORE 28 Apr 1852
          Native of King & Queen Co. VA. Left widow,
          6 sons, 6 daughters.

HENDRICKS, James of Boone Co., poisoned. His wife and   MORE 26 Apr 1847
          Samuel Grubb arrested.

HENING, James died in Alexandria, Clark Co., in 39th yr.   MORE 27 Jan 1851

HENING, John G. died at the home of his son in his 74th   MORE 18 Apr 1845
          year -- St. Francisville, MO on 4 April.

HENNESY, Rev. Richard, president of St. Vincent College   MORE 11 July 1853
          in Cape Girardeau, died 9 July.

HENRALTY, Hugh died 1 Nov. age 39. (HENRATTY?)   MORP 3 Nov 1845

HENRY, Andrew died at his home in Harmony Twp., Washington   MORE 18 June 1833
          Co., 10 June. Had been a fur trader.

HENRY, Isaac N. died 1 January after a short illness.   MORE 3 Jan 1821
          "Conducted to grave by Masonic brethren."

HENRY, Dr. Julian formerly of Philadelphia died 23 Sept.   MORE 25 Sep 1848
          Funeral from St. George's Church.

HENSLEY, Donata (?) murdered in Carondelet 19 Aug. by   MORE 25 Aug 1848
          two Germans. (This might be a woman.)

HEPBURN, Lieut. George O., formerly of Potosi, killed in   BRUNS 8 June 1848
          Mexican War. Mother of New York.

HERDITCH, Louis Vilar, son of Joseph, died 26 July in   MORE 10 Aug 1846
          his 24th year in Ste. Genevieve.

HEREFORD, William S. died 25 Jan. in his 25th year.   MORE 26 Jan 1853
          Interred Bellefontaine.

HERNDON, George died in Howard Co. 3 Apr. in his 75th yr.	COMB 15 Apr 1847
HERNIESEN, George died in St. Louis Tuesday 5 September.	MORE 7 Sep 1837
HERREFORD, Dr. T. A. formerly of St. Louis died in Los Angeles 7 January.	MORE 7 Mar 1852
HERRIN, Owen B. of Boone Co. died 9 June leaving wife and 4 children.	STGAZ 27 July 1853
HERSEY, Benjamin, formerly of Lyndburgh VA, 4 May, age 62.	MORE 9 May 1838
HESS, A. D., yesterday, about 40.	JINQ 24 July 1845
HESS, Capt. Henry died 19 Apr. Interred Catholic Cemetery.	MORE 20 Apr 1851
HESTER, Thomas -- St. Clair Co. Sale of his slaves.	OSIN 25 Dec 1852
HEWETT, James W. formerly of Lynchburg died in Glasgow 20 February.	LEXP 1 Mar 1854
HEWITT, W. T. of Saline Co. died 3 April in 53rd year. Mason. Husband, father. (Probate: Waterman T.)	BRUNS 21 Apr 1849
HIATT, John W. drowned while trying to cross Bonne Femme Creek.	MIN 18 June '22
HICKAM, John, died in Boone Co. 27 February age 74. One of the first settlers in 1816.	BRUNS 9 Mar 1848
HICKCOX, Major died 13 Feb. age 60. Detroit, Buffalo, New York City please copy.	MORE 16 Feb 1848
HICKMAN, Francis died at his residence in St. Ferdinand Twp. 27 March in his 93rd year.	MORE 2 Apr 1845
HICKMAN, Capt. James of Franklin died in Boone Co. 13 Sep.	MIN 21 Sep 1826
HICKMAN, Thomas late of Maryland died in Dover 14 Oct. age about 70.	LEXP 18 Oct 1854
HIGBEE, Anderson died "in this place" last night.	MIN 21 Aug 1829
HIGBEE, Joseph died "last Sunday in this place."	MIN 14 Aug 1829
HIGDON, Gustavus A. died 6 Jan. age 25. Formerly of Washington DC.	MORE 9 Jan 1849
HIGGINBOTHAM, Thomas died at Montauk, Dent Co. 11 Nov. in his 87th year.	MORE 27 Nov 1851
HIGGINS, Morris, late of New Orleans, born in Ireland, died in the Hospital age 52.	MORE 20 June 1840
HIGGINS, William, a merchant, died yesterday.	MORE 13 July 1830
HIGGS, John of Ray Co. died 6 June near Ft. Kearney age 39. Left wife, 7 children.	MORE 7 Oct 1850
HIGNETT, Charles G. formerly of Baltimore Co. MD died of cholera age 51.	MORE 21 June 1851
HILL, Alexander died at his residence in Carroll Co. 12 April, professor of religion for more than 26 years. Cumberland Presbyterian.	LEXP 29 Apr 1845
HILL, William, murderer of Wm. Perry at Lambert's Diggings, captured in Texas.	MORE 23 Nov 1825

HILL, William C., late of Louisville, died of lockjaw 21 April. Resided Elm St. betw. 6th & 7th. — MORE 23 Apr 1841

HILL, William died of cholera Wednesday week. — BRUNS 28 June 1849

HILL, Col. William died this morning at half-past two at the Union Hotel. Of the firm of W. and J. B. Hill, commission merchants. — MORE 23 July 1836

HILLHOUSE, William -- St. Clair Co. Petition to sell his real estate by the publ. adm. — OSIN 18 Jan 1851

HILLYER, Apollas died 18 Nov. at the residence of Dr. S.W. Adreon. Native of Granby CT. Age 28, in St. Louis about 3 years. Funeral Presbyterian Ch. — MORE 21 Nov 1837

HINKLE, Ephraim died in St. Louis. — MORE 29 Mar 1831

HINKSON, John M. Esq. died 25 December last, a young gentleman of distinguished merit much lamented by all his friends and acquaintances. — MORE 22 Jan 1814

HINSON, Harrison committed suicide in Jefferson Co. on 26 May while temporarily deranged. — MORE 31 May 1847

HINTON, Rev. I.T. former pastor of the St. Louis Baptist Church died in New Orleans 28 August. — MORE 6 Sep 1847

HITE, Isaac -- St. Clair Co. Final settlement by Abraham Hite. — OSIN 25 Dec 1852

HIX, F. W. died at his home on Bowling Green Prairie on 1 May. "Old and esteemed citizen." Born Prince Edward Co. VA. Never married. — BRUNS 4 May 1848
" 11 " "

HIX, Dr. John A. died at Marshall, Saline Co., Saturday. — BRUNS 5 July 1849

HOBBS, Price (Brice?) died at Cantonment Bellefontaine on 1 Nov., son of Nicholas of Frederick Co. MD. — MORE 7 Nov 1812

HOBBS, Thomas said to have been murdered by Robert Turk on 30 Aug 1844. — JINQ 15 May 1845

HOCKER, R.D. died of cholera at Harrisonville. — LEXP 2 Aug 1854

HOCKER, Samuel B. died 11 April; born in Mercer, now Boyle Co. KY. Died in 39th year; born 18 Dec. 1812. Member Methodist Church, buried Methodist cemetery. Lexington & Danville please copy. — BOBS 29 Apr 1851

HODGE, Joseph L. died near Franklin age about 45. Formerly of RI. Providence RI please copy. — BOLT 25 Apr 1840

HODGE, Col. William died, late editor of Vandalia Free Press. — LEXP 4 Feb 1845

HODGES, Rev. (?) died at Bonhomme 29 August. Presbyterian. From probate, Coleman Hodges. — MORE 3 Sep 1840

HOFFA, Henry died last Friday, native of Pennsylvania. Osburn Chaney was charged with his murder. — MORE 3 Oct 1825
" 12 Dec "

HOFFMAN, Henry T. died of cholera Friday last, age about 40. A mechanic. — BRUNS 12 July 1849

HOFFMAN, William H. formerly of Abbottstown, Adams Co. PA, died age 28. — MORE 19 Jan 1853

HAGAN (or HOGAN), Dr. Sylvester died at Paris, Monroe Co. on 19 Sept. in his 36th year.	MORE 5 Oct 1836
HOGAN, Thomas died last Thursday.	MORE 14 Mar 1825
HOLBERT, Joseph -- St. Clair Co. Final settlement by Jesse Applegate.	JINQ 26 Aug 1841
HOLEBROOK, Jacon died 11 Oct. in his 40th year.	MORE 13 Oct 1851
HOLBROOK, David L. of St. Louis died Wednesday night.	MORE 6 Sep 1844
HOLDEN, Edward M. of Perryville died 6 May.	MORE 7 June 1850
HOLIDAY, Erasmus Dallan died 18 January in his 20th year at the home of his guardian Wm. S. Boxley.	MORE 4 Feb 1845
HOLLIDAY, George, late of Clark Co. KY, died 30 September.	MIN 14 Oct 1820
HOLLIDAY, L.L. died 17 July of consumption.	COMB 23 July 1846
HOLLIDAY, Capt. R.T. of Hannibal died in Sacramento 25 Feb.	MORE 28 Apr 1850
HOLLAND, Charles H. died 26 March in his 22nd year. Formerly of Walpole NH.	MORE 27 Mar 1849
HOLLAND, Henry -- Chariton Co. Final settlement by R. Holland.	BRUNS 5 July 1849
HOLLAND, John D. died 26 Nov. 4 miles west of St. Louis, son of William and Elizabeth. Late of Prince Edward Co. VA.	MORE 28 Nov 1836
HOLLAND, Matthew died "a few days ago."	MORE 15 Feb 1817
HOLLAND, Nathaniel "a young man" died in Brunswick 21 Oct.	MODE 4 Nov 1846
HOLLIMAN, Thomas "old and worthy citizen" died 16 Sept.	PWH 23 Sep 1843
HOLLOWAY, John C. of Col. Price's Reg. died at Santa Fe 5 November.	MODE 13 Jan 1847
HOLLOWAY, Thomas, father of a man of the same name who died a short time since, died Sunday.	BRUNS 24 May 1849
HOLMAN, Dr. John died in Chariton (town) Monday last.	MIN 30 Nov 1826
HOLMES, Jacob died 1 April age 32. Funeral from the residence of John Cavender, 3rd below Cedar.	MORE 2 Apr 1853
HOLMES, John Martin late clerk of the Columbus, age 39.	MORE 11 Jan 1852
HOLMES, Capt. R. died at Jefferson Barracks 4 November.	MORE 5 Nov 1833
HOLMES, Samuel L., Deputy Sheriff, killed by Elijah Mallerson at latter's grocery store, St. Charles Co. He had facetiously accused Mallerson of swindling a customer of "two bits."	MORE 10 Dec 1838
HOLMES, William died 29 Sept. in his 34th year. Funeral from home of his brother Robert betw 6th-7th. Westchester PA please copy.	MORE 30 Oct 1846
HOLRAH, Mr. ___ killed in St. Charles by Mr. Reynolds of KY.	HIM 16 Nov 1854
HOLT, Dr., member of legislature from Platte Co.	BOLT 19 Dec 1840
HOMER, James, merchant of St. Louis, died 27 Sept. at the residence of C. Rhodes.	MORE 29 Sep 1838

HONEY, Charles Augustus son of John W. and Mary S. died   MORE 6 Sep 1844
    in Hillsboro 23 August age about 14.

HONEY, Capt. John W. died at his residence in Jefferson Co.   MORE 11 Sep 1832
    4 Sept. after a severe illness of several weeks.

HOOE, J. T., died, formerly of Prince William Co. VA.   MORE 27 June 1849

HOOK, Elijah of Franklin died aboard the *Far West* Tuesday. MORE 27 Aug 1835

HOOPER, Capt. ___ of the *New Haven* died Tuesday of typhoid. SWERE 14 Oct 1844

HOOPER, Clark, invitation to his funeral from Mrs. Whaley's   MORE 1 Mar 1841
    Boarding House, #80 Myrtle. Presbyterian cemetery.

HOOPER, Joseph, native of Maryland, died 4 Feb. in 24th yr.   MORE 7 Feb 1846

HOOVER, Jonathan of Taney Co. died 7 June at Ash Hollow,   MORE 7 Oct 1850
    age 45. Left a wife.

HOPKINS, Elliot R., "collector of this port." Funeral   MORE 19 Sep 1842
    from the Virginia Hotel.

HOPKINS, Francis Henry died 17 August age 28.   MORE 24 Aug 1826

HOPKINS, Major Wm. M. died at the residence of Charles   MORE 9 Oct 1839
    Cabanne Saturday last. "Highly respected."

HOPKINS, William -- Montgomery Co. Final settlement   MORE 15 Sep 1829
    by Isaac Hopkins.

HOPKINSON, N.G. died Sunday 16 Feb. in his 23rd year at   MORE 18 Feb 1845
    the residence of Dr. N.B. Atwood.

HOPPER, Edmund, in Lt. Col. Willock's command, died on   MODE 13 Jan 1847
    the way to Santa Fe.

HOPPER, Mr. ___ (Raleigh) died, representative from Decatur. MORE 6 Nov 1844

HORD, Robert of Boonville died age 33.   MIN 24 Aug 1833

HORD, Willis L. died at the residence of Wm. Gardner Esq.   MORE 3 Sep 1833
    in St. Ferdinand Twp. Formerly of Mason Co. KY.

HORDS, Henry died in the *Car of Commerce* disaster.   MORE 27 May 1828
    (He was a black crewman)

HORN, Thomas, late sheriff of Greene Co., died 22 Sept.   JINQ 2 Nov 1843

HORN, Wiley of Johnson Co. murdered by a negro.   MORP 8 May 1845

HORNICAN or HONNICAN, David, a blacksmith, died 12 Sept.   PWH 17 Sep 1846

HORNSBY, Henry age about 21 died at the residence of his   MORE 5 Oct 1851
    brother in St. Louis Co.

HORTON, John age 11 son of Mrs. Mary died 11 March.   PWH 30 Mar 1848
    William age about 18 " died 21 March.

HOUGH, Silas died 17 October at Jefferson City.   COMB 29 Oct 1847

HOUGHLAND, Wm. G. died in St. Louis 29 January.   MORE 6 Feb 1836

HOUX, Jacob died near Pilot Grove in Cooper Co. age 71y   LEXP 1 Feb 1854
    8m 10d. Emigrated to MO 1817.

HOWARD, Asa -- Gentry Co. Final settlement by John C.   STGAZ 27 July 1853
                                         Williams.

HOWARD, David died 10 April age 65 (? - blurred), resident   MORE 12 Apr 1849
    of Charrette, Warren Co., for more than 30 years.
    Methodist.

HOWARD, John, shot by gunsmith F. Hellinghaus, not expected   MORE 10 June 1844
    to live. Native of New Hampshire. (Shown in
    later story as Amanzo Howard.)

HOWARD, ____ executed for murder at Boonville last Friday.   MORE 10 Aug 1841

HOWARD, John S. died in California MO 18 Apr age 36.   MORE 24 Apr 1851

HOWDESHELL, John died 17 Jan. in St. Ferdinand.   MORE 22 Jan 1853

HOW, Harvey of P--- Co. died at Chimney Rock in June.   MORE 7 Oct 1850
    Age 45. Survived by wife.

HOW, Dr. James Samuel died in his 22nd year. Funeral from   MORE 15 June 1849
    his father's residence, St. Charles betw 8-9.

HOWELL, Samuel "an old resident advanced in years" committed   BGRAD 11 June 1842
    suicide in a field near the Middle Fork of the
    Salt River.

HOWLAND, Alfred, formerly of New York, Friday age 32.   SCOMB 6 July 1836

HOWLETT, L. V. Nelson died of erysipelas 8 August en route   MORE 4 Dec 1851
    to Oregon. His family arrived there safely in Sept.

HOYLE, L. killed in the Big Hatchee explosion at Hermann.   MORP 25 July 1845

HOIT, Albert L., formerly of Georgetown NH died 11 Oct.   MORP 13 Oct 1845
    age 22, of typhoid.

HUBBARD, Dr. Jabez died 4 Feb. age 41.   MIN 18 June 1821

HUBBARD, Rev. Thomas died at the home of his son Asaph E.   MIN 30 Dec 1823
    in his 75th year, in Howard Co. Baptist.

HUBBLE, John, murdered. Formerly of Harrisonville,   MODE 8 Dec 1847
    Van Buren Co.

HUDSON, Abner -- DeKalb Co. Letters of administration to   STGAZ 28 July 1848
    David Thompson 12 July.

HUDSON, Baley -- DeKalb Co. Letters of administration to   STGAZ 27 Nov 1846
    A. H. Skidmore 2 November.

HUDSON, John W. died near Sibley in Jackson Co. 10 Apr.   LEXP 22 Apr 1845
    age about 34. Eldest son of Samuel decd.,
    formerly of Mason Co. KY. Wife, 3 children.

HUFFMAN, David -- St. Clair Co. Letters of administration   JINQ 4 May 1843
    to J. Applegate & L.R. Ashworth, 16 March.

HUGHS, Andrew died Sunday last age 45 or 50.   BRUNS 27 Sep 1849

HUGHES, Benjamin died Saturday in this county.(Howard)   BOLT 13 Sep 1845

HUGHES, Fleming P., a painter, died 11 July. Left wife   BRUNS 19 July 1849
    and one child.

HUGHES, Henry died 29 June age 45. Lived on Morgan St.   MORP 30 June 1845

HUGHES, James M., Co. N., Col. Price's Reg., died 11 Nov.   MODE 13 Jan 1847
    at Santa Fe.

HUGHES, William Sr., formerly of Jessamine Co. KY, died 10 January age 67. — MIN 25 Jan 1828

HUGHES, Dr. Joel died 3 March age about 40. — BGRAD 9 Mar 1844

HUGHES, John C. died age 21. Funeral at Mrs. E. Hughes'. — MORE 3 July 1851

HUGHES, Paschal of Cole Co. died Monday, age about 30. — JEFRE 14 May 1842

HUGHES, W. of Howard Co. died 25 June at the crossing of South Fork age 40. — MORE 7 Oct 1850

HUKEMAN, Bernard of Jefferson City, Infantry Battalion, died on the way to Santa Fe. — MODE 13 Jan 1847

HULAGAN, John, native of Dublin, died last Monday. — SCOMB 12 Aug 1835

HULETT, George died "Thursday last"; fell from a horse. — BGRAD 13 Aug 1842

HULL, Jephtha of Cape Girardeau Co., 18 June, age 29. — MORE 7 Oct 1850

HUMBERT, Adam -- Dallas Co. Letters of administration to Joseph Moad, 4 November. — SPAD 15 Nov 1845

HUMMULTY, Hugh, killed by lightning near Manchester 21 Aug. — MORP 23 Aug 1845

HUMPHREYS, Francis died 20 July age about 30, formerly of Harrison Co. KY. Wife, 4 children. — PWH 23 July 1845

HUMPHREYS, John, late of Birmingham, Eng. died age 26. Son of James. Resided on Pratt Ave. — MORE 9 May 1849

HUMPHRIES, Joseph died near Smith's Landing, of cholera, returning from St. Louis. — FULT 4 May 1849

HUNSDON, Alexander H. died in New Orleans 23 April. Funeral Presbyterian Church, burial Presb. cemetery. — MORE 8 May 1847

HUNT, James drowned when the ferry sank at Savannah Landing. — STEGPD 21 May '53

HUNT, Lieut. Samuel W. died at Jefferson Barracks 11 Sept. — MORE 22 Sep 1829

HUNT, Theodore Esq., for many years Recorder of Land Titles, died Saturday evening age 54. — MORE 24 Jan 1832

HUNT, Wilson P., an old inhabitant, many years postmaster, died yesterday. Resided 7th & Olive. — MORE 14 Apr 1842

HUNT, Thomas died at Bellefontaine at the mouth of the Missouri on 17 July. Col. of the 1st Reg of Infantry. — MORE 24 Aug '08

HUNT, Winson of Scott Co. died "10 miles this side of Fort Kearney" of lung fever, age 40. Wife, 1 child. — MORE 7 Oct 1850

HUNTER, Charles -- DeKalb Co. Final settlement by William Hunter. — PLAR 25 Feb 1848

HUNTER, Joseph of Scott Co. died Tuesday, Dec. 2-, an old resident. Revolutionary soldier, at Valley Forge. — INP 10 Jan 1824

HUNTINGTON, George P. died in Fulton Co. IL, age about 29. Late resident of St. Louis, native of Hudson NY. — MORE 26 Mar 1840

HURT, Jubal died "last night." — MIN 23 Oct 1829

HUSSEY, Charles Stetson died 8 May age 22 at the residence of his father. Bangor ME pls copy. — MORE 10 May 1853

HUDGINS, HUTCHINS, Parke or Parks -- killed by Indians.　　MORE 18 Mar 1815

HUTCHINS, Nicholas M., formerly of Baltimore Co. MD, died　　MORE 13 Sep 1836
　　　Friday 9 September.

HUTCHERSON, James son of John died of pneumonia in his 15th　　PWH 1 Jan 1846
　　　year. (two sisters also died within 4 days)

HUTCHINSON, Samuel L. died 14 Feb. at the residence of John　　MORE 6 Aug 1847
　　　Campbell, St. Louis Co. Formerly of Monroe Co. VA

HUTTON, ____ shot and killed by a neighbor, ____ Asher, in　　MORE 14 Sep 1843
　　　Platte Co. "last Friday." Asher claimed self-
　　　defense; they had been quarreling for a year.
　　　Both men were over 60.

HYDE, George A., city recorder, formerly of Georgetown DC,　　MORE 29 Jan 1853
　　　died 28 Jan. Funeral, St. Patrick's Church.

HYDE, John B. died in St. Louis 13 Nov. in his 27th year.　　MORE 16 Nov 1838

INGLISH, Amon died Friday evening last in Moniteau Twp.,　　JINQ 22 Dec 1842
　　　Cole Co. Left wife, 8 children.

INGRAM, Arthur, a St. Louis merchant, died in his 29th year　　MORE 23 Sep 1828
　　　"after 18 months' suffering of the severest kind."
　　　At residence of father near Pittsburg.

INGRAM, Thomas J. died at Mr. Wiggins' residence 13 August.　　MORE 15 Aut 1834

INSKEEP, Rev. J. M. C. died at Liberty 14 Nov. age 38.　　FULT 7 Dec 1849

IRVIN, ____ died after a fight with James Brooke and　　PLAR 27 Oct 1848
　　　his son in Newmarket.

IRWIN, James died in St. Louis last Friday.　　STCHMO 19 Sep 1821
　　　William, oldest son of James, died Wednesday.　　MORE 13 Oct 1819

IRVIN, John died at Mr. Harmon's of Porch's Prairie last　　BRUNS 28 June 1849
　　　Friday. Had taught school in Carroll Co.

IRVING, Richard died yesterday age 30 (31?)　　SWERE 6 Mar 1848

IRWIN, John of St. Louis age 40 died at Panama 4 March.　　MORE 3 May 1853

IRWIN, William A., formerly of Winchester VA, died 14 May　　MORE 3 May 1851
　　　in Shelbyville MO in his 27th year.

ISOM, Dr. William died at his home in St. Michaels, Madison Co. MORE 14 June '27

IVERS, Charles, 1st engineer of the Car of Commerce, killed.　　MORE 27 May 1828

IZARD, James F. died at Ft. Leavenworth, a 1st Lieut.　　MORE 31 May 1836

JACKS, John died 21 March near Glasgow, age about 45. He had　　BRUNS 31 Mar 1849
　　　blood poisoning from a thorn prick.

JACKSON, Edmund, native of Dublin, died 2 Nov. in 23rd year.　　MORE 4 Nov 1851

JACKSON, Edward W. died in Callaway Co. 6 Sept. age 21.　　JINQ 19 Sep 1844

JACKSON, Eli died in Peno Twp., Pike Co., Tuesday last in　　BGDB 27 Dec 1845
　　　his 50th year.

JACKSON, Gabriel S. died in his 30th year at the residence　　BOLT 19 Apr 1845
　　　of his father, Monday last.

JACKSON, Rev. J. M. murdered at Clarksville by __ Moon.	MORE 23 Nov 1846
JACKSON, James died in Fayette 28 June in his 27th year. Left relatives and friends. I.O.O.F.	BOLT 4 July 1845
JACKSON, E. G. son of the late George E., died 27 May in his 22nd year. Resided Ste. Genevieve Co.; accidentally shot himself.	MORE 15 June 1841
JACKSON, John of Howard Co. died 17 Sept. age 73. An early settler, he was in the Battle of New Orleans.	BRUNS 27 Sep 1849
JACKSON, Julius died in Shelby Co. 28 March in 56th year.	PWH 20 Apr 1848
JACKSON, Thomas M. died age 22y 5m. Lexington KY. pls copy.	MORE 27 June 1849
JACOBS, Daniel of Benton Co., of Col. Price's Regiment, died on the way to Santa Fe.	MODE 13 Jan 1847
JAMES, William, originally from England, died while en route to St. Louis from Louisville.	MORE 24 Apr 1834
JANNERET, __ --advertisement by Hariette Janneret to persons who had left watches for repair by "my late husband."	MORE 13 Oct 1830
JANNEY, N.E., several years a prominent resident of St. Louis, died on the *Alice* while en route home. Interred Pittsburgh.	MORE 10 Oct 1848
JARRETT, Abraham of Herculaneum died 17 April in his 75th year in Louisville KY.	MOAR 12 May 1837
JASPER, Merrel died at his residence near Oregon, Holt Co. on 25 August. Age about 35, native of KY, "short time among us." Wife, children.	STGAZ 26 Sep '45
JEFFRIES, Dr. __ died in Perryville.	MIN 31 Aug 1833
JEFFREY, Palmon, late of Morgantown VA, adm sale of pers. property in Cooper Co.	BORE 2 Jan 1844
JENKINS, William M., a farmer formerly of Baltimore Co. MD died of apoplexy 20 July.	PWH 23 July 1846
JENNINGS, __ shot by storekeeper Cleff at Lexington.	BOLT 4 Apr 1846
JENNINGS, Jacob died in this county 18 March in his 48th year. (Cooper Co.)	COMB 25 Mar 1847
JENNINGS, John A. died in Monroe Co. 10 November.	MODE 17 Feb 1847
JENNINGS, John H., Co. O., Col. Price's Regiment, died 11 Nov. at Santa Fe.	MODE 13 Jan 1847
JESSER (JASSER), F.L. died 25 Sep. Resided 171 S. 2nd. "An old resident." (Frederick L. Jasser)	MORE 26 Sep 1848
JESSUP, A., a passenger, died in the *Car of Commerce* tragedy.	MORE 27 May '28
JESSUP, G. "	
JETTE, __ from Saline Co., Doniphan's Regiment, died at Santa Fe.	MODE 13 Jan 1847
JETTER, Horace died 7 Nov. in his 28th year.	MORP 8 Nov 1845
JEWETT, O.P. died at Hillsboro 1 March.	MORE 15 Mar 1853

JOHNSON, Abner -- Chariton Co. Sale by exr. Henry Shannon.   BOLT 6 Nov 1841

JOHNSTON, Alexander of Cooper Co. died "the 23rd" from a   WEM 28 Mar 1839
    fall from a carriage.

JOHNSON, Alexander died at the residence of his brother in   MORE 30 July 1847
    Springfield MO 9 July age 39. Native of Co.
    Tyrone, 18 years in the US.

JOHNSON, Benjamin N. son of B.S. died in his 20th year.   PWH 15 Oct 1842

JOHNSON, Benjamin Sr. died in Jefferson Co. age about 75.   MOAR 3 Feb 1837
    Formerly of Louisville, in MO since about 1802.

JOHNSON, Benjamin of Berkshire NY died in St. Louis age 22.   MORE 6 Mar 1840
    (His brother John lived in St. Louis.)

JOHNSON, Capt. C. D. W. died in Cooper Co. 9 August, from   OSIN 27 Aug 1853
    MD in 1832. Methodist, Mason, I. O. O. F.

JOHNSON, Claiborne died 22 Aug. at the residence of his   BOLT 29 Aug 1840
    son Reuben near Fayette. Age about 80, a
    veteran of the Revolution.

JOHNSON, Ezra, a saddler of Westport, formerly of Glasgow,   BRUNS 14 June '49
    died of cholera the 24th.

JOHNSON, Edward, "for many years a highly respected   MORE 6 June 1851
    citizen;" funeral from Christ Church.

JOHNSON, George died Wednesday last in St. Louis Hospital   MORE 12 Apr 1844
    from wounds received at the German Ball on
    Christmas Eve.

JOHNSTON, Henry and Alexander, sons of Thomas of Bon Homme,   MORE 2 Jan 1811
    died on 27 December.

JOHNSON, Henry died at the home of his father George A. in   MORE 4 Apr 1843
    St. Charles Co. 22 March in his 22nd year.

JOHNSON, Horatio died 3 February in his 28th year, a   MORE 7 Feb 1811
    native of Maryland.

JOHNSON, Hugh died "last Saturday."   MORE 8 Aug 1825

JOHNSON, Jeremiah died 8 January. (Canton, Lewis Co.)   CAMP 12 Jan 1849

JOHNSON, John died at Cape Girardeau 19 Sept., several   MORE 29 Sep 1838
    times representative from that county.

JOHNSTON, Laban of Cooper Co. died 25 Dec. in his 70th year.   WEM 17 Jan 1839
    Born in VA in 1760, father early removed to PA.
    Was at Redstone Fort in 1776. Joined the
    Methodist Church in 1800.

JOHNSTON, Peter found guilty of the murder of John Spahr   MORE 7 June 1810
    (Ste. Genevieve), to be hanged 3 August.

JOHNSON, Dr. Peyton T. died 2 October. Late of Natchez MS   BGRAD 7 Oct '43
    and formerly of Lexington KY.

JOHNSON, Reuben an old and highly esteemed citizen died   GLWT 31 July 1851
    near Fayette Saturday.

JOHNSTON, Robert youngest son of Samuel Sr. died 9 Sept.   MORE 11 Sep 1853
    age 24. Philadelphia pls copy.

JOHNSTON, Robert died in Fayette 19 Dec.   MIN 29 Dec 1832

JOHNSTON, Thomas died in Little Rock 14 January.   MORE 27 Jan 1835

JOHNSON, William, age about 45, died 21 Nov. Late resident   MORE 23 Nov 1847
of Nelson Co. KY. Beardstown please copy.

JOHNSON, William F. of Lafayette Co. died at Scott's Bluff   MORE 7 Oct 1850
16 June age 26.

JOHNSON, D.C. of Palmyra died of smallpox near Ash Hollow   MORE 7 Oct 1850
15 May.

JOHNSON, William -- Montgomery Co. Final settlement by   MORE 29 May 1832
John Baker.

JOHNSON, ___ "a former Methodist clergyman who had fallen   MORE 19 Apr 1843
into evil ways" died in the calaboose, drunk.

JONES, Dr. ___ murdered by ___ Gibson, all of Rockhouse   STGAZ 23 June 1848
Prairie.

JONES, Alex and Joshua, both of Boonville, died in Mexico.   COMB 16 Dec 1847

JONES, Asa, body found in Mississippi River.   SWERE 9 Sep 1844

JONES, Benjamin, killed in a milling accident, St. Francois Co.   JEFRE 21 Dec '33

JONES, Charles, died at Chariton in Howard Co.   MORE 27 Feb 1818

JONES, David found dead near Lexington 24 May. Miller, late   MORE 10 June 1843
of Beardstown IL. Believed suicide. Had $300
and some deeds with him.

JONES, F., 2nd clerk of the *Kit Carson*, died of cholera   BRUNS 19 May 1849
"a few days since." Buried Glasgow.

JONES, Henry, blacksmith at Brunswick, died Monday last.   BRUNS 24 Feb 1849

JONES, Hugh murdered at Ste. Genevieve by Charles Heath.   MORE 29 Feb 1812

JONES, James of Monroe Co. thrown from horse and killed.   MORE 29 Apr 1849

JONES, James died in Boone Co. 14 June.   MORE 2 July 1844

JONES, John Rice died in St. Louis last Sunday, Judge of   SLINQ 3 Feb 1824
the Missouri Supreme Court.

JONES, Dr. John of Marthasville, Warren Co., shot dead in   MORE 4 Feb 1842
his own yard 21 Jan. Age about 53, native of KY,
graduated from Transylvania. Emigrated about
24 years ago. Arrests have been made.

JONES, Joseph H., "two years past" a merchant of St. Louis,   MORE 10 Mar 1829
died a suicide in Philadelphia 16 Feb. Native of
England.

JONES, Joseph, brother of William H., died yesterday age 24.   MORE 6 Apr 1844
Shot from a house by an unknown rioter in 5th Ward.

JONES, ___ of Callaway Co., Doniphan's Reg., died at Santa Fe.   MODE 13 Jan '47

JONES, Levin from Adair Co. died 13 Sept. en route to Santa Fe.   " 17 Feb 1847

JONES, Levi of Randolph Co. of Col. Price's Regiment died   MODE 13 Jan 1847
on the way to Santa Fe.

JONES, Lewis of Louisville KY died in St. Louis.   MORE 6 Sep 1831

JONES, Col. Myers F., formerly member of the Legislature   MORE 26 Jan 1847
    from Washington Co., died in San Felippe Tx.

JONES, Nathan died at his residence in Bonhomme Twp. in his   MORE 26 Nov 1851
    59th year yesterday. "Old and respected."

JONES, Dr. Samuel L. killed in Buchanan Co. 18 June by   MODE 18 July 1848
    George P. Gibson, with a butcher knife.

JONES, Thomas E. died at the residence of Ferdinand Kennett   MORE 5 Sep 1845
    4 Sept. in 26th year. Natchez please copy.

JONES, William died in Callaway Co. 23 Sept. at the residence   JEFRE 26 Sep '40
    of Mr. Yount, age about 60. One of the first
    aettlers of Jefferson City.

JONES, William P. at Dubuque's Mines in 25th year. US Navy.   MORE 5 Aug 1834

JORDAN, William S. oldest son of Andrew died 23 July near   BGRAD 27 July '44
    Louisiana age about 22.

JORDAN, Mr. and family shot and scalped in the upper   MORE 10 Apr 1813
    settlement of St. Charles.

JOY, W.P. of Camden Co. died 10 June 60 miles west of   MORE 7 Oct 1850
    Fort Kearney age 20.

JUCKET, William a soldier in the 6th Reg., Inf., died   MIN 22 Apr 1820
    at Cantonment Missouri 6 April.

JUDLIN, Richard formerly of Baltimore died 13 July in 29th y.   MORE 15 July '53

JUZBUG, August, native of Germany, died age 33. Funeral   MORE 6 July 1842
    from residence, 137 S 2nd below Poplar.

KAVANAGH, Dr. Charles died Tuesday last.   MIN 28 Aug 1821

KEELER, Lt. Samuel, 6th Reg. Inf., at Council Bluffs 27 May.   MIN 24 June 1820

KEEGAN, Patrick died of consumption 9 April in his 45th y.   MORE 11 Apr 1853
    Buried Rock Springs.

KEENE, Pollard, a native of KY, died 20 April. "Was at   MORE 3 May 1817
    River Raisen." A merchant.

KEENER, Charles S. of Baltimore died at the Prairie House.   MORE 3 July 1832

KEENEY, Dr. Christopher H., son of Mrs. Mary Lisa, died   MORE 7 July 1829
    Friday age 22. Interred family burying ground
    5 mi. from St. Louis.

KEENEY, Michael -- Montgomery Co. Letters of administration   MORE 2 Oct 1840
    to William S. Wyatt.

KEESACKER, John died Saturday last.   MORE 8 Sep 1829

KEISER, Capt John W., a steamboat developer, died in   BRUNS 30 Aug 1849
    Rocheport 18 August.

KELLAR, Isaac "an aged citizen" died Saturday. Methodist.   PWH 13 Aug 1845

KELLOGG, Capt. Edwin died in St. Louis 17 Feb. age 28.   MORE 20 Feb 1844

KELLY, F.K. died yesterday. Resided 81 Market St.   MORE 4 Feb 1845

KELLY, Jacob -- Wayne Co. Final settlement by Isaac E. Kelly.   INP 15 Dec 1826

KELLY, Washington, formerly of Baltimore Co. MD, died 16 Aug. at the home of James Griffith, Newark. — PWH 25 Sep 1844

KELSO, Edward W. died in Warren Co. in his 42nd year. Many years a resident. Louisville please copy. — MORE 28 Mar 1850

KELTON, William, funeral notice. — MORE 12 Jan 1851

KEMBLE, James, drowned, deckhand on the Fayaway. — MORE 27 June 1849

KENDRICK, Major James died in his 56th year. Born in VA, later moved to KY. — PWH 26 Sep 1840

KENNEDY, James died 29 May in his 37th year. Resided 7th St. Between Morgan and Franklin. — MORE 30 May 1848

KENNEDY, William A., late of Pittsburgh, died "last night" at Mr. Newman's boarding house, age about 30. — SWERE 29 Oct 1848

KENNEDY, Thomas -- Montgomery Co. Final settlement by Sarah Kennedy. — MORE 13 Apr 1826

KENNEDY, ___ badly scalded at McKee's steam flouring mill and little hope for his recovery. — MORE 21 Nov 1844

KENNER, Winder H. died in Warren Co. VA, notice to his brother Rhodam somewhere in Missouri. — PWH 4 Dec 1841

KENNERLY, James age 48 interred O'Fallon Burying Ground. — MORE 27 Aug 1840

KENNETT, Wilson P. died at Herculaneum 20 October. (Faded: in his 15th or 45th year.) — MORE 23 Nov 1837

KIMMICK, KEOMICK __ a storekeeper murdered at Valle's Mines in Jefferson Co. in a robbery "last week." (John G. Keomick in probate record) — MORE 27 Dec 1844

KERR, David W., on of Maj. Wm. H., age 17. — JEFRE 24 Aug 1839

KERR, James died in the district of St. Charles, formerly of Mercer Co. KY. — MORE 16 Nov 1811

KERR, John Esq. died Wednesday in his 49th year. Resided 5th & Market. — MORE 21 Dec 1843

KERRY, Asa died in Randolph Co. Born 29 Feb. 1768. — MORE 31 Mar 1851

KETCHUM, Major D. at Jefferson Barracks 31 August. 6th Reg. US Inf. Left "sons." — MORE 2 Sep 1828

KEYTE, James, of Brunswick, native of Manchester, Eng. died at Jefferson City 26 August. — SWERE 9 Sep 1844
James O'Fallon, son of the late James, killed by a falling tree, age 15. — MORE 4 Feb 1846

KIBBE, Amos -- Montgomery Co. Letters of administration to Publ. Adm. J.P. Wiseman, 1 December. — FULT 7 Dec 1849

KIBBY, Col. Timothy died at St. Charles leaving "a disconsolate widow and a number of children." — MORE 13 Feb 1813

KICE, Jacob formerly of Augusta Co. VA died 21 Feb. in 69th y. — LEXP 16 May '48

KIENLEN, C.F. of Central Twp. died 31 December 1851. — MORE 1 Jan 1851

KIGER, Jacob A. died 30 May in his 48th year. Native of Winchester VA. — MORE 31 May 1848

KILLAM, W. S. of Lincoln Co. died aboard the <u>Corn</u> en route   MORE 10 May 1850
    to CA. Age 35, formerly of VT.

KIMBALL, Ansel S. "victim of the arson and murders of 17 Apr."
    1st Engineer Union Fire Co., killed by falling
    debris. Born Concord NH, to MO 1836. Left wife.   MORE 19 Apr 1841
    Interred Presbyterian cemetery.

KIMBROUGH, William died at the home of Mr. Hackney, age 20.   SPAD 6 Sep 1845

KING, William B. died at City Hotel. Interred Presb. cemetery.   MORE 14 Oct '41

KING, Glen drowned in the Missouri near the mouth of the   MORE 24 Mar 1841
    Lamine. Father James King asks that anyone finding
    the body notify him. Glen was 17.

KING, Isaac and wife died of cholera at Harrisonville.   LEXP 2 Aug 1854
    Nathan and wife   "   "

KING, John died 10 September age about 40, "one of the   INJN 12 Sep 1844
    oldest and most respected citizens."

KING, John killed in a street fight. Michael Bernard
                            acquitted.   MORE 21 Feb 1849

KING, Preston -- Montgomery Co. notice by Jacob Groom, adm.   MIN 10 Dec 1819
    Moses -- ". Letters of administration 18 Oct. by   MIN 26 Oct 1826
    John King, Chariton.

KING, Robert died at the home of his son-in-law in Merrimack
    Twp. 5 March in 56th year. Formerly of Mason Co. KY.   MORE 11 Mar 1853

KINGSBURY, Capt. James. Funeral from St. Xavier Church.   MORE 27 June 1853

KINGSBERRY, Noah died 24 May in his 35th year.   GLWT 29 May 1851

KINGSBURY, Robert, son of Jerre of Boone Co., age about 13,
    accidentally shot by his brother Leonard at the   BOLT 6 Jan 1844
    home of their brother-in-law Mr. Stapleton,
    while preparing for a deer hunt.

KINGSLAND, Lawrence, formerly of Pittsburgh, died 15 Oct.   MORE 16 Oct 1847
    age 70. Interred Bissell Burying Ground.

KINKEAD, Andrew Esq. of Bonhomme Twp. died 30 Mar. age 65.   MORE 10 Apr 1818

KINNEER, Robert died Saturday age 42, "old & respected."   MORE 16 July 1844

KINNEY, James died Tues. at the home of D. Ballentine.   COMB 18 Feb 1847

KINNEY, John, native of Scotland, died at the home of   CANE 12 Jan 1854
    Peter Cline, Scotland Co., 3 Nov. 1853.

KINNEY, Thomas died 10 Sept. on passage to Louisville on the   MORE 11 Dec 1832
    <u>Columbus</u>. Supposedly lived in Louisiana MO.

KIRK, James murdered in Mercer Co. by Benjamin Smothers.   MODE 11 Nov 1846

KIRKLAND, Abraham killed by a falling log at a house-   PWH 22 Apr 1847
    raising in Monroe Co. "old & respected."

KIRKLAND, Hugh A. -- Wright Co. Letters of administration   SPAD 30 Mar 1847
    to H. H. Lea, 9 March.

KIRKPATRICK, Rev. David M. died at the home of Wm. Grant   MIN 22 Feb 1834
    in Callaway Co. 12 January.

KIRKPATRICK, Sgt. Alexander A. fell at the Battle of Sacramento. Harrison Lodge, I.O.O.F.	MODE 12 May 1847
KIRKPATRICK, John G. found dead in bed in Paris MO Sunday.	COMB 20 June 1846
KIRKPATRICK, Dr. William died of consumption 21 Feb. in his (30th or 36th) year.	MORE 27 Feb 1851
KIRTLEY, Jeremiah died at Lexington 7 Feb. in his 61st yr. Long a resident of St. Louis county or city.	MORE 16 Feb 1844
KITCHEN, John, living in the eastern part of Chariton Co., drowned at Switzer's Mill 16 May. "Worthy old gentleman."	BRUNS 31 May 1849
KITZMILLER, William Esq. died 24 Sept. age 42.	MORE 21 Sep 1851
KIVEN, ___ killed in an "affray" at a drinking house on the levee owned by Philip Rock.	MORE 15 Dec 1841
KLIENARD, Wm. Franciscus died 5 May age 32. Left widow and infant child. Frederick City MD please copy.	SWERE 14 June 1847
KLUNE, KLUNK, Joseph died Saturday last.	MORE 13 Jan 1835
KNAPP, Rev. Azel L., Baptist minister, died at the home of Ira T. Nelson in New Hope, Lincoln Co., 16 Aug. Native of Maine, in Lincoln Co. 10 years.	MORE 23 Aug 1844
KNAPP, William died at Savannah MO 25 April age 45. Late of New York.	MORE 13 May 1844
KNAUDER, Rudhowe or Reinhold. Resided 2nd & Almond. KNAUBER	MORE 27 June 1851
KNIGHT, John died of cholera Thursday.	MORE 30 Oct 1832
KNOTTS, William K. died at Oakville, St. Louis Co., in his (57th? 37th?) year. Baltimore please copy.	MORE 27 June 1849
KNOX, Edward B. murdered by Thomas McLaughlin. Reward for McLaughlin offered by Walter Knox.	MOAR 10 July 1839
KNOX, George of Rocheport, "merchant & legislator," Thurs.	BRUNS 24 May 1849
KOERHER, John A., age 42, 16 Mar. Resided 2nd & Myrtle.	MORE 17 Mar 1853
KOUFE, Andrew H. of Col. Price's Regiment, died 10 Nov. at Santa Fe.	MODE 13 Jan 1847
KRAGER, John killed on Bond St.; murder being investigated.	MORE 10 Oct 1844
KREIDER, Philip, a German baker, drowned in a pond while watering his horse.	MORE 5 June 1848
KRIDER, Hiram E. died of consumption of the brain 12 Feb. at the home of Mr. Gage, age 35.	MORE 13 Feb 1851
KRILL, Thomas murdered by Barnhard Baumaster.	MORE 27 Sep 1843
KRITZER, Joseph -- Chariton Co. Petition to sell his real estate by Jacob Tschippat, adm.	BRUNS 16 Mar 1848
KUYKENDALL, Isaac of Boone Co. died in Oregon 18 Dec. age 27.	MORE 1 Apr 1851
KYLE, ___ of Saline killed by brother David in fit of insanity. Near Cambridge, 4 April.	GLWT 14 Apr 1853

KYLE, David died in St. Louis Saturday, a merchant. MORE 17 Feb 1835

LACKLAND, Benjamin F., son of George L. of St. Louis Co., MORE 26 Feb 1847
　　died in Santa Fe 29 Dec. age 27. Price's Reg.

LACOMB, Francois, native of Canada, died 31 August. MORE 19 Sep 1811

LACY, Edward son of George and Mary Ann of Austin, MO, late MORE 5 Oct 1848
　　of Quincy IL, of smallpox, 4 Oct., in his 23rd year.

LADD, John S., a printer, originally from Detroit, died at SWERE 3 Aug 1846
　　City Hospital 1 Aug. in his 29th year. Consumption.

LA FETRA, Peter A. died 12 June. Philadelphia please copy. MORE 16 June 1849

LAGSTEIN, John of Saline Co. died 16 June near the Crossing MORE 7 Oct 1850
　　at Scott's Bluff, age 27.

LAIDAIN, Joseph, formerly of Boston, died 17 March age 37y 8m. MORE 18 Mar '43
　　Funeral from #38 Elm St.

LAKE, Ballard died 16 August in his 20th year at the PWH 20 Aug 1846
　　residence of John Keach. Baptist.

LALOR, Patrick, native of Wexford, died 15 December. MORE 23 Dec 1828

LAMARQUE, Etienne died at his home in Old Mines, MORE 20 Nov 1851
　　Washington Co., 10 November.

LAMME, Francis, soldier of Capt. Craig's Company, killed in a MORE 27 May 1815
　　skirmish with Indians, Lower Cuivre Ferry.

LAMME, Samuel C. "killed lately by Indians on his caravan MIN 11 Dec 1819
　　on the prairie trace between Missouri and Santa Fe."

LAMONT, Daniel died of apoplexy at Fayette on his return to MORE 1 Feb 1837
　　St. Louis from the west. Resided Chestnut St.;
　　interred Presbyterian cemetery.

LAMPHER, George, died at Fredericktown, Madison Co. MO, on MORE 30 Oct 1845
　　16 October. Late postmaster.

LAMKIN, James C., late of KY, died 6 October. Interred in PWH 9 Oct 1845
　　Lewis Bryan burying ground.

LANAHAN, Michael, fell from the Hannibal and drowned. MORE 13 Aug 1845

LANDREVILLE, Andre died 12 September. MORE 16 Sep 1834

LANE, Dr. Henry committed suicide "Monday morning last." MORE 17 Sep 1838
　　John Francis, oldest son of Dr. Henry of Ste. Genevieve　" 20 July 1826
　　died 16 July age 14.

LANE, John -- Chariton Co. Final settlement by George F. Adams. BRUNS 6 Sep '49

LANE, Micajah M. died yesterday of bilious fever. "Worthy." SLINQ 23 Aug 1823

LANE, Presley Carr, native of VA, died in Carroll Co. in MORE 23 Sep 1846
　　his 25th year. Planned to settle in MO.

LANE, Victor Ralph Carr, son of Dr. William Carr Lane, died MORE 25 Aug 1846
　　in Lexington KY 19 August, age about 16. (Only son)

LANGHAM, Major Angus L., formerly of St. Louis, died very MORE 9 Sep 1834
　　suddenly at Little Rock on 20 August.

LANGLEY, James died 28 June of cholera. FULT 6 July 1849

LANGLEY, John, deckhand on the <u>Charles Carroll</u>, killed 27 Nov.   MORE 29 Nov 1847
when crushed by a falling hogshead of sugar.

LANHAM, George H., formerly of Prince George Co. MD, died at   MORE 29 July 1834
his plantation 29 January age about 70.

LANHAM, Richardson died in Boone Co. 29 March age 63.   MORE 10 Apr 1832

LANHAM, Stephen, County Court Justice, died yesterday at   MORE 29 Sep 1841
his residence near Manchester.

LANIUS, Jacob, presiding elder of the M. E. Church south,   WEPT 18 Oct 1851
died at Fayette 5 Oct. Left wife, 7 children.

LANSDALE, Isaac and two of his children, of cholera, Palmyra.   MORE 28 June 1833

LANSDOWN, Lawrence J., formerly of VA, at his father's home   JEFRE 5 Oct 1839
on the Osage River, 19 September.

LARKIN, Edward, body found on bank of slough near Outrander's   MORE 19 Nov 1840
steam mill. Verdict: death by freezing.

LATHAM, William -- Chariton Co. Letters of administration   BRUNS 7 Apr 1849
to John C. Cavanah, 19 March.

LATRESSE, Frederick died yesterday age 38.   SWERE 28 Aug 1848

LATREZE, Edward, age 42, native of St. Louis, died 26 Aug.   MORE 27 Aug 1851

LATOUR, Amable P. died 11 January. Resided on Convent St.   MORE 12 Jan 1848
between 3rd-4th. Interred Catholic cemetery.

LAUDERDALE, J. H. of Lafayette Co. died in Diamond Springs CA   MORE 5 Feb 1852
on 22 November.

LaVALLE, Charles A., Jr. killed by lightning at New Madrid   MORE 27 Aug 1845
8 Aug. in his 17th year. Son of Charles & Sarah.

LAVEILLE, Col. Joseph C., more than 20 years a citizen of   MORE 20 Sep 1842
St. Louis, "yesterday age 57." Episcopal cemetery.

LAWLER, Edward, native of Co. Kildare, 27 June age 25.   MORE 29 June 1852

LAWLESS, Bradford "in Cooper Co. a few days since."   MIN 16 Sep 1820

LAWLESS, Luke E. Esq. "died in this city Saturday."   SWERE 21 Sep 1846

LAWRENCE, Daniel, a native of Hollis NH and formerly of   SWERE 10 July 1848
Natchez, died yesterday.

LAWRENCE, George died of cholera in St. Joseph 9 August.   MORE 19 Aug 1851

LAY, Daniel, many years a resident, 4 Sept. age about 65.   MODE 22 Sep 1847

LEACH, John died 22 October age about 35.   MODE 10 Nov 1847

LEACH, William, native of Scotland, died 19 June age 53.   MORE 27 June 1843
Had been in St. Louis 3 years.

LEAKE, Floyd, lately a resident of Ralls Co., died in   PWH 22 Mar 1849
Shelbyville 25 February.

LEAKE, Thomas "an Englishman believed to have died in St.   MORE 22 Nov 1848
Louis sometime after June 1841." Information wtd.

LEAMAN, E. P. of St. Louis died in Hannibal 1 September   MORE 6 Sep 1844
of congestive fever.

LEAR, Col. John, Judge of the Marion Co. Court, at Palmyra   PWH 27 May 1847
    23 May. Born Mason Co. KY 1798, to MO 1819.

LEATHERBERRY, George W. died in St. Charles Saturday at the   SLINQ 22 Sep 1822
    home of George Collier. Relatives in MD.

LEAVENWORTH, Seth M., father of Dr. L., pioneer and resident   MORE 4 Apr 1853
    of Indiana 40 years, died 2 April.

LeBARON, Col. William, late of Wheeling VA, died age 45.   MORE 13 Dec 1838

LE BEAU, Francois died in St. Louis Wednesday last.   MORE 14 May 1833

LE BLOND, Joseph, of Carondelet; funeral notice.   MORE 28 Dec 1846

LECKEY, Dr. James G. died at his residence in St. Ferdinand   MORE 3 Sep 1841
    Twp. age 26. Native of Ireland; recently of
    Rockbridge Co. VA.

LE CLERK, Rev. Louis died 24 July.   MORE 26 July 1833

LE COMPTE, Guillaume Hebert, age 72, died 17 February.   MORE 22 Feb 1809

LE DUC, Joseph died "on Monday last."   MORE 24 May 1810

LE DUC, Marie Philip died at the residence of Hypolite Papin   MORE 19 Jan 1843
    15 January age 70. Born St. Denis, resided in Paris.

LEE, Carey A. of McCoys & Lee died in Independence 3 Sept.   LEXP 10 Sep 1844
    in his 34th year.

LEE, General Elliott died 25 February.   MORE 26 Feb 1851
    (A story in MODE 17 March 1846 says that a "General
    Elliott" of St. Louis was murdered in Taos.)

LEE, John "an illustrious citizen" died last week.   MORE 24 Aug 1816

LEE, Noah of Cooper Co., formerly of Howard Co., died 2 Sep.   GLWT 25 Sep 1851

LEE, Thomas Laycock, son of Rev. James (Methodist) died of   MORE 11 Jan 1853
    scarlet fever 8 January in his 16th year.

LEE, William -- Dallas Co. Final settlement by William   SPAD 13 Apr 1847
    Montgomery.

LEECHMAN, A. J. of Grundy Co. died 16 June.   MORE 7 Oct 1850

LEEPER, Samuel -- Chariton Co. Final settlement by   BOLT 20 Feb 1841
    Nancy Leeper.

LEGUERRIER, Charles Sr. died 16 Aug. in Jackson Co. age 68.   SLINQ 7 Sep 1846

LEIGHTON, Dr. Jonathan died in Manchester (IL?) 15 Jan.   MORE 31 Jan 1837
    age 32.

LEIPER, Francis died in Green Co. 20 May at the home of   WEM 13 June 1839
    his mother.

LEITCH, Arthur died age 57. Resided #142 7th St.   MORE 1 Oct 1847

LEITENSDORFER, Col. Eugene, age 75, died at Carondelet 11   MORE 14 Mar 1845
    March. Funeral from home of Joseph Pease.

LELAND, Judge John D. died near Boonslick Sunday night.   BOLT 23 June 1847
    Born Northumberland Co. VA 10 Nov 1797, moved to
    MO in 1836. In Saline Co. until 1840. Admitted
    to the Bar in 1819.

LELAND, John died January last of typhoid fever in El Passo,   MODE 14 Apr 1847
    NM in his 21st year, eldest son of Col. John D. of
    Howard Co. In Doniphan's Regiment, MO Volunteers.

LEMON, William of Boone Co. died last Sunday.   MIN 1 Oct 1831

LENNAN, Dr. Francis died in St. Charles.   MORE 6 Oct 1819

LEONARD, Nathaniel died 20 Feb. in his 76th year at the home   BOLT 24 Feb 1844
    of his son, A. Leonard. Was a Capt. in the 1st Reg.
    Artillery in the late war with Great Britain.

LEONARD, Patrick, born Ireland, a resident of Washington Co.,   BEA 8 July 1828
    died at Fever River IL in April. Notice to heirs.

LEONARD, William, "one of our oldest residents," Wednesday last.   PWH 13 Sep '49

LESSLEY, Andrew died 23 January leaving a large circle of   HIM 25 Jan 1855
    relatives and friends.

LESPERANCE, Damase R., native of Canada, died in his 26th   MORE 19 Sep 1844
    year at St. Louis Hospital, 18 Sept. Funeral
    from home of Mrs. Picott, Vine & Washington.

LESSIEUR, Francis Esq. died at Portage des Sioux, where he   MORE 10 Feb 1844
    had lived 44 years, on 30 Jan. in his 72nd year.

LESTER, John C. executed for the murder of his brother-in-law   MORE 15 Dec 1845
    King B. Scott, at Clinton.

LEWIN, A. C., postmaster at Fredericktown. (No other data.)   MODE 13 Nov 1848

LEWIS, Alexander, a native of Scotland, died Sunday at the   MORE 21 June 1852
    home of his brother-in-law David Reid.

LEWIS, Andrew J. died at the home of his father in Marion   PWH 27 Mar 1841
    Co. 22 March age 26.

LEWIS, James Howell, son of Warner, died yesterday at the   MORE 24 Mar 1838
    residence of Capt. Robt. Freeland. Age about 28.

LEWIS, Jasper died 28 August.   PWH 2 Sep 1843

LEWIS, Jeremiah died in Clark Co. 20 Oct. in his 56th year.   PWH 30 Oct 1841

LEWIS, John P. W., son of Warner of St. Louis, died at his   MORE 16 Oct 1839
    temporary residence at Princeton KY where we was a
    student at Princeton College. Age 20.

LEWIS, Joseph, age about 20, died Sunday last.   STCHMO 25 July 1821

LEWIS, Edmund died in Saline Co. on 5 April in his 58th   MODE 10 Apr 1848
    year. Native of VA, to Howard Co. about 19 years ago.

LEWIS, Henry P. died near Grand River, of cholera, age   BRUNS 12 May 1849
    about 28. "Had walked up from Glasgow a day previous."

LEWIS, Richmond, son of Rev. Lewis of Howard Co., shot him-   BOLT 10 Jan 1846
    self near Platte City. "Partially deranged for some time."

LEWIS, Thomas died Friday "old and respected citizen."   PWH 17 Dec 1846

LEWIS, Thomas A. died at Milton, Randolph Co., 18 Aug., age   BRUNS 26 Aug 1848
    about 40. Oldest son of Judge Lewis of Howard Co.

LEWIS, Stephen Walker died at Monticello, Howard Co., in his   BOLT 28 Sep 1844
    48th year. Native of Buckingham Co. VA. To MO in
    1834 from Lynchburg. Husband, father. Mason.

LEWIS, Thomas H. died at Cape Girardeau 18 May, "old, respected." MORE 28 May '45

LEWIS, Warner, late of Goochland VA, died 6 Oct., a few miles from St. Louis. SLINQ 14 Oct '20

LICHER, Jurgen Henry died 9 May. Emigrated from Germany 1845. Born in Henimern, Gronenberg, Hanover. MORE 12 May 1847

LIGHTNER, Isaac of "the Foundry" died of cholera. BRUNS 12 July 1849

LIMBER, John, deckhand on the Constitution, killed in an accident while shoving off. MORE 18 Aug 1848

LINCH, David killed in sinking of ferry at Independence. MORE 30 June 1834

LINDELL, John "of the firm of John Lindell & Co., died at the village of Louisiana, Upper Mississippi." SLINQ 23 June 1821

LINDELL, John died yesterday morning of congestive fever in his 26th year. Funeral from mother's home, 181 3rd St. MORE 25 Aug 1845

LINDSEY, James died in Buffalo Twp., Pike Co., Thursday age 22. BGRAD 10 Aug 1844

LINDSY, Sterling -- Dallas Co.
Letters of administration, Ezekiel Lindsy. 20 May. SPAD 13 June 1846

LINDSEY, William, at his father's home near St. Charles, age 21. STCHMO 22 July '20

LINN, ___ "one of the rangers at Cap au Gris." MORE 6 May 1815

LINN, Barnabas, recently from New Orleans, died yesterday. BEA 15 Aug 1829

LINVILLE, Squire died 2 April, age about 22, as a result of a fall from a horse. JEFRE 7 Apr 1838

LIPPINCOTT, Samuel Esq. of Ralls Co. died at Rio Brassos TX 6 July age 42.(Widow, daughter) Atkinson Rose, his son, died at the same place 31 July age 18. (Mother, sister) MORE 19 Oct 1826

LISA, Manuel died "on Saturday evening last at the Sulphur Springs near this place." MORE 16 Aug 1820
Manuel his son died at Louisiana, Pike Co. in 17th y. MORE 10 Aug 1826

LISLE, Gen. B. M. died at Jefferson City 18 February. MORE 21 Feb 1845

LITTLE, George M., died in St. Louis 14 April. MORP 21 Apr 1845

LITTLE, John, a native of Ireland, believed born in Co. Down, near Bainbridge, died in August. Notice to heirs. SLINQ 30 Aug '20
" 28 Apr 1821

LITTLE, John, died "Sunday last." Left a large family. INP Nov 1826

LITTLETON, Capt. William, funeral notice: today, from his residence at the corner of 10th and Olive. SLINQ 22 Jan 1849

LIZENBY, James -- Chariton Co. Letters of administration to Publ. Adm. on 23 September. BRUNS 28 Oct 1847

LOCKHART, Jeremiah J. died in Brunswick 5 Oct. in 39th yr. GLWT 16 Oct 1851

LOCKWOOD, Isaac died 7 June. Buried Presbyterian cemetery. MORE 8 June 1849

LOGAN, John died at Perryville in his 59th year. Many years a resident, formerly of KY. MORE 21 May 1850

LOGAN, Dr. Robert, watchmaker, died Monday evening.	MORE 27 Oct 1819
LOISE, Edward F., formerly of Council Bluffs, died 12 May 1847 age 43.	MORE 13 May 1851
LOMON, Henry died about 15 September/at the house of Johnson Clay in Platte Co. Born Germany, no known heirs	PLAR 5 Jan 1849
LONERGAN, Capt. Kennedy died 9 August in his 45th year.	MORE 20 Aug 1851
LONG, Dr., of Carrollton, killed by riding under a partly fallen tree. He was knocked from his horse.	BRUNS 26 Aug 1848
LONG, Henry C. "in this city only a short time."	BRUNS 2 Sep 1848
LONG, Horatio of St. Louis, in Hopkinton NH 21 Sep. age 32.	MORE 15 Nov 1841
LONG, John "the younger" executed for the murder of George Gordon "last Saturday."	MORE 20 Sep 1809
LONG, Reuben, of Liberty, died at the residence of Dr. Nathaniel Hutchison at Boonville Sunday and was interred in the Methodist cemetery there.	WEM 10 Jan 1839
LONG, Reuben -- Gentry Co. Final settlement, James Long.	STGAZ 27 July 1853
LONG, Samuel, of Boone Co., accidentally shot at Ballard's (formerly Holt's) mill, Callaway Co., 12 May.	BRUNS 1 June 1848
LONG, James H. died at Bonhomme 5 August in his 30th year. Wife, child.	MORE 8 Aug 1843
LONG, William Oliver, son of William and Elizabeth, died at Gravois 31 July in his 23rd year,	MORE 3 Aug 1843
LONG, William Esq. died at his residence in Bonhomme on 27 December "one of the oldest and most respected citizens of that settlement."	MORE 2 Jan 1836
LOOKER, Benjamin F., late of Harrison, Hamilton Co. OH, died 9 September. Resided Almond betw 2-3rd. Cincinnati and Ft. Madison IA please copy.	MORE 10 Sep 1844
LOOMIS, Samuel Richardson, eldest son of Sarah, died 5 Mar. age 17. Resided at #71 Pine.	MORE 6 Mar 1847
LOONEY, Isam -- St. Clair Co. Petition to assign dower.	OSIN 18 Jan 1851
LOUKS, Jacob, father of John of Carondelet, 26 Aug. age 81.	MORE 27 Aug 1853
LOVELACE, Zachariah R. Sr. died in Hartford Twp., Pike Co. 18 Jan. in his 80th year; his wife Lucy had died 13 Hours before. They had lived together 55 years and were buried in the same grave. On the 25th their eldest son James died in his 50th year, leaving a large family. All died of pleurisy.	BGRAD 3 Feb 1844
LOVELAND, Truman age 21 died 1 September.	MORE 3 Sep 1853
LOVETT, D. B. of Mercer Co. died 13 June, 60 mi. west of Ft. Kearney, age 29.	MORE 7 Oct 1850
LOVING, Burwell, only son of John, died 28 December age 25.	STCD 10 Jan 1852
LOWDERMILK, A. of Lewis Co. died 16 June near Cottonwood Springs age 28. Left wife and child.	MORE 7 Oct 1850

LOW, Nathaniel, an auctioneer, died 25 June. He was shot by Edward Ford, who was charged with his murder. — MORE 19 June 1844

LOWER, Jacob, formerly of Oneida Co. NY, age about 50. He resided on Locust between 4th-5th. — MORE 9 May 1849

LOWRY, Charles F., member of the St. Louis Bar, resident of St. Louis 3 years, died at the home of his father in Springfield IL age 24. — MORE 17 May 1837

LOWREY, Thomas, late of Jefferson Co. VA died 31 Oct. at the house of Col. Samuel Hammond in St. Louis. — MORE 8 Nov 1820

LUCAS, Adrian -- Montgomery Co. Letters of administration to W. Lucas. Final settlement, W. Lucas -- — MORE 23 Mar 1830 / JEFRE 8 Mar 1834

LUCAS, Charles, son of J.B.C., killed in a duel with Thomas Hart Benton. — MORE 27 Sep 1817

LUCAS, John B. C., late Judge, age 84y 16 d, a resident of St. Louis for 37 years. — MORE 30 Aug 1842

LUCAS, James Jr., in Brunswick 21 Feb. after a short but severe illness, in his 31st year. — BRUNS 24 Feb 1848

LUCAS, James of Carroll Co. died at the residence of John Grimsley 18 January in his 69th year. — BRUNS 27 Jan 1848

LUCAS, Robert, son of J.B.C., a career army man, died at French Mills, River St. Lawrence, on 8 February. — MORE 9 Apr 1814

LUIS, Antoine "an old inhabitant of this town" died Thurs. — MORE 25 Apr 1812

LUNA, Peter died of cholera 13 July. Pittsburgh pls copy. — MORE 14 July 1851

LUNARD, Hugh died at the house of Alexander Browne near John H. Howe's salt works. Said to have been born in Ireland, age about 34, no known relatives. — MIN 28 Sep 1826

LUSK, Robert McClure died age 26, native of Cumberland Co. PA. — JINQ 15 Aug 1845

LUSK, William, senior editor of the Jefferson <u>Inquirer</u>, died 10 October. — JEFRE 14 Oct 1843

LUTTRELL, James, native of Ireland, died Wednesday. — MORE 12 Sep 1835

LUX, John died of lockjaw yesterday. He had broken his leg the week before while jumping from a buggy. — MORE 30 Oct 1844

LYBRAND, S. (prob Samuel); name found on clothing of a body taken from the river. — MORE 25 May 1840

LYLE, James S. -- notice of his decease on 7 March. — MORE 24 Mar 1834

LINCH, David killed in the sinking of the ferry at Everett's Ferry near Independence 16 June. — SOV 4 July 1834

LYNCH, James C., "many years a resident," died 22 Sept. age 53. — MORE 24 Sep 1845

LYNCH, John, brother of James, died yesterday age 41. — SWERE 8 Jan 1849

LYONS, Matthew died Saturday, 16 October. — MORE 19 Oct 1840

McAFEE, John Sr. died in Shelby Co. in his 60th year 19 Aug. — PWH 28 Aug 1841

McALEER, James died of consumption 18 Aug. in his 33rd year. Philadelphia please copy. — MORE 20 Aug 1845

McALISTER, Rev. Alexander died 25 March at Rushville IL. MORE 31 Mar 1834
    Methodist, resident of St. Louis many years.

McALISTER, Capt. James, formerly of KY, resident of St. Louis MORE 23 July 1833
    Co. more than 21 years, died age 71.

McALISTER, Green P. R. age about 25 died at his father's BGRAD 31 Aug 1844
    residence in Cuivre Twp., Pike Co.

McALISTER, John died Sunday week, age 56. Formerly of BRUNS 14 Apr 1849
    Page Co. VA.

McALLISTER, John, formerly of Louisville, died 27 April age SWERE 30 Apr 1849
McCALLISTER   about 48. Late mate of the Missouri. Lived
    Mullanphy betw Main & Broadway. Methodist cemetery.

McARTHUR, John Hosford, son of John Esq., died on 15 Oct. MORE 1 Nov 1833
    in Ste. Genevieve age 17.

McCABE, Dr. C.B.N. died 24 January in Bloomfield. Left CGWE 2 Feb 1849
    several children. Interred Cape Girardeau.

McCAGG, R.C. died 12 May. I.O.O.F. Episcopal cemetery. MORE 16 May 1849

McCALL, James, an attorney, yesterday; formerly of NY. STCHMO 12 Sep 1822

McCANN, Capt. Joseph died in Fayette. MIN 24 Aug 1833

McCAN, Patrick, a native of Ireland, died in LaGrange in CAMP 13 Apr 1849
    August 1847. No known heirs.

McCARDLE, John, engineer at Conner's Mill, Cooper Co., was BOLT 27 Dec 1845
    killed 10 Dec. when his coat caught in the MORE 25 Dec 1845
    gearing. Native of Liverpool, about 38. Family.

McCARRY, John of Cape Girardeau died 15 June at Scott's MORE 6 Oct 1850
    Bluff of cholera, age 21.

McCARTAN, Thomas, St. Louis merchant, died 29 July. MORE 2 Aug 1831

McCARTHY, Charles, late of Co. Kerry, died at Fee Fee. MORE 27 Aug 1851
    Funeral from St. Patrick's Church.

McCARTHY, Peter, in a factory accident; badly mangled. MORE 12 Sep 1845

McCASH, David, formerly of Cincinnati, died yesterday MORE 23 Mar 1852
    age 35. I.O.O.F. rites.

McCASKRIE, Reuben died on the way to CA, between Council BRUNS 5 July 1849
    Grove & Independence.

McCASKA, William, age 34, died at the residence of MORE 17 Nov 1851
    William Hamilton. Wheeling VA please copy.

McCAUEL, Thomas -- Montgomery Co. Letters of administration MORE 27 Aug 1823
    to John Reynolus (sic)

McCAUSLAND, John died in St. Louis 18 September age 40. MORE 21 Sep 1843

McCAY, Robert deceased, late of New Madrid Co., notice to MORE 10 July 1843
    his heirs.

McCLAIN, Matthew -- Dallas Co. Final settlement by SPAD 6 Apr 1847
    Caleb Williams, publ. adm.

McCLAIN, William C. "an intemperate man" died suddenly HANT 27 July 1852
    Sunday in South Hannibal.

McCLELLAND, Col. Elisha died at Nashville, Boone Co. He had   MORE 26 Mar 1839
    been a resident of St. Louis for several years.

McCLELLAND, Col. James died last Sunday in this city (Columbia) MIN 13 July '33

McCLELLAND, James J., "long a resident" of St. Louis died at   SWERE 1 Nov 1847
    City Hospital 29 October age about 55.

McCLELLAND, Capt. Robert "well known to those officers who   MORE 23 Nov 1815
    followed Anthony Wayne" died Wednesday last.

McCLOUD, Robert died 1 May in his 37th year of consumption.   MORE 8 May 1832

McCLUER, J. A. died at the home of his mother in St. Ferdinand   MORE 2 Nov 1842
    30 Sept. in his 25th year.

McCLUER, William, late of Bedford Co. VA, died at his home   MORE 27 Aug 1833
    in St. Louis Co. 31 July.

McCLURE, Andrew, grandson of George Knox, died ? August.   MIN 5 Aug 1822

McCLURE, James, formerly of Vincennes, died 25 June age 37.   MORE 4 July 1825

McCLURE, James -- Chariton Co. Letters of administration   BRUNS 7 Oct 1848
    to Wm. J. White.

McCLURKEN, Samuel died 28 March age 33. Buried in   MORE 29 Mar 1853
    Washington Co. IL.

McCOLLUM, Lewis -- Chariton Co. Letters of administration   BRUNS 28 Oct 1847
    to the publ. adm., 23 September.

McCORD, Major William died at his residence near Versailles,   MORE 25 Oct 1839
    Morgan Co. 17 October, age 41 leaving a
    "deeply afflicted family."

McCORMICK, ___ killed in a skirmish with Indians near Fort   MORE 27 May 1815
    Howard, on lower Cuivre ferry. Capt. Craig's Co.

McCORMICK, ___, a teamster, died in the Santa Fe country.   MODE 13 Jan 1847

McCORMICK, John of Pettis Co. died 29 March 40 miles west   MORE 7 Oct 1850
    of Ft. Kearney, age 24, of cholera.

McCORMICK, Joseph, resident of Concord Twp., Washington Co.,   MORE 6 Nov 1840
    died 4 Nov. in his 62nd year. Native of NC, in
    MO 25 years. Wife, numerous children.

McCORMACK, James died 19 Jan. at his home on Platin Creek,   MORE 29 Jan 1846
    Jefferson Co., in 54th year. Wife, several children.

McCORMACK, Peter B. died in Jefferson Co. 1 March age 87.   MORE 14 Mar 1840
    Born in Ireland (Dublin), Revolutionary soldier.
    Numerous offspring.

McCORMACK, Enoch, son of James, died at Selena, Jefferson   MORE 26 Oct 1843
    Co., in his 28th year.

McCORMIC, James died at his residence on Gravois Thursday   MORE 25 May 1830
    age 68.

McCORMIC, John S. died at Gravois 13 July in his 23rd year.   MORE 16 July 1844

McCOY, Samuel, a discharged US Army soldier, died at the   MIN 9 Oct 1829
    house of Zachariah Clevenger, Ray Co., in fall of
    1825. Supposedly born VT, age about 25.

McCRACKEN, Cyrus, formerly of Woodford Co. KY, died   PWH 13 Aug 1845
    Saturday night last.

McCRACKIN, Smith A. -- Gentry Co. Final settlement by   STGAZ 19 Jan 1853
    James Thompson.

McCREDIE, George P. died at his residence in Callaway Co.   MORE 27 Jan 1837
    on 1 January. Late of Richmond VA.

McCULLEY, ____ killed 28 March in Daviess Co. when digging   BRUNS 13 Apr 1848
    out a mill seat, Taylor's Ferry, Grand R.

McCULLOCH, Roderick -- St. Clair Co. Letters of admini-   OSIN 9 July 1853
    stration to Wm. H. MucCulloch, 11 May.

McCULLOH, Thomas B. died 20 July age 27. Funeral from home   MORE 21 July 1843
    of father-in-law, R.B. Fife, Walnut-8th-9th.

McCULLOUGH, John, age 24, formerly Albemarle Co. VA,   JEFRE 7 Sep 1839
    "one editor of the *Inquirer*."

McCULLOUGH, Robert, formerly of Allegheny Co. MD, died   MORE 2 Aug 1841
    1 Aug. in 23rd year. Funeral from residence
    of William Cooper on Broadway.

McCULLUM, J. of Taney Co. died 18 June 40 miles west of   MORE 7 Oct 1850
    Ft. Kearney, age 13.

McCUNE, John died in Pike Co. 31 Jan. Father of Mr. McCune   MORE 7 Feb 1852
    of McCune, Gaty etc., St. Louis.

McCURDY, John B. of Danville, member of the medical class   MORE 16 Nov 1846
    at St. Louis U., died 13 November.

McCURRY, Edward -- Ozark Co. Letters of administration   SPAD 14 Mar 1846
    to Wm. M. Brown, 3 February.

McCUTCHAN, James Darst died in St. Charles Co. 24 March   MORE 15 Apr 1848
    in his 15th year, son of James, decd., and
    grandson of Isaac and Phebe Darst.

McCUTCHEON, William, formerly of Augusta Co. VA, died   MORE 10 Jan 1852
    8 January in his 63rd year.

McDANIEL, Eli "recently" at Gentryville. A Mason.   STGAZ 25 May 1853

McDANIEL, John, formerly of Philadelphia, in St. Louis.   SWERE 9 Mar 1846

McDANIEL, Richard B., only son of George H., died in his   PWH 29 July 1843
    13th year on 26 July.
    George H. died at his residence near Palmyra   PWH 19 Mar 1846
    Tuesday of inflammation of the brain.

McDANIEL, Jacob Esq., representative from Chariton Co.,   STGAZ 6 Oct 1852
    died Thursday last of cholera.

McDEARMON, James R. of Jefferson City, auditor of Public   MODE 4 Apr 1848
    Accounts, died 21 Mar. (James P.?)

McDONALD, Andrew Jackson died 27 Mar. in his 35th year.   STGAZ 14 Apr 1852

McDONALD, Capt. Henderson, formerly of Pittsburgh, 3 Mar.   MORE 4 Mar 1852

McDONALD, James R., many years a broker, died 12 May.   MORE 17 May 1849
    Pittsburgh and Ohio please copy.

McDONALD, J. St. Clair died age 38, native of Albany NY.   MORE 11 June 1849

McDONALD, Maj. John D. died in St. Louis Saturday, formerly   MORE 16 Apr 1839
of Mason Co. KY. "Father, husband, friend."

McDONALD, James -- estate of Joshua McDonald, who died   MORE 29 Mar 1824
in 1810, shows that James had died and the new
administrator was Elizabeth McDonald.

McDONALD, John died at the residence of R.S. Holliday near   MORE 5 Mar 1838
St. Louis. Originally from Winchester VA.

McDONALD, Peter "wounded with an ax by Washington Butcher"   MORE 4 June 1845
evening before last, will not recover.

McDONALD, Samuel H. died at the home of his brother James R.   MORE 27 Oct 1845
in Jefferson Co. 21 Oct. in his 31st year of
congestive fever. Formerly of Nashville; buried
in St. Louis. Franklin PA please copy.

McDONALD, Dr. Simon died in Savannah 22 August.   STGAZ 31 Aug 1853

McDONALD, William, of Herculaneum, died in St. Louis in   MORE 13 Oct 1830
his 54th year "Sunday evening last."

McDONALD, William I., died about 1 August at the home of   MORE 23 Sep 1836
Samuel Gibson, Franklin Co. No known heirs.

McDONOUGH, Patrick died yesterday age 66. His friends and   MORE 13 Jan 1845
those of James Timon invited to funeral at his
late residence, 118 S. Main.

McDONOUGH, William Stephen, formerly of St. Louis, died   MORE 7 Mar 1852
near Sacramento 25 January.

McDOUGAL, James, killed when accidentally caught in a   MORE 7 June 1824
flywheel at a rolling mill "in an instant
crushed to atoms." Blacksmith. Left family.

McDOWELL, John of Ray Co. died 18 June near Chimney Rock   MORE 7 Oct 1850
age 34.

McDOWELL, John, clerk of the <u>Vandalia</u>. Date and age not   MORE 13 July 1838
shown. Wheeling and Boston, please copy.

McELROY, James, "aged and respected" died 20 September.   PWH 25 Sep 1841

McELROY, William, Sunday evening last, age about 40.   PWH 22 Aug 1840

McENNIS, John, sexton of the Catholic cemetery, 3 August.   MORE 4 Aug 1846

McEVOY, Joseph, native of Ireland, age 97, died 26 Apr.   MORE 27 Apr 1846
Resident of St. Louis 12 years. Funeral
from home of son-in-law William Lindsay.

McEWING, Hugh died at Huntsville 12 March age about 50.   MODE 21 Mar 1848
Native of Scotland.

McEWEN, Robert, an engineer, died of pneumonia 6 April.   MORE 9 Apr 1853
Wife, 3 children. Louisville please copy.

McFAUL, Charles, died 27 July age 25. Brother-in-law of   MORE 28 July 1851
Cornelius Noonan.

McFALL, John "aged and respectable" died last night.   BRUNS 9 Mar 1848

McFARLAN, George W. -- Chariton Co. Final settlement by BRUNS 9 Mar 1848
    Clark Banning.

McFARLANE, James, stabbed and killed by Vincent I. Hudson BOLT 16 Sep 1843
    at Hannibal.

McFARLAND, Rev. John died in Ste. Genevieve 29 Sept. Born MORE 3 Oct 1846
    Richmond Co. NC. Methodist.

McFERRON, Joseph J., junior editor of the Jackson *Review*, BRUNS 9 Dec 1848
    died near Cape Girardeau 19 Nov. age 28.

McFERRON, Joseph Esq. died Sunday 4th ult. at his residence MORE 7 Mar 1821
    near Jackson in his 41st year. Born Ireland.
    Clerk of the Cape G. Circuit Court and of the
    Supreme Court, 4th Judicial Circuit.

McGAIGAN, John died in Ste. Genevieve Co. 26 April in his MORE 4 Oct 1845
    31st year. Formerly of Philadelphia.

McGAHAN, George died at his home in St. Ferdinand 2 Dec. MORE 22 Dec 1848

McGARVIN, Dennis -- Montgomery Co. Letters of administration
    to Matthias McGirk, 7 July. FULT 13 July 1849

McGHEE, Charles, in St. Louis "Wednesday evening last." MORE 9 Aug 1833

McGHEE, Dr. Lynch A., died at his residence on 5th St. MORE 14 Feb 1844
    11 Feb. age 64.

McGIN, Patrick died in St. Louis 3 Nov., of a bilious MORE 7 Nov. 1821
    complaint, in 24th year. A resident of Pittsburgh
    for many years. A butcher.

McGINNIS, Neal died at Rocheport 3 Jan. age 41. LEXP 1 Feb 1854

McGIRK, Isaac, attorney, died last night. MORE 16 Feb 1830

McGIRK, George died in Howard Co. last Tuesday. MIN 1 Apr 1826

McGIRK, Judge Mathias died 14 August at his residence near MORE 3 Sep 1842
    Loutre Island, Montgomery Co., in 58th year.

McGOVERN, John died Tuesday in his 40th year. Formerly of SOV 14 Mar 1835
    Elleshardra Parish, Co. Cavan.

McGREADY, Dr. James Hardage, son of Dr. Israel, died at MORE 19 Dec 1845
    Potosi 7 Dec. age 29.

McGUIRE, Rev. Allen died in Boone Co. 30 March age 67. MIN 4 Apr 1835

McGUIRE, Philip, representative from Washington Co. in the MORE 16 Feb 1815
    General Assembly, died at Mine-a-Breton "a few
    days ago."

McGUIRE, Thomas died 15 December. MORE 23 Dec 1828

McGUIRE, Thomas J., a printer, died Wednesday. MORE 3 Aug 1830

McGUNNEGLE, Capt. James of the US Army died "few days ago." SLINQ 2 Sep 1822

McGUNNEGLE, Wilson of Hill & McGunnegle died "this morning" MORE 23 June 1829
    after an illness of a few hours.

McHARGUE, John -- Chariton Co. Final settlement by BRUNS 30 Mar 1848
    Joseph McHargue.

McHENRY, John, Representative from Bates Co., died at Mrs. Luck's in Jefferson City 8 January. — BRUNS 20 Jan 1849

McILVENNY, Hugh, a deckhand, drowned. — MORE 17 June 1847

McINTYRE, Charles S. died at Mine la Motte in Madison Co. about 19 October. — MORE 30 Oct 1841

McJARRETT, David, native of Armagh, 22 February age 38. — SLDU 23 Feb 1847

McKAY, Patrick died Friday last in St. Charles. He was 22, only son of Patrick McKay who emigrated in 1794 from Dublin to New York City where he resided many years. Leaves aged father, mother, two sisters. — MORE 29 Dec 1829

McKAY, Dr. Robert died in New London 11 March. — PWH 23 Mar 1844

McKEE, Capt. Henry died in St. Joseph 27 Jan. in his 45th year. Formerly of Lexington KY. Left wife, two small boys. — MORE 12 Feb 1849

McKEE, James died in St. Louis Friday morning. — MORE 3 Feb 1835

McKEE, James of St. Louis died in New Orleans 29 Feb. Funeral from his mother's residence. — MORE 10 Mar 1852

McKEE, James G. formerly of Lexington died in St. Louis 26 Sept. Buried Lexington. — LEXP 27 Sep 1854

McKEE, John died 26 August on "the road between this place and Bellefontaine." A house carpenter from Pittsburgh, taken ill on boat bound for Boonslick. Went ashore to seek help, died before reaching it. — MORE 4 Sep 1818

McKEE, Samuel died in St. Louis Wed. "many years a citizen." — MORE 19 Apr 1836

McKENNA, James "many years a resident" died 19 Nov. — MORE 20 Nov 1851

McKENNY, Richard died Tuesday last. — MORE 3 July 1834

McKENNY, Samuel T., a mechanic, Saturday. — SCOMB 27 July 1835

McKENZIE, Calvin died at the home of his father, Allen, opposite Ross Old Ferry 17 February, formerly of Cape Girardeau Co. — INP 4 Mar 1826

McKIBBEN, Dr. Thomas age 32 died 10 Sept. Formerly of Zanesville OH. — MORE 11 Sep 1853

McKINLEY, John died 13 August age 32. Philadelphia and New Orleans please copy. — MORE 14 Aug 1851

McKINNEY, A. died of congestive chills in Huntsville 6 Oct. — GLWT 9 Oct 1851

McKINNEY, Capt. Alexander died in Warren Co. 7 Dec. age 53. Left wife and large family. — MORE 1 Jan 1841

McKINSTRY, Alex, formerly of St. Louis, died 9 Sept. in Santa Fe age 37. — MORE 26 Sep 1848

McKINSTRY, Charles died at Port Perry, Perry Co., on 4 April. Native and resident of Hudson NY, only a few months in Port Perry. — MORE 25 Apr 1841

McKINSTRY, Elisha Williams son of Alexander H. died 2 Feb. in Santa Fe where he had gone for his health. NY City and Hudson please copy. — MORE 16 Apr 1847

McKNIGHT, William died Sunday morning age 40. — MORE 4 Jan 1831

McLALLEN, Philemon age 27 died 4 June. Ithaca NY and San Francisco please copy. — MORE 5 June 1853

McLANE, M. M., a merchant at Ashley, died Sunday last age about 40. — BGRAD 9 Nov 1844

McLAUGHLIN, John -- Texas Co. Letters of administration to Hiram King, executor, 28 July. — MORP 30 July 1845

McLAUGHLIN, Thomas died 7 April at his home on S. 2nd. Funeral at St. Louis Cathedral. — SWERE 9 Apr 1849

McLEAN, Charles died in Randolph Co. 17 September. — BOLT 27 Sep 1845

McLEAN, James sentenced to die 31 March for the murder of Major Floyd. — MORE 10 Jan 1843

McLEAN, Dr. William B. died Saturday last in Randolph Co. in his 52nd year.
(MORE 16 Jan 1846 gives initial as C.) — BOLT 10 Jan 1846

McLEARIN, Neil -- Montgomery Co. Final settlement by N. Dryden. — MOAR 14 June 1839

McLURE, William R., proprietor of the City Hotel, died Friday in his 47th year. Wheeling and Pittsburgh please copy. — MORE 25 July 1853

McMAHAN, D. died aboard the *President* 16 October between Vicksburg and St. Louis. — MORE 5 Dec 1842

McMENNEY, Samuel died Sunday evening last. — MORE 28 July 1835

McMILLEN, John -- Bates Co. Deceased 19 April 1844. Letters of adm. to Marcus W. Garrison. — LEXP May 1844

McMILLAN, John, from near Dayton, OH fell on a stanchion while boarding a steamboat. Killed. — MORE 22 Oct 1838

McMULLEN, James, killed by Indians. — MORE 18 Mar 1815

McMUNN, James died "in this town" Thursday age about 50. — MIN 21 Aug 1824

McMURTRIE, William, age about 25, died in Shelbyville 2 September. — PWII 16 Sep 1843

McNAIR, Major Alex died at Independence 24 October. Of St. Louis, age 37. — BRUNS 11 Nov 1848

McNAIR, D. D., late sub-agent for the Osage Indians, was killed by lightning Thursday 2 June. — MORE 5 July 1831

McNAIR, Fred B. of St. Louis died of yellow fever in New Orleans 28 August. — MORE 17 Sep 1833

McNAIR, Capt. Washington late of St. Louis died in New Orleans 16 July in his 30th year. — MORE 25 July 1853

McNAUGHT, Capt. George died at the residence of his brother-in-law R. C. Vaughn in Saline Co. in his 36th year. — MORE 11 Aug 1853

McNEIL, Joseph died yesterday evening age 27. — MORE 8 Dec 1846

McNEIL, Joseph brother of John died 7 (?) age 27. SLDU 5 Dec 1846

McNULTY, Patric died Tuesday. "A little over 18." Sons BRUNS 21 Apr 1849
    of Temperance invited to funeral.

McPHETERS, Charles died Thursday last in Lewis Co. PWH 9 Oct 1845

McPHERSON, Major Charles, resident near Franklin, died MIN 1 July 1824
    age 36. Husband, father.

McPIKE, William Esq. died in Pike Co. 9 September, of MORE 14 Sep 1841
    yellow fever, in his 51st year.

McQUAIG, Alexander, native of Scotland, died 15 June. MORE 18 June 1851

McQUIE, Edward T., late of this county, died near SALT 29 Aug 1840
    Marion, Iowa Ter., about 9 August.

McQUILLAN, William killed by bank of earth falling on him MORE 15 Aug 1844
    while excavating. Formerly of PA, driven
    from home in American Bottom by recent flood.
    Family now destitute. Lived near Big Mound.

McQUIDDY David of Clay Co. died in Louisville 29 Sept. MORE 5 Oct 1851

McREA (McREE, MACREA), Col. William, recently surveyor- MORE 17 May 1833
    general of MO and IL, veteran of the late war,
    died in St. Louis Wednesday last.

McCREA, Lt. Col. William died of cholera aboard the MORE 13 Nov 1832
    Express en route from Louisville 3 Nov. age 65.

McSARK, J. of Howard Co. died 18 June 100 mi. west of MORE 7 Oct 1850
    Fort Kearney, age 28.

MABRY, Joel -- Taney Co. Letters of administration to SPAD 25 Apr 1846
    Maximillian Mabry 30 March.

MACKEY, James Esq. died 16 March at his residence SLINQ 23 Mar 1822
    near St. Louis.

MACKEY, John Sr. died at his residence in Pike Co. in BGRAD 13 Jan 1844
    his 74th year on 9 Jan. Settled there 1810.

MACKAY, Resin, son of Capt. Thomas, killed by a slave PWH 8 May 1841
    in his 20th year.

MACKEY, Thomas A. died at Liberty, Clay Co. 23 May MORE 10 June 1842
    age 22. Late of Virginia.

MADDEN, John fell from the *Narragansett* last Monday MORE 22 Nov 1843
    evening and drowned. Left wife and two
    children in St. Louis.

MADDEX, Aquila died in Shelby Co. 8 Dec. in 61st year. PWH 28 Dec 1848

MADDOX, James Adams died at the residence of his father, PWH 16 Oct 1844
    William A., 2 Oct. in his 20th year.

MAGENIS, Arthur L., resident of St. Louis many years, SWERE 27 Mar 1848
    died in Boston 10 March. Native of Antrim.

MAGENIS, Michael, reward notice by widow, Mary. "She has MORE 19 Mar 1842
    reason to believe that his death on 16 Dec. last
    was not an accident and that he was murdered."

MAGHEE, L., a laborer, fatally shot by Owen P. Crow. MORE 25 Aug 1843

MAGILL, Samuel died in Florissant 15 Aug. age 70. MORE 16 Aug 1831

MAGNONETT, John, a Frenchman, no known heirs, drowned MORE 1 Apr 1845
    in the Miss. near the mouth of Plattin Creek
    21 Feb. 1845. A stonecutter.

MAGRUDER, Denis died 29 Sept. age about 35. PWH 1 Oct 1842

MAHAFFY, Samuel of St. Louis died 18 June. MORE 20 June 1835

MAHAN, Judge James F. of Palmyra died age 60. Louisville MORE 29 Mar 1852
    and Frankfort please copy.

MAHON, Bernard, 1st Engineer of the *Big Hatchee*, killed STGAZ 15 Aug 1845
    in the explosion of the boat at Hermann 23 July.

MAIZE, George murdered by John W. Steward in Perry Co. BEA 27 June 1829
    on 11 May. Reward offered.

MAJOR, Benjamin P., Senator from Benton, Saline & Pettis MORE 20 Mar 1844
    counties, killed at Warsaw 2 March by Col. E.
    Cherry in a political argument.

MALLORY, C. P. died 5 July age 22. Native of Plattsburg NY. SWERE 15 July 1844
    (age given by MORE as 27) MORE 10 July

MALLORY, William -- DeKalb Co. Letters of administration STGAZ 3 May 1854
    to Lanze Mallory 3 April.

MALONE, Albert of Plattsville accidentally shot himself MORE 7 Oct 1850
    while taking a rifle from a wagon on the way
    west, 14 May. Age 50.

MANDERS, Mr. H. and two children died of cholera in
    Palmyra. MORE 28 June 1833

MANLEY, John killed by Indians on the way to Boone's Lick. MORE 18 Mar 1815

MANLY, John died 10 July age 25. Indianapolis pls copy. SWERE 19 July 1847

MANNING, Alonzo F., Judge of the Criminal Court of MORE 31 May 1847
    St. Louis Co. No other data.

MANNING, William died in Scott Co. 22 ? in his 47th year. MORE 21 Feb 1853

MANSFIELD, N. of Shannon Co. died 22 June on the Big Blue MORE 7 Oct 1850
    River, age 36.

MANSKER, Lewis, age 40, died on Hubble's Creek 28 August. INP 6 Sep 1823
    Left wife and 6 children.

MANSUR, Charles died at Grape Grove (Ray Co.?) 12 August MORE 30 Aug 1847
    age 42. Boston & Philadelphia please copy.

MARCH, Clement, a resident many years, died Thursday. MORE 30 Nov 1830

MARGUERON, Philip "one of our oldest and most MORE 7 Jan 1846
    respected citizens" funeral notice.

MARS, Mr. ___ thought to have been of Boon Co. died on MIN 21 Oct 1823
    the expedition to Santa Fe.

MARS, Augustus of Johnson Co. died of typhoid 6 November LEXP 22 Nov 1854
    in Lexington, age 22.

MARS, Isaac, a passenger on the St. Louis, bound for　　　MORE 17 Apr 1834
　　　Galena, was killed 12 April.

MARSH, Richard died Sunday 22 December.　　　MORE 25 Dec 1839

MARSHALL, John -- Montgomery Co. Letters of administration　MORE 25 Nov 1828
　　　to Nathaniel Hart & Wm. Clyce.

MARSHALL, P. V. (or Francis V.) of the firm of Riggs &　　　MORE 16 Oct 1832
　　　Marshall, died Sunday (probably of cholera).

MARSHALL, Washington, of St. Louis, died 16 July.　　　MORE 7 Oct 1850
　　　(Presumably on the western trail.)

MARTIN, Bernard, a gardener, formerly of Louth, Scotland.　　　MORE 25 Feb 1851

MARTIN, G. Earl died yesterday at Planter's House, late of　　　MORE 6 Sep 1843
　　　Rodney MS. Member St. Louis Lodge #20.

MARTIN, Jesse died at the home of his son Thomas G. on　　　MORE 30 May 1848
　　　27 May in his 60th year. Resident of Monongahela
　　　City PA, had two sons in St. Louis. Had come with
　　　his wife and youngest daughter for a visit. Was
　　　20 years Ruling Elder, Presbyterian Church.

MARTIN, John died 25 Sept. near Versailles, Morgan Co.　　　MORE 2 Oct 1847
　　　Formerly of Morgan Co. KY. In his 44th year.

MARTIN, John C. of Dublin, Ire. died at Lexington MO　　　COMB 20 May 1847
　　　of lockjaw. Date not shown.

MARTIN, Joseph died at Marion 27 Sept., age about 30.　　　JEFRE 5 Oct 1839

MARTIN, Lewis, a Revolutionary soldier, died 10 July　　　MORE 15 July 1834
　　　in St. Ferdinand Twp.

MARTIN, Lewis E. died at his home near Bridgeton Sunday　　　MORE 11 Jan 1844
　　　leaving a large family. His daughter Mrs. ___
　　　Kennedy died at the same time.

MARTIN, Lewis H. died 13 June in his 28th year. Funeral　　　MORE 14 June 1851
　　　from Fee Fee Church.

MARTIN, Louis, funeral sermon to be preached 17 April　　　MORE 12 Apr 1853
　　　at 4th Baptist Church.

MARTIN, Orsen of Cooper Co. died at Bluffton.　　　WEM 22 Sep 1827

MARTIN, James killed by Jennings Hulsey in a quarrel　　　BRUNS 13 Jan 1849
　　　over cards at Richwoods, Washington Co.

MARTIN, Conolen Daniel, formerly of Virginia, died 2 Aug.　　　MORE 6 Aug 1844
　　　Long a resident of MO. Left widow, 5 children.
　　　In his 44th year. Lynchburgh please copy.

MARTIN, John Q. died 29 Dec. aboard a steamboat from New　　　MORE 10 Jan 1849
　　　Orleans. Many years resident of St. Louis. Left
　　　wife, 2 children. Member I.O.O.F.

MARTIN, Thomas J., no date given; had been Public　　　BRUNS 25 May 1848
　　　Administrator of Livingston Co.

MARTIN, Thomas, formerly of Jefferson City, now about　　　MORE 11 Feb 1845
　　　4 miles in the county, thrown from horse and
　　　killed Wednesday last.

MARTIN, William, son of Dr. J.B. of New Madrid, accidentally shot himself.	STEGPD 11 June 1853
MARTIN, William A. -- Gentry Co. Letters of administration to James C. & Isaac A. Patton 25 Aug. 1851.	STGAZ 7 Jan 1852
MARTYR, William H. died of lockjaw 31 July in his 32nd yr.	GLWT 4 Aug 1852?
MARVIN, Joseph B., recently of Hampshire Co. VA, died Thursday last.	PWH 17 Oct 1840
MASON, Mr. ___ died at Plum Creek 16 June.	MORE 7 Oct 1850
MASON, Isaac, a free man of color, drowned in Chouteau's Pond when he drove in with a horse and wagon.	MORE 18 Aug 1845
MASON, James, late receiver of public monies at Edwardsville, IL, died in St. Louis Saturday.	MORE 7 July 1834
MASON, John, died, no other data. His administrator was Thomas Hempstead.	MORE 9 Apr 1814
MASON, Capt. John T. of Howard Co., formerly of Lynchburg VA, died age "50 or 60."	BRUNS 14 Apr 1849
MASON, Littleberry, one of the first settlers of MO and a member of the MO senate, died 29 June.	HANT 24 July 1852
MASON, Dr. Richard died last night.	MORE 12 Apr 1824
MASON, Robert Esq. died in Lafayette Co. in his 31st year, late of Mason Co. KY. Wife, two small children.	MORE 29 Aug 1839
MASON, Thomas Jr. died near Manchester, St. Louis Co., on 17 July age 24. Widow and orphan.	MORE 23 July 1823
MASON, William G. died in St. Louis 2 November.	MORE 3 Nov 1845
MASSIE, David died in his 74th year.	MORE 14 Apr 1851
MASSEY, Capt. William "died in this county."	SLINQ 26 May 1821
MASSIE, Thomas died at the residence of Dr. T.P. Massie in St. Charles Co. 23 August in his 23rd year. Louisville & Maysville KY please copy.	MORE 31 Aug 1846
MASSEY, Woodbury was shot by Capt. Wm. B. Smith and son at Dubuque 7 September. A lawsuit triggered the attack. Left wife, four children.	MORE 22 Sep 1835
MASSEY, Capt. ___ died of cholera at Palmyra.	MORE 23 June 1835
MASSEY, Henry L. of Potosi was accidentally shot by a boy hunting birds "little hope for his recovery."	MORE 15 July 1843
MASSIE, Samuel Smith "died yesterday." Funeral from his residence, Walnut between 8th & 9th.	MORE 12 July 1843
MASSIE, Theodorick died 17 September.	PWH 25 Sep 1841
MASTERSON, James, stabbed on the levee "in a precarious situation." Assailant fled.	MORE 9 Sep 1843
MATKIN, David -- Ripley Co. Final settlement by Welborn Matkin.	SPAD 20 Sep 1845
MATHEWS, C. S. died at the residence of his brother-in-law Capt. John P. Moore.	NERA 25 May 1848

MATTHEWS, Mr. ___ was murdered by Dr. Coolidge (who was sentenced to hang) at Augusta.   MORE 7 Apr 1848

MATHEWS, Edward of Jefferson City died on the way to Santa Fe. Infantry Battalion.   MODE 13 Jan 1847

MATTHEWS, Greenfield -- DeKalb Co. Final settlement by Isaac N. Shambaugh.   STGAZ 21 Dec 1853

MATHEWS, Henry "an aged and respectable citizen" died of consumption Monday last.   PWH 3 Aug 1848

MATTHEWS, Jacob died in Fabius Twp. 22 July, "old and respected."   PWH 29 July 1843

MATTHEWS, John R. died Thursday 13 Aug. at the house of George Willing. Native of Somerset Co. MD. Age about 35.   MORE 15 Aug 1840

MATHEWS, John S., Esq., Clerk of the Circuit and County Court, Jefferson Co., died at Hillsboro Sunday. Native of MD. Baltimore please copy.   MORE 1 Oct 1845

MATHEWS, Thornton of Pike Co. died in Shasta CA 1 May.   MORE 17 June 1853

MATTHEWS, Victor; he had been murdered and Elisha Baldwin convicted but the verdict was reversed.   MORE 29 Oct 1848

MATSON, William died of cholera in Palmyra.   MORE 28 June 1833

MAULSBY, Hamilton P. Esq. died at Walnut Grove near New Madrid Sunday in his 45th year. Native of VA. Wife, 4 children. Mason.   MORE 3 May 1849

MAUPIN, Alexander drowned in the South Fabius River on 20 June. Left wife and two children.   PWH 26 June 1841

MAUPIN, Garland D., many years a citizen of Howard Co., died 13 March. Formerly of KY.   BRUNS 24 Mar 1849

MAUPIN, Granville, a teamster, died in the Santa Fe country.   MODE 13 Jan 1847

MAUPIN, William J. died near Glasgow 27 July in 31st yr.   BRUNS 9 Aug 1849

MAWSON, John, native of England, found dead.   MORE 6 Feb 1849

MAXFIELD, Wyatt accidentally killed while hunting near Paris with friend Oliver Smith.   PWH 2 Aug 1849

MAXWELL, Rev. Mr., thrown from horse and killed. Pastor of congregation in and adjacent to Ste. Genevieve.   MORE 4 June 1814

MAXWELL, John died in Indian Creek Twp., Pike Co., on 6 Sept. age about 30.   BGRAD 2 Dec 1843

MAXWELL, John "of James Old Ferry." No date.   MORE 13 Feb 1818

MAY, Lieut. Charles died at Jefferson Barracks age 21. Fell in a duel. 6th Reg. U.S. Infantry.   BEA 27 Jan 1830

ME, MEE, Major Augustus "blew his brains out with two pistols" Saturday last. Had been a teacher in a military school, was very ill of bilious fever and had not been expected to live.   MORE 19 Sep 1821

MEAD, George Esq., Recorder of the City of St. Louis, died 19 February.	SWERE 21 Feb 1848
MEANS, John, resident of Franklin, killed by robbers on the way back from Santa Fe.	MORE 28 Oct 1828
MEDLEY, Matthew, a barber, killed in warehouse fire.	MORE 2 Sep 1839
MEEGAN, Terrence, late of Galena, brother of James of St. Louis, died 28 July.	MORE 29 July 1853
MEEKER, Mr. _____ died 8 January.	CAMP 12 Jan 1849
MEING, George C., age about 27, died 8 April at the home of his brother-in-law J. J. Wilshusen.	MORE 9 Apr 1853
MENNIFEE, Capt. John died Thursday of inflammation of the lungs.	PWH 4 Feb 1847
MERCER, William R. (B?) died in Knox Co. 8 March in his 48th year. Native of Mercer Co. KY.	MORE 19 Mar 1851
MEREDITH, A. of Camden Co. died 10 June at the Crossing of the South Fork of the Platte, age 27.	MORE 7 Oct 1850
MEREDITH, Campbell D. died at Hannibal 22 January.	PWH 3 Feb 1844
MEREDITH, Hamilton D. died in Hannibal in his 20th year. Brother of H. Meredith of Florida, Monroe Co. Buried at his brother's.	MORE 9 Oct 1839
MEREDITH, W. W. killed in Independence by Wm. H. Harper. Interred Episcopal Cemetery, St. Louis.	MORE 12 June 1846
MERIAM, Samuel died of consumption 27 Feb. in his 24th year. Formerly of Ware, MA. In St. Louis three years.	MORE 28 Feb 1848
MERRILL, Edward S. died in Fayette 13 Sept. of bilious fever. Of Chariton Co., formerly of Charleston, ME.	BOLT 19 Sep 1840
MERRITT, Meltritimal, late of Hannibal, born in New Hampshire, died in St. Louis Hospital age 30.	MORE 20 June 1840
MERRIWEATHER, Francis, a young man, died at the home of his father, Walker, 20 January.	SALT 7 Mar 1840
MICHAU, A.A. died yesterday at the home of Mrs. Saugrain, age 47. Interred Catholic cemetery.	MORE 25 Aug 1838
MICHAU, J. died 15 May. Buried from Mrs. Saugrain's.	MORE 16 May 1835
MICHAU, St. Amant died 16 March at his home 5 miles from St. Louis (south) age 48. 30-year resident.	MORE 19 Mar 1845
MICHEAU, John "yesterday at the advanced age of 81 years."	MORE 30 June 1819
MIDDLETON, Lewis, bound for St. Joseph with wife and two children, taken from the <u>Mary Blane</u> to the hospital and died 6 May.	MORE 7 May 1849
MIFFLIN, Henry, late of Philadelphia, formerly of the US Navy, died 20 February.	MORE 22 Feb 1841
MIGGET, John died 16 May age 29 from injuries received four days before in explosion of soda fountain.	SWERE 17 May 1847

MIGNAULT, Telesphore Gregoire, formerly of St. Denis,   MORE 8 Feb 1842
    Dist. of Montreal, died age 27. In St. Louis
    5 years. Resided Pine betw 6-7. Catholic.

MILBURN, Marcus J. died at the Jefferson House on his way   MORE 14 Nov 1842
    to settle in Collinsville. Native of NY. Left wife.

MILLAN, William L. died yesterday noon in his 26th year.   PWH 19 Mar 1846

MILLER, Andrew, a baker, died near Herculaneum 9 Sept. 1820.   MORE 7 Mar 1828
    Born near Strasbourg, Flanders. Served under
    Bonaparte.

MILLER, George, son of Lewis of the Glasgow vicinity,   GLWT 3 Mar 1851
    died recently in California.

MILLER, George C., body found in Lindell's Field 3 miles   MORE 12 Nov 1838
    from St. Louis. A cooper. Apparent suicide.

MILLER, Capt. James died in Cooper Co. 26 Sept. in 74th y.   WEM 30 Oct 1839

MILLER, Maj. James died at Wellsburg VA, 12 Feb. Father   GLWT 17 Mar 1853
    of John of the Glasgow vicinity, brother of late
    Gov. John of MO. Born 1784.

MILLER, John, son of Samuel, drowned 29 August. Family   MORE 30 Aug 1846
    lived on Olive St.

MILLER, John, former governor of MO, died 10 March at   SWERE 23 Mar 1846
    the home of Major R. Graham, St. Louis Co.

MILLER, Isaac, Chariton Co. -- letters of administration   MIN 2 Nov 1826
    to John Humphreys 23 October.

MILLER, James P., an inhabitant of Franklin, killed by   MIN 25 Sep 1820
    lightning 23 September.

MILLER, Richard, a teamster, died in the Santa Fe   MODE 13 Jan 1847
    country.

MILLER, Samuel, deck passenger on the *Alton*, died on the   MORE 21 Dec 1839
    New Orleans-St. Louis trip in November.

MILLER, Thomas Jefferson, proprietor of the St. Louis   MORE 22 Jan 1833
    Times, died Tuesday evening last.

MILLER, William died in Benton Co. 13 December age 55 or   BORE 11 Jan 1845
    56. Presbyterian.

MILLIGAN, Thomas died at the house of Mr. Heitkamp 5 Nov.   MORE 13 Nov 1844
    Said he had a brother in Ohio.

MILLINGTON, Dr. Jacob died at the home of Seth Millington   MORE 20 Apr 1830
    in St. Charles 11 Apr. Of Herkimer Co. NY.

MILLINGTON, Ira died in St. Charles 8 July, many years   MORE 15 July 1834
    a resident there.

MILLINGTON, Dr. Seth died at his home near St. Charles   MORE 8 Aug 1834
    on 4 August age 48. Formerly of Herkimer Co.
    NY, resident of MO since 1809.

MILLINGTON, Jeremiah died at St. Charles age about 55.   MORE 17 Sep 1847
    New York please copy.

MILLS, Henry L. died at Portage des Sioux on the morning of the 28th September. (Probably cholera)	MORE 16 Sep 1832
MILLS, John died in Bonhomme 8 September.	MORE 27 Sep 1824
MILLS, John died at his home about 10 miles west while working in his garden, about 12 o'clock yesterday, negro called "Free Big George" supposed murderer.	MORE 19 Aug 1834
MILLS, Micklebury and Patsy, man and woman, son and daughter of James of the Fayette vicinity, died Wednesday.	BOLT 3 Oct 1840
MILLS, William M. died 1 April at the home of Joseph A. Wherry, St. Louis. Of St. Charles, age 33, native of Columbia Co. PA.	MORE 22 Apr 1841
MILNER, Charles died age 27. Interred Bellefontaine.	MORE 12 Aug 1853
MILLUM, Solomon -- Gentry Co. Letters of administration to William A. Childers, 7 January.	STGAZ 22 Feb 1854
MILNER, ____, a soldier, drowned crossing the Mississippi in a small boat.	MORE 22 Nov 1817
MILTENBERGER, John P. Esq., late counsel, French section at this port, died 1 March.	MORE 4 Mar 1843
MILTON, Frederick, formerly of Henry Co., died in El Dorado Co. 17 April. Left wife, 8 children.	MORE 11 June 1852
MILTON, George age 43 died 8 Jan. Palmyra pls copy.	MORE 11 Jan 1853
MIMMS, L. D. died at the residence of T. M. James in Kansas City, in his 13th year. Formerly of Russellville, Union Co. KY.	KCEN 22 Mar 1856
MINARD, Rev. Peter, late rector of St. Paul's Church, died of consumption age 39.	MORE 6 Oct 1840
MINOR, Col. William C. died at Jefferson City 20 Feb. age 45.	MORE 22 Feb 1851
MITCHELL, Dr. Charles L. died 6 August and his wife died on the 7th.	MIN 26 Aug 1823
MITCHELL, James Cary died 19 August. Here several months, formerly of Clarke Co. VA.	COMB 27 Aug 1846
MITCHELL, John died in his 36th year, 4 miles east of Bowling Green, on 8 July.	SALT 11 July 1840
MITCHEL, C. L. died this morning. (NOTE -- probably same as Dr. Charles L., above.)	MORE 6 Aug 1823
MITCHEL, G. M. of Perry Co. died at Scott's Bluff 24 June age 22.	MORE 7 Oct 1850
MITCHELL, Solomon P. died at Fayette 14 Nov. age about 60. Buried by Masonic fraternity.	BRUNS 25 Nov 1847 MODE 24 Nov 1847
MITCHELL, Thomas died in St. Francois Co. 28 October leaving a wife and children.	MORE 4 Nov 1843
MITCHELL, William died at the house of Richard W. Newell in Pike Co., 1819. Born London, lived in Philadelphia, to St. Louis in 1818.	STCHMO 4 July 1822

MITCHELL, William K. Esq. died in St. Louis 29 August. SWERE 6 Sep 1847

MOCK, George died Wednesday in Spencer Twp. age 55. (His BGRAD 31 Aug 1844
    wife died Sunday age about 50.)

MOFFATT, George M., engineer and machinist, died 18 Feb. MORE 20 Feb 1836
    Originally from RI.

MOFFAT, Thomas, young clerk of St. Louis, died 20 July in MORE 27 July 1846
    Glasgow. Buried private graveyard of Capt. John Bell.

MOFFATT, William A. of St. Louis died near Louisville MORE 27 Sep 1851
    20 September.

MOLLOY, Anthony died in Florissant 14 November. MORE 15 Nov 1838
    Interred Catholic cemetery.

MONROE, Col. Joseph Jones, youngest brother of Pres. Monroe,
    died 14 July at his residence in Howard Co. SLINQ 19 July 1824
    (MODE 26 July gives death date as 6 July)

MONROE (MUNRO), William, "one of the earliest settlers" MODE 15 Mar 1846
    died 3 March in his 64th year. Emigrated from
    KY in 1809, settled near Ft. Hempstead. Methodist.

MONTAGUE, Samuel E. Esq. died 13 June in Chariton Co. MORE 24 June 1850

MONTGOMERY, John died at his residence in Barry Co. SPAD 6 Apr 1847
    30 March age 65.

MONTGOMERY, Joseph D. -- Wayne Co. Erasmus Ford JASO 13 Oct 1838
    resigns letters of administration.

MONTGOMERY, Timoleon son of Col. J. J. died 30 April age 24. MORE 3 May 1852

MOODY, Joseph drowned near David Lemasters' on the Missouri
    River, age 44. Reward to person finding and STCHMO 17 Mar '21
    burying him and returning his watch and pocket book
    to his widow in Montgomery Co. near Pinckney.

MOORE, J. of Ray Co. died 16 June, 100 mi. west of Fort MORE 7 Oct 1850
    Kearney, age 37. Left wife and children.

MOORE, James S. was killed at Lebanon by John J. Edwards. MORE 22 Sep 1846

MOORE, James Jr. died "last Sunday." MORE 13 Sep 1827

MOORE, John "many years a citizen" died Monday. BEA 10 Feb 1831

MOORE, Jonah died in Chariton Co. 17 September, "old GLWT 25 Sep 1851
    and respected."

MOORE, Col. William died in Ray Co. 8 April in his 65th LEXP 12 Apr 1854
    year, native of Lunenbergh Co. VA. Came to MO
    in 1845.

MOORE, Maj. Zachariah died in Femme Osage, St. Charles Co. MORE 7 Sep 1837
    on 28 Aug. Revolutionary soldier.

MOREHEAD, John N. late of Richmond died of typhoid near MORE 26 Apr 1850
    Sacramento 29 November 1849.

MOORHEAD, W. of Ray Co. died 24 June near Ft. Laramie MORE 7 Oct 1850
    age 22.

MOORMAN, Robert A. died at the home of his brother-in-law MORE 13 Mar 1834
    Capt. James C. Anderson 7 March. Late of
    Lynchburgh VA.

MORELAND, James died in Franklin Tuesday last.	MIN 29 Jan 1821
MOREN, Charles -- Ripley Co. Public Administrator took over his estate.	SPAD 9 Jan 1847
MORGAN, Capt. Asa died at Boonville Friday morning last.	MIN 25 Sep 1821
MORGAN, Martin -- Chariton Co. Letters of administration to Elizabeth Morgan.	BRUNS 25 May 1848
MORGAN, William O. -- Chariton Co. Final settlement by Aquilla Cavanah.	BRUNS 30 Mar 1848
MORGAN, Capt. Willoughby died at Fort Crawford 4 April.	MORE 24 Apr 1832
MORIN, Antonio Vincent was killed in a steamboat disaster in Mexico, age 25.	MORE 4 July 1842
MORIN, James died 8 Feb. at the house of James K. Dickson, Platte City. Said to have been from Split Rock NY.	PLAR 17 Mar 1848
MORRIS, John, native of Ireland, died age 38.	MORE 5 Apr 1852
MORRIS, Judge John P. died 5 July in Texas at the house of Capt. Rodgers. Traveling for his health.	MODE 12 Aug 1846
MORRIS, John P. Jr. died of consumption 10 August age 21y 10m.	MORE 13 Aug 1838
MORRIS, Richard, formerly of Wexford Ireland died age 73.	MORE 14 Jan 1851
MORRIS, Thomas W. of Glasgow died "Tuesday week" in his 33rd year. Buried by Sons of Temperance.	BRUNS 14 June 1849
MORRISON, Col. James died at St. Charles 27 Sept. in his 83rd year. Formerly resided at Boonslick and managed the salt works.	MODE 24 Oct 1848
MORRISON, James J., of J. & W. Morrison, died at the home of George Collier near St. Louis yesterday.	MORE 16 Oct 1832
MORRISON, Robert, resident of Concord, Callaway Co., died of cholera in St. Louis.	FULT 6 Apr 1849
MORROW, George died 7 February in his (?44th?) year.	MORE 21 Feb 1832
MORROW, James, engineer of the Circassian, drowned. Left wife and children in Pittsburgh.	MORE 20 Nov 1846
MORROW, James died in Marion Co. 15 October, formerly of Trumbull Co. OH.	MORE 2 Nov 1830
MORROW, Robert died 9 April.	SPAD 13 Apr 1847
MORROW, Robert, engineer of the St. Louis, "Sunday last."	BEA 5 Aug 1830
MORSE, John -- Chariton Co. Final settlement by John Watson.	BRUNS 4 May 1848
MOSELEY, James W. died in Hannibal 4 Sept. in 24th year.	MORE 10 Sep 1853
MOSS, Luke died Friday morning last. "highly respected."	PWH 5 Nov 1846
MOSS, Peter died 23 October near Spencerburg. Baptist. Left 13 children. (His wife died 20 October.)	BGRAD 11 Nov 1843
MOSS, William died at the home of his uncle Jesse on 27 March age 28. Native of KY.	BGDB 4 Apr 1846

MOSS, Dr. Woodson J. died at his home in Liberty, 1 Dec.	MORE 12 Dec 1843
MOSS, Major ____ killed by Richard P. Phillips in St. Francisville, Clark Co.	MORE 13 Mar 1844
MOTHERSHEAD, Clifton Esq. died 23 Sept. in Jefferson Co. in his 38th year.	MOAR 27 Sep 1838
MOWYER, David age about 45 died at the house of Augustus Leflet 6 January. Native of Northumberland Co. PA. Resident here 7 years.	PWH 8 Jan 1846
MUHR, Jacob died 26 February age 29.	SWERE 6 Mar 1848
MUIR, Douglas, of Cooper Co., near Boonville, died at the home of Mr. Shaw in St. Louis, on his return from Virginia Springs. Left wife and family.	MORE 29 Aug 1845
MULCAHY, William, native of the parish of Castletown Roache, Co. Cork, died yesterday age 65.	SWERE 14 Aug 1848
MULDROW, James, an old citizen, died Tuesday last.	PWH 27 June 1848
MULDROW, Dr. Milton died 9 September at the residence of his father. Born 1830.	PWH 14 Sep 1848
MULHERIN, Elder J. D. died in Pike Co. 29 Aug. in 46th y.	MORE 3 Sep 1851
MULLANPHY, Michael died at the home of Charles Chambers on 9 Sept.	MORE 15 Sep 1840
MULLANPHY, John Esq. died yesterday afternoon.	MORE 30 Aug 1833
MULLIGAN, Hugh died in St. Louis Sunday.	MORE 14 Apr 1829
MULLINS, ____, a gambler, died in Keytesville Saturday.	BRUNS 14 June 1849
MULLINS, Dr. Lewis J., of Warsaw, Benton Co., died 10 October. Formerly of KY.	MORE 21 Oct 1843
MUNRO, Daniel Sr. died "near this place" 8 August. Revolutionary soldier, in his 73rd year.	MIN 14 Aug 1824
MUNRO, John son of William died 13 May age 19.	MIN 26 May 1826
MUNSEY, James died at Chillicothe Saturday, a Mason.	BRUNS 9 Sep 1848
MURPHY, John, deckhand on the LaSalle, drowned yesterday.	MORE 1 June 1844
MURPHY, Dennis died 13 January in his 57th year. Resident St. Louis 27 years. Catholic. Lived on Green St.	MORE 14 Jan 1848
MURPHY, Isaac -- Franklin Co. Final settlement by Nancy Hart (late Murphy) and Isaiah Todd.	MORE 2 Mar 1830
MURPHY, James died 9 Sept. in his 30th year. Buried at Rock Springs. New York please copy.	MORE 10 Sep 1853
MURPHY, Morris died in St. Louis 25 November.	MORP 28 Nov 1845
MURR, C. of Green Co. died 10 June at Court House Rock, age 26.	MORE 7 Oct 1850
MURRAY, Hugh W., of A. Oakford & Co., died 23 August.	MORE 26 Aug 1839
MURRAY, James L., formerly of St. Louis, died recently in Alexandria VA.	MORE 23 Dec 1837

MURRAY, William Riley, formerly of KY, died 10 January in Savannah age 22. — SASE 24 Jan 1852

MURROW, Joseph died of cholera at Paynesville, Pike Co. Longtime resident. — MORE 25 July 1851

MUSICK, Absalom died at Columbia (?) 2 January. — SLINQ 5 Jan 1820

MUSICK, Elder T. R. died 2 December in his 85th year. — MORE 7 Dec 1841

MUSICK, Joel died 25 Sept. at his home in Florissant, a representative-elect to the state legislature. — MORE 2 Oct 1832

MUSICK, Joseph killed by accidental discharge of pistol. — MORE 31 July 1846

MUSICK, Lewis and wife drowned when a keelboat sank. — MORE 4 May 1826

MUSSETT, Rev. Alvin, formerly of Glasgow, died 21 Dec. in California. — GLWT 3 Mar 1851

MEYER, ___, a German farmer, drunk, nearly froze to death Saturday, not expected to live. — BRUNS 24 Feb 1849

MYER, A. of St. Louis died on the Little Blue River 4 June age 40. Left wife, 3 children. — MORE 7 Oct 1850

MYERS, Charles, mate of the *Annawan*, drowned near Liberty, left pregnant wife and one child. — MORE 11 Mar 1844

MYERS, John W. Esq. died in Boone Co. 14 Oct. in 45th yr. — MORE 20 Oct 1851

MEYER, John C. died in his 31st year. — MORE 6 July 1851

MYER, Mattois, a stonemason from St. Louis employed at Ft. Smith, drowned in the Arkansas River. — MORE 31 Dec 1845

NALLY, Joseph A. died in Pike Co. 5 Sept. age about 30. — BGRAD 9 Sep 1843

NANSON, John died in Glasgow Wednesday. Native of England, came here in his youth. — BOLT 24 Oct 1846

NAPIER, Mr. ___ died in Fulton last Sunday. — MIN 7 Apr 1832

NASH, Francis died at his home in St. Ferdinand Twp. Member of the legislature for several years. — MORE 8 Nov 1833

NASH, Dr. John T. died 29 October age 43 leaving a widow and 5 children. — MORE 5 Nov 1825

NAVALLES, Joseph died Saturday age 60, a resident for about 33 years. — MORE 4 Jan 1841

NAYLOR, Samuel, native of England, died 22 March from excessive drinking. Resided 112 Green St. — MORE 23 Mar 1849

NEALE, Arthur, of Cote sans Dessein, died in the *Big Hatchee* explosion at Hermann 23 July. — STGAZ 15 Aug 1845

NEAL, Joab -- Gentry Co. Letters of administration to James M. Howel, 22 February. — STGAZ 29 Mar 1854

NEAL, Reubin died in St. Louis 19 November. — SLINQ 25 Nov 1820

NEAVES, Orrin D., eldest son of Thomas B. and Margaret, died age 17y 3m 2d. — SPAD 4 Apr 1846

NECHT, Nathaniel died 31 December, formerly a resident   MORE 4 Jan 1842
    of Ingen (Bingen?) Germany.

NEIDLET, Stephen of St. Louis died 30 Apr. of cholera.   STGAZ 19 May 1852

NEILL, Jeremiah died in Montgomery Co. of winter fever on   MORE 3 Mar 1843
    6 February in his 56th year. Came to MO in 1818, a
    Captain in the "last war." Formerly of Lee Co. VA.

NELSON, William H., resident of St. Louis the last 7 years   MORE 12 July 1844
    died yesterday age 45. Native of Staunton VA,
    formerly of Cincinnati.

NESBIT, Robert died 23 January at the home of Mrs. Eliza   PWH 22 Feb 1849
    Anderson in Shelby Co., age 75y 10m.

NEVILL, James died at the home of his father near   SALT 15 Feb 1840
    Frankford 5 Feb., age about 19.

NEVIN, John -- Montgomery Co. Final settlement by   MORE 11 May 1826
    Mathias McGirk.

NEW, William, a merchant of Carrollton, died on the   BRUNS 31 May 1849
    Sacramento between Glasgow and Brunswick, of
    cholera, age about 35. A Mason.

NEWELL, Lewis died at his farm in Illinois opposite the   MORE 17 Aug 1838
    upper ferry. Of St. Louis.

NEWTON, Peter, native of Ireland and many years a   COP 14 Oct 1842
    resident of Columbia, died 6 October.

NEYFIELD, Capt. Charles, an officer in the Polish Revo-   MORE 13 Aug 1838
    lutionary army, died Friday night last.

NICOL, James died 15 November. Resided 7th below Spruce.   MORE 16 Nov 1848
    Interred Presbyterian cemetery.

NICHOLS, Mack P. -- Montgomery Co. Letters of administration
    to Philip T. Nicholas 29 June.   SALT 29 Aug 1840

NICKERSON, S. R. of Glasgow died in Mexico.   COMB 16 Dec 1847

NICHOLSON, Peter, a Scotsman, fell from the revenue cutter   MORE 5 June 1849
    and drowned, age 23. "Man of intelligence."

NIDELEY, Stephen died 28 April age 24y 10m 25d.   MORE 5 May 1851

NINEMIRE, ___ killed in Daviess Co. 28 March when digging   BRUNS 13 Apr 1848
    out a mill seat at Taylor's Ferry, on the
    South Fork of Grand River.

NISBET, William T., son of William and Mary S., died in   MORE 14 Sep 1853
    his 25th year on 13 September.

NOLAND, Martin, of Co. L., Col. Price's Reg., died at   MODE 13 Jan 1847
    Santa Fe 9 November.

NORMAN, Oliver died 17 June at his home in Davis (sic) Co.   STGAZ 29 June 1853
    age 53. Maysville KY please copy.

NORMAN, Rosey died at the house of George Myers at   MORE 13 Dec 1833
    Clarksville 11 June. Nativity not known.

NORRIS, C. C. was accidentally killed. No details.   MORE 23 July 1847

NORRIS, Nelson died in his 64th yr. Lived 124 N. 6th St.   MORE 28 June 1849

NORTON, Sheldon died at St. Francisville, Clark Co., on 12 Sept. Agent for the American S.S. Union. Oscar, his son, died a week later.   MORE 1 Oct 1838

NOSTRAND, Stephen L., formerly of St. Francois Co., died at Logan's Creek, Shannon Co., on 10 March.   MORE 8 Apr 1846

NOWEL, Abraham said to have been murdered in Benton Co. 18 Oct. 1842 by Isham Hobbs.   JINQ 6 June 1845

NIE, NYE, Benjamin died in the Jefferson City neighborhood Sunday last of bilious colic.   JEFRE 20 July 1833

NYE, Joseph of Platte Co. died of cholera 17 June.   MORE 18 June 1851

NYE, Joseph W., formerly of Sandwich MA, died 8 November.   MORE 9 Nov 1838

OAKLEY, Timothy died 16 Sept. in his 32nd year. Funeral from his home on Main St. opposite Bank of MO.   MORE 17 Sep 1838

O'BANNON, Capt. Joseph died in his 65th year. Native of VA, in Missouri about 5 years.   INP 18 Dec 1824

OBER, Samuel R. died last Sunday.   MORE 28 Sep 1826

OBERMEYER, Lewis, Jefferson City merchant, died "Tuesday week."   BRUNS 21 June 1849

O'BRIEN, Hugh died 6 January in his 52nd year. Citizen of St. Louis 20 years. Resided Broadway & Wash. Interred Catholic cemetery.   MORE 7 Feb 1848

O'BRIEN, John, deck passenger on the Persian, died in an explosion on 7 November.   MORE 14 Nov 1840

ODEAM, Willis, a Revolutionary soldier, died at the home of his son-in-law in Barry Co. age about 90.   SPAD 6 Apr 1847

ODELL, Jeremiah C. was murdered in Georgetown, Pettis Co. on 3 July by Davis L. Owen.   BOLT 11 July 1840

O'DONNEL, James -- Ripley Co. Public administrator took over his administration.   SPAD 17 Oct 1846

O'FALLON, Major Benjamin died at his home in Jefferson Co. age 49. Funeral from home of Col. John O'Fallon to the family burying ground.   MORE 20 Dec 1842

O'FERRALL, John D. age 31 died at his residence north of Tully on 10 December.   CAMP 15 Dec 1848

OGLESBY, John P. died 3 Feb. in his 25th year at the home of his father; had returned from CA 10 days ago.   BOBS 12 Feb 1851

OGLESBY, Reuben-- according to testimony in a divorce case James Mellsaps was indicted for his murder in Crawford Co. Date not given.   MORE 30 Nov 1838

O'HARA, Edward age about 24 died this morning. Funeral from home of his brother John Young. (They were half-brothers.)   MORE 20 June 1852

O'HARA, M. died 11 May age 34. Resided 151 N. 7th St. SWERE 14 May 1849

O'HARA, William M. Esq. died at the Post of Arkansas on 21 July. Native of NJ, resident of St. Louis about 3 years. Left mother, wife, 4 children. MORE 29 Aug 1821

O'HEELEY, Alexander died Saturday. Of Teyhorney, Ireland. MORE 15 Dec 1819

OLDENBURG, Louis died Tuesday last in St. Louis. MORE 10 Mar 1835

OLDHAM, Jefferson died of congestive fever Thursday. PWH 16 Oct 1841

OLDHAM, Samuel G. died 24 Dec. "respected and worthy." PWH 31 Dec 1841

OLDHAM, William B. died at the home of his mother 26 Aug. as a result of injuries received in a fall from a building. PWH 27 Aug 1846

OLIS, Michael, deckhand on the *Autocrat*, drowned 15 Aug. MORE 16 Aug 1847

OLIVER, Benjamin, late clerk of the Ray Co. Circuit Ct., died in Richmond 12 April age about 33. LEXP 15 Apr 1845

OLIVER, Isaac died suddenly in Callaway Co. 11 Dec. age 73y 11m 12d. Formerly of Halifax Co. VA. MORE 19 Dec 1848

OLIVER, Thomas, judge of the probate court and clerk of circuit court, died in Ste. Genevieve 17 November. MORE 5 Dec 1825

O'NEIL, Henry died 14 November age 29. MORP 17 Nov 1845

O'NEIL, Hugh Sr. died 29 March in his 67th year, citizen of this city many years. SCOMB 30 Mar 1836
SOV 2 Apr 1836

O'NEIL, Hugh Esq. died Thursday, representative of this county in the state legislature. "Brief career in this community." Interred Catholic cemetery. MORE 5 June 1841

O'NEILL, Thomas, postmaster at Florence, Morgan Co., son of Charles of New Franklin, killed last Friday by Claiborne Young. MODE 1 Sep 1830

ORMSBEE, Daniel G. died 10 Oct. age 31. Formerly of MA. Boston and Barre please copy. MORE 12 Oct 1840

O'ROURKE, John, many years a resident, died 4 June age 62. Funeral from the Cathedral. MORE 5 June 1845

ORR, Matthew, a young man, died this morning. MORE 16 Sep 1815

ORR, Philip and Thomas his son; Philip died age 50 and the son a few days later. Cumberland Presbyterians. BGRAD 13 Apr 1844

ORR, Robert died near Ashley age about 55. Early settler. BGRAD 3 Aug 1844

ORTLEY, H. K. died Wednesday at Major Brant's residence. MORE 12 Apr 1836

OSBORN, Mahlon, formerly of Westfield NJ, died 3 April of erysipelas age 35. Interred Bellefontaine. MORE 4 Apr 1851

OSGOOD, Alfred, St. Louis merchant, died yesterday. MORE 10 Jan 1852

OSTRANDER, John E. died yesterday age 40. Resided Christy-11ths St. Presbyterian cemetery. SWERE 14 May 1849

O'TOOLE, L.M. drowned while crossing the river in a skiff at Jeffersonville. SWERE 9 Apr 1849

OVERLY, Henry, a Revolutionary pensioner, died 15 June at Shamrock, Callaway Co., in his 84th year.	SPAD 12 July 1845
OVERSTOLTZ, William died 13 May age 74. Funeral from home of his son Henry to Methodist cemetery.	MORE 14 May 1853
OVERTON, Robert W., son of William, died during the Mexican War.	PWH 27 May 1847
OWENS, ___, Callaway Co., in Doniphan's Regiment, died at Santa Fe.	MODE 13 Jan 1847
OWENS, ___, son of Berry, was thrown from a horse and killed, near Keytesville.	MODE 8 Sep 1847
OWEN, James M. -- Gentry Co. Letters of administration to James W. Owen & Wm. A. Patton, 29 Aug. 1851.	STGAZ 7 Jan 1852
OWENS, William C., clerk of the Franklin Co. Court, shot down by unknown assailant who waited concealed. (Issue of 28 Nov. states a man named Jones charged.)	MORE 21 Nov 1834
OXLEY, Major of Randolph Co. died in Santa Fe about 1 Jan.	BRUNS 14 Apr 1849
PACA, John, many years a resident of St. Louis, died in his 61st year. Baltimore Patriot please copy.	MORE 30 Aug 1841 " 4 Sep "
PACKARD, Capt. G. H. died 15 Feb. in his 49th year.	MORE 18 Feb 1846
PADDOCK, Gaius died Thursday 11 Aug. "in this city."	MORE 16 Aug 1831
PAGAUD, Horace died at his father's home age 28. New Orleans, Petersburg, Norfolk please copy.	SWERE 26 June 1848
PAGE, Benjamin, a soldier, died at Bellefontaine.	MORE 15 Jan 1814
PAGE, James age 76 died at his home on Park Ave. in St. Louis Co.	MORE 29 July 1853
PAINTER, Alexander -- Montgomery Co. Final settlement by James Caldwell.	FULT 24 Nov 1848
PALMER, Alexander died at Richwoods (Washington Co.) 1 Aug. age 37.	MORE 10 Aug 1853
PALMER, Capt. Bennet, Clerk of the Circuit Ct. of Lincoln Co., died in Monroe Wednesday last.	STCHMO 22 Aug 1821
PALMER, William, late of London, died yesterday in his 40th year. Resided 12th & Gay. New York pls copy.	MORE 14 Sep 1848
PALMER, Capt. Zalmon C. died at Hillsboro, Jefferson Co., on 23 May.	MORE 3 June 1842
PAPIN, Hypolite died at his home on St. Charles Rd., age 54. Funeral from Renard home on 2nd St.	MORE 21 Dec 1842
PAPIN, Joseph M. died yesterday morning at an advanced age.	MORE 19 Sep 1811
PARK, William -- Dunklin Co. Letters of administration to Nancy C. Park, 2 April.	NMJ 24 June 1853
PARKER, A. E. M., a teamster, died in the Santa Fe country.	MODE 13 Jan 1847
PARKER, Capt. Alonzo R. died 29 April age 35. Late of New Bedford MA.	MORE 12 June 1851

PARKER, Charles T., an attorney, native of Boston, died   MORE 16 July 1833
    Sunday evening last in his 25th year.

PARKER, John M., an old resident of St. Louis, died in New   MORE 23 Jan 1849
    Orleans 8 Jan. age 37. Methodist. Wife, 4 children.

PARKER, Oliver Esq. died in Columbia 20 May.   COP 28 May 1842

PARKER, William, native of New York, fell dead yesterday   MORE 19 Sep 1843
    at a ball alley near the drydock.

PARKINSON, William, died in St. Charles 23 March age 22.   MORE 12 Apr 1842
    Had been thrown from a horse. Late of
    New Kent Co. VA.

PARKMAN, Samuel, formerly of Westborough MA, died age 22.   MORE 24 June 1847

PARKS, D. D. of Lexington died of cholera Wednesday last.   LEXP 9 Aug 1854

PARKS, Joseph -- Montgomery Co. Letters of administration   MORE 26 Oct 1843
    to William Parks.

PARMELEE, Sylvanus, "many years a resident" died 26 Aug.   MORE 1 Sep 1829

PAROLE, _____, killed in the Car of Commerce disaster.   MORE 27 May 1828

PARISH, Henry decd. -- Montgomery Co. Notice to heirs,   SALT 24 July 1841
    Wm, Martha, John G. & Philip Parish and
    Achille and Mary F. Quisenberry.

PARSONS, _____ of Howard Co. died 10 June at Ft. Laramie.   MORE 7 Oct 1850

PARSONS, David C. M. died at his residence in Ashley, Pike   MORE 2 Aug 1844
    Co., 30 July. Formerly of Augusta Co. VA.
    Emigrated about 1828. In state legislature.

PARSONS, George W. died at New Hope 14 July. Left wife,   SALT 24 July 1841
    4 children. Methodist.

PARSONS, James, a resident of Gasconade Co., died 26 Mar.   MORE 13 Apr 1852
    age 58y 1m 26d. Formerly of VA.

PARSONS, James of MO died at the home of James Parsons in   PWH 15 Apr 1847
    the vicinity of Romney VA 19 Mar. age about 45.

PARSONS, James D. died in Shelby Co. 14 April age 42.   MOCHA 5 May 1853
    Left wife and one son.

PASTINES, James B. of St. Louis died 25 November aboard   MORE 11 Dec 1847
    the Rowena.

PATCHETT, Henry, drowned from the New Haven. Lived on the   MORE 30 Dec 1846
    Missouri R. near St. Charles. Left a family.

PATRICK, Maston of MO died at Kaskaskia 16 Dec., about 35.   BEA 27 Jan 1831

PATRICK, Robert died 13 Aug. age 51y 7m 11d. "For some   MIN 17 Aug 1826
    time a citizen of Howard." Left family.

PATTERSON, Henry died 23 August.   PWH 28 Aug 1841

PATTERSON, James died 27 Sept. in Calumet Twp. (Pike Co.)   BGRAD 12 Oct 1844
    age about 50.

PATTERSON, John, mortally wounded at a battle on the lower   MORE 27 May 1815
    Cuivre ferry near Ft. Howard. Capt. Craig's Co.

PATTERSON, John died 31 Jan. age 79, resident of St.   MORE 9 Feb 1839
    Louis Co. for 40 years.

PATTERSON, John H. -- Dallas Co. Letters of administration   SPAD 8 Apr 1845
    to Lewis L. & Mary Patterson, 6 March.

PATTERSON, Nathaniel died 3 Nov. age 44. Funeral from   MORE 4 Nov 1846
    his home, #62 4th St.

PATTERSON, T. M. died in St. Louis 9 Dec. Of Pittsburgh.   MORE 11 Dec 1843

PATTERSON, Samuel, native of Downpatric, Co. Down, died   MORE 6 Oct 1840
    age 22.

PATTERSON, Solomon died 21 May in his 79th year at the home   MORE 28 May 1842
    of his son-in-law R. McCracken Esq. in IL.

PATTON, Jacob -- Montgomery Co. Final settlement by   FULT 24 Nov 1848
    Jacob Patton.

PATTON, John, a printer, many years' resident, Thursday.   MORE 25 Nov 1828

PATTON, Rev. W. W. died 6 July at St. Louis. Presbyterian.   BRUNS 26 July 1849

PAUL, Jeremiah, formerly of NJ, a portrait painter, died   SLINQ 15 July 1826
    near St. Louis last Thursday.

PAUL, Nathan, of Paul & Ingram, died Friday last.   MORE 8 Oct 1823

PAUL, Rene -- a very long tribute.   MORE 21 May 1851

PAUL, Julius son of Rene died 31 July in his 21st year.   MORE 2 Aug 1847

PAUL, Gabriel, native of Santo Domingo, died 10 August   MORE 11 Aug 1846
    age 70. Interred Catholic cemetery.

PAULDING, James, age 40, formerly of NY, 18 June.   SCOMB 22 June 1836

PAULSEL, Henry P. died of cholera Wed. in Jefferson City.   FULT 27 Apr 1849

PAXON, James died 13 Oct. in Lincoln Co. Late of KY.   MORE 18 Oct 1827

PANE, Enos A. of Co. M., Col. Price's Reg., died at   MODE 13 Jan 1847
    Santa Fe 6 November.

PAYNE, J. W. of New Hope, Lincoln Co., died of injuries   MORP 19 July 1845
    12 July. (Stark Fielder and Wm. Hammock charged.)

PAYNE, John Esq., attorney, died in his 24th year.   MIN 25 Sep 1821
    Native of Culpepper Co. VA.

PAYNE, Robert Esq. died 28 August.   MIN 30 Aug 1827

PAYNE, John died 25 July. (No other data.) (Tribute)   INP 31 July 1824

PAYNE, John -- Chariton Co. Final settlement by   BRUNS 14 June 1849
    Wm. Scriviner.

PAYNE, Robert Van Cliff, originally of Bath Co. VA, late   MORE 2 Dec 1842
    of St. Louis, died at the home of Johnson Foreman
    in Beatie's Prairie, Cherokee Nation.

PEACHER, George age about 13 and Martha about 7 drowned in   BRUNS 13 Apr 1848
    Sulphur Creek 3 April. Children of Reuben of
    Boone's Lick Twp., Howard Co.

PEACHY, John D., formerly of Portland ME, died 29 August.   MORE 2 Sep 1840

PEAKE, Dr. _____ of Palmyra killed by husband whose wife he   MORE 23 Nov 1842
    had seduced. Husband followed him to Columbia.
    Dr. left wife. Husband not named.

PEAKE, William died of cholera at Warsaw.   BRUNS 14 June 1849

PEARCE, George died Friday last.   MORE 16 July 1833

PEARSON, Isaac Esq., native of NJ, died 9 June.   PWH 17 June 1843

PEARSON, John died at Franklin 23 Sept. in his 69th year.   BOLT 4 Oct 1845
    Native of Westmoreland, England.

PEARSON, Thomas H. of Linn Co. died 20 May in his 38th y.   BOLT 30 May 1846

PEAS, Augustus, late of Hartford CT, in Monroe Co. 5 Jan.   MORE 17 Jan 1843
    age 49.

PECK, Charles Esq., several years resident of St. Louis,   MORE 8 Mar 1848
    died 14 Feb. of consumption in Charleston SC.
    Left widow and infant daughter.

PECK, Hon. James H., Judge of the US District Ct., died   SCOMB 2 May 1836
    in St. Charles 29 April.

PECK, Ruloff Esq. died last Saturday in St. Charles.   MORE 7 Jan 1828

PEEBELS, John S. son of Mrs. Mary of this place died at   MIN 15 Oct 1822
    St. Francisville in August in his 20th year.

PEEBELS, Thomas died in this place (Franklin) Sunday.   MIN 9 July 1819

PEERS, Henry C., son of Valentine and Julia, died aboard   MORE 30 July 1853
    the _Atlantic_ 29 July age 20y 5m 4d. Funeral in
    St. Louis.

PEERS, John D., Esq. died in Farmington, St. Francois Co.   MORE 3 Aug 1846
    on 27 July, age 50. Son of Valentine Peers, a   "   24 Aug "
    Revolutionary soldier. Late of Maysville KY.

PEERY, Joseph D. -- Montgomery Co. Final settlement   FULT 10 Aug 1849
    by Thomas Perry.

PELTIER, Antoine, killed in a skirmish with Indians on the   MORE 27 May 1815
(PELKY) lower Cuivre ferry near Ft. Howard. Capt. Craig's Co.

PEMBERTON, William S. died 18 August in Lewis Co.   PWH 21 Aug 1841

PENDEGRASS, Robert, resident of MO, where his family   SLINQ 18 Aug 1821
    resides, died in Carlisle PA.

PENN, Gamaliel, formerly of Dayton OH, died 1 June of   MORE 6 June 1845
    bilious congestive fever, age 71.

PENN, Shadrach Jr., editor of the Missouri _Reporter_,   MORE 17 June 1846
    died age 56. Formerly of KY. Resided 8th & Pine.
    (COMB 20 June 1846 says he was born near
    Frederick MD, served in the War of 1812.)

PENROSE, Clement B. Sr., Esq. died Friday morning last.   MORE 12 May 1829

PERKINS, Maj. Archelaus died at the home of his son-in-law   BRUNS 19 May 1849
    James Herndon of Carroll Co. in his 89th year.
    Formerly of Goochland VA.

PERKINS, Enoch -- Montgomery Co. Final settlement by Wells E. Marvin. — MORE 1 Sep 1829

PERKINS, Capt. Joseph, formerly of US Army, died Saturday. — MORE 26 Jan 1824

PERKINS, Luther, funeral notice by I. O. O. F. — MORE 27 July 1853

PERKINS, Col. William K. died Tuesday in Buffalo Twp. (Pike Co.) in 53rd year. Paducah please copy. — BGRAD 3 Jan 1845

PERKINS, _____, engineer of the St. Louis, bound for Galena, killed 12 April. — MORE 17 Apr 1834

PERKINSON, John F. -- Chariton Co. Final settlement by Eliza Perkinson. — BRUNS 30 Mar 1848

PERRIN, Dr. Henry, Secretary and Supt. of the MO Silk Co. died near St. Louis 4 September. — MORE 7 Sep 1839

PERRY, _____ of western Ralls Co. drowned in Salt River in the floods. — BRUNS 31 Mar 1849

PERRY, Capt. Andrew died 26 April in Washington Co. — MORE 17 May 1831

PERRIE, Dr. John, formerly of MD, died 14 July. — LEXP 26 July 1854

PERRY, Robert of Platte Co. died on the way to Santa Fe. Infantry Battalion. — MODE 13 Jan 1847

PERRY, Samuel of Potosi died 12 March in his 48th year. — MORE 28 Dec 1830

PERRY, Dr. Thomas H., pastor of New Jerusaleum Church Society in St. Louis the past two years, died 7 April age 34. Formerly in US Navy. — SWERE 14 May 1849

PERRY, Thomas J. Esq., nominee for County Court Justice, died Tuesday. Of St. Ferdinand. — MORE 18 June 1842

PERRY, William killed at Lambert's Diggings 17 Sept. by William Hill. — MORE 23 Nov 1825

PESCAY, _____ drowned. Came to St. Louis last summer. Left disconsolate mother. — MORE 31 Jan 1811

PETER, a French boy, died in Car of Commerce disaster. — MORE 27 May 1828

PETERS, John killed by Johan Brannon, a free negro, in a quarrel over cards. — MORE 7 Feb 1845

PETERSON, William, a printer, died 30 May age 44. Interred Episcopal cemetery. — MORE 31 May 1853

PETTIBONE, Rufus, of St. Charles, died last Sunday. — MORE 8 Aug 1825

PETTIT, Ralph P. died at his home in Louisiana, Pike Co. 8 June age 31. Formerly of Chester Co. PA. — BGRAD 24 June 1843

PEYTON, William of the Glasgow vicinity died recently in California. — GLWT 30 Jan 1851

PFEIFER, Edward, late from Germany, died 29 September. — JEFRE 3 Oct 1840

PFOUTS, Major George died 24 June, age about 50, in Oregon, Holt Co. Member of Bar, formerly OH legislator. — STGAZ 4 July 1845

PHARR, William C., eldest son of Rev. Samuel of Pike Co., died at the home of his uncle V.K. Pharr in IN. Cumberland Presbyterian. — SALT 16 May 1840

PHILIPS, Charles Esq. died 29 July at St. Charles, formerly MORE 6 Aug 1823
    from the Canadian provinces.

PHILLIPS, Charles Howard, formerly of Boston, died yesterday. MORE 1 July 1845

PHILLIPS, John of Linnaeus died at Boonville on his way home BRUNS 14 Oct 1848
    from St. Louis.

PHILLIPS, John Yerby of Boone Co. died 24 Sept. of typhoid. MODE 6 Oct 1847
    Born Northumberland Co. VA 12 Aug. 1797, came to
    Mo 1816/17 and married. Large family of children.

PHILIPSON, Joseph Jr. died Monday. MORE 11 Sep 1822

PHILIPSON, Philip died at Lexington 24 Sept. on returning MORE 7 Oct 1834
    from the Rocky Mountains. Son of Simon, St. Louis.

PHILIPSON, Simon Esq. died 29 June age 75. MORE 1 July 1841
    William Hymen youngest son of Simon died of MORE 23 July 1833
    cholera Sunday age 14.

PICKENS, George of Pettis Co. died on the Big Blue River MORE 7 Oct 1850
    7 June age 20.

PICKETT, Sandford died 17 Dec. in Shelby Co. in 79th year. PWH 22 Jan 1846

PIERCE, Peter H. Jr. died in his 24th year. Left wife. BOLT 24 Aug 1844

PIERCE, Thomas of Taney Co. died at Chimney Rock 19 June MORE 7 Oct 1850
    age 12.

PIGOTT, John, native of Dublin, many years a resident BEA 3 Nov 1831
    of St. Louis, died 25 October.

PIGOTT, William died yesterday in St. Louis. MORE 17 Apr 1838

PIGGOTT, William, a druggist, died 2 Oct. in his 24th yr. MORP 3 Oct 1845
    Resided Franklin & Wash. Catholic cemetery.

PILCHER, Beverly "many years a resident" died 6 March. MODE 14 Mar 1848

PILCHER, ____ of Boons Lick died on the road from MODE 15 Mar
    Santa Fe. 1846 OR 1847

PILE, John killed last Friday at Carrollton by Dr. Haden. MODE 15 Sep 1847

PINER, John died 5 April at the home of Elijah Foster. JINQ 8 June 1843
    Born Halifax VA. (Notice to heirs.)

PIPER, Samuel died 5 March in his 27th year at the home SPAD 14 Mar 1846
    of his mother in Bolivar, Polk Co.

PITMAN, John age 88 died at the home of his son David K. MORE 12 Jan 1839
    in Dardenne Twp., St. Charles Co.

PITZER, George died in St. Charles Co. age about 60. MORE 30 Jan 1835

PLAIN, John died on Sunday night last, late of NY, MORE 15 Sep 1819
    interred with Masmichmacs (?).

PLASTER, Joseph died at the home of Joseph Pilcher, SWERE 24 July 1848
    5th & Locust, yesterday.

PLASTER, William of Boone Co. died in CA 25 Feb., about 23. MORE 10 May 1852

PLEASANTS, ____, killed in a duel. T. Ritchie, his MODE 29 Apr 1846
    seconds and others acquitted.

PLUMMER, Joseph killed by his brother Philemon (with a   MORE 7 May 1839
    pitchfork) in Lincoln Co. on 28 April. (A
                        family quarrel.)

PLUMP, Capt. Erich of Jefferson city died Wednesday week.   BRUNS 19 Dec 1848

POE, Simon H. died in Cape Girardeau 1 May. Death resulted   STEGPD 21 May 1853
    from his attempt to go down into his well but the
    details are not clear.

POINDEXTER, _____ died of cholera in Palmyra.   MORE 28 June 1833

POINTER, John Leonard died 5 January. Funeral from home of   MORE 6 Jan 1844
    his mother, Market between 6th-7th. Age 29.   "   9 Jan   "
    Interred Methodist cemetery. Wife, 2 children.
    I.O.O.F. Cincinnati, Lynchburg VA, Richmond VA
                        please copy.

POINTER, John, formerly of Lynchburg VA, died 23 Sept.   MORE 27 Sep 1831
    in his 54th year. "Nearly 30 years a Methodist."
    Left wife and children.

POLHILL, John C., Judge of the Ocmulga Circuit, died in   MORE 17 Sep 1838
    Cass Co. 26 August. (Possibly Illinois?)

POLLARD, Elijah died at the home of his father in Shelby Co.
    Thursday evening last.   PWH 11 Jan 1840

POLLARD, William, a Revolutionary soldier, died 5 June   PWH 12 June 1841
                        in his 81st year.

POLLARD, William S. died 21 April in his 21st year.   PWH 4 May 1848

POOL, Samuel died at the home of his son Thomas Esq.   PWH 5 Mar 1846
    in Monroe Co. 25 February in his 62nd year.

PORCH, Henry, of Porch's Prairie, Chariton Co., died Thurs. BRUNS 9 Dec 1848

PORTER, Henry died 6 February in Calumet Twp. (Pike Co.)   BGDB 14 Feb 1846
                        age about 40.

PORTER, Levi Van Camp, son of John S. and Elvira, died at   LEXP 21 June 1854
    St. Louis when returning from California.
    Age 18y 6m 19d.

PORTER, William, a resident of St. Louis for 12 years, a   MORE 26 Dec 1848
    native of CT, died 25 Dec. at the home of
                        Joseph Harding.

PORTER, William C. -- Camden Co. Final settlement by   JINQ 10 Apr 1845
                        Nathaniel Porter.

POST, Justus, formerly of St. Louis, native of VT, died   MORE 16 June 1846
    near Caledonia, Pulaski Co. IL 14 March.

POSTON, Col. Henry died at his home in St. Francois Co.   MORE 13 Apr 1840
    26 Jan. in his 55th year. "Husband, parent."

POTEET, John D. died Friday.   MORE 7 Aug 1822

POTTER, Willis -- Grundy Co. Letters of administration   PLAR 14 July 1848
    to John and Thomas L. Potter.

POTTS, John H., surgeon dentist, died 14 July age 36, near   BRUNS 26 July 1849
    Rocheport. Formerly of Fayette, then St. Louis.
                        Mason, I.O.O.F.

123

POTTS, Rev. William, pastor of 1st Presbyterian Church, died age 48. MORE 29 Mar 1852

POWELL, Anderson died in Bowling Green 27 Dec. in 66th yr. BGDB 3 Jan 1846

POWELL, Fielding stabbed to death by his brother Will at Glasgow Sunday last. BRUNS 15 July 1848

POWELL, George H., formerly of Eastern Shore MD, died at St. Charles 23 July. MORE 28 July 1829

POWELL, James -- Montgomery Co. Final settlement by William Newlane. MORE 27 Mar 1832

POWELL, Gen. Joseph died 7 March. SPAD 9 Mar 1847

POWELL, Peter, of St. Louis, died in New Orleans 18 Nov. of consumption, age 49. MORE 28 Nov 1846

POWELL, Peter, of Macon Co., died 13 July in his 75th yr. Formerly of NC. BRUNS 26 July 1849

POWELL, Willis J. died yesterday age 60y 4m. Funeral from his residence, 3rd between Olive & Locust. MORE 21 Oct 1846

POWARS, Moses died 29 November. MORE 2 Dec 1841

POWERS, Samuel died in Union, Franklin Co., in June 1835. Believed to have relatives in Carlyle PA. Age about 25. (Notice to possible heirs.) MORE 29 Jan 1839

POWERS, William, son of James, drowned in Chouteau's Pond. Funeral from residence, 5th St. opposite Convent. MORE 27 May 1846

PRATER, Jeremiah accidentally shot himself at Bolivar. STGAZ 15 Dec 1852

PRATHER, Dr. J.V., president of trustees of St. Louis U., died at the home of David Tatum in St. Louis. BRUNS 6 Sep 1849

PRATHER, Thomas died 30 September. MODE 14 Oct 1846

PRATHER, Thomas died of cholera 20 May (in a letter from Vermilion Creek). BRUNS 21 June 1849

PRATTE, General Bernard "one of our most estimable and opulent citizens" died yesterday. MORE 2 Apr 1836

PRATTE, Evariste E. died in Fredericktown 13 Feb. age about 50. MORE 19 Feb 1849

PRATT, Julius H., formerly of Buffalo NY, died in this city 8 November age 27. MORE 10 Nov 1845

PRATT, Samuel A., age 22, late of Woodstock VT, died 9 Sept. "Here with uncle Nathaniel Simonds and lady." JEFRE 11 Sep 1841

PRATTE, Sylvestre, son of Gen. B., died several months ago at the headwaters of the Platte, near the mountains. MORE 30 Sep 1828

PRATT, Virgil, formerly of Knox Co., died near Marysville CA 12 February. CANE 29 Mar 1855

PRAY, William died at Newington NH 28 December. MORE 27 Jan 1846

PRESTON, Berry -- Gentry Co. Letters of administration to Ann Berry, exr., 27 December. STGAZ 18 Jan 1854

PRESTON, Elijah listed among the casualties of a steamboat catastrophe in Livingston Co., age 31.	MORE 4 July 1842
PREWITT, Joel Sr. died Monday last.	MODE 20 Oct 1847
PRUITT, Larkin of Capt. Hudson's Co., under Maj. Clark, died at Santa Fe beteen Nov. 1-Nov.15.	MODE 13 Jan 1847
PREWITT, Patrick H. died at his father's home near Fayette Tuesday in his 22nd year.	BOLT 12 Nov 1842
PREWITT, Price of Howard Co. died suddenly 9 February.	MIN 15 Feb 1827
PRICE, Edwin C., formerly of Baltimore, died at the home of Daniel S. Robbins near Bellefontaine 10 Aug. in his 23rd year.	MORE 19 Aug 1840
PRICE, Harrison died in Buffalo Twp. (Pike Co.) 17 March in his 23rd year.	BGDB 21 Mar 1846
PRICE, ___ killed in a runaway on St. Charles Road while returning to his home in Callaway Co.	MORE 29 May 1841
PRICE, James, age about 29, of Newton Co. died 8 Feb. on the middle fork of the Calaveras.	MORE 16 Apr 1852
PRICE, Lemuel killed by Joseph Kincade in a fight at the house of H. C. Mills near Camp Branch.	MORE 9 Feb 1820
PRICE, Miles -- Montgomery Co. Final settlement by Alphonso Price.	MORE 20 Mar 1837
PRICE, Moses -- Montgomery Co. Final settlement by Alphonso Price.	MORE 26 Nov 1836
PRICE, Capt. Risdon "many years a resident of MO" age 65.	MORE 23 Dec 1845
PRICE, Samuel -- Montgomery Co. Letters of administration to Alexander McKinney.	MORE 1 Nov 1827
PRIMEAU, Paul died 11 September in his 76th year.	MORE 12 Sep 1851
PRINGLE, Norman Esq., formerly of CT, died recently at his residence in Hickory Grove, Montgomery Co.	MORE 28 July 1836
PRITCHART, William died in Lexington. PRITCHETT (state not shown, probably Missouri)	MORE 5 Oct 1830
PROCTOR, John died Monday last.	MODE 12 May 1847
PROVENCHERE(R), John Louis died yesterday. Funeral from late residence, 7th & Spruce, to Catholic cemetery. "An old resident."	MORE 13 July 1839
PROVENCHERE, Pierre died 8 Sept. age 55, native of France.	MORE 13 Sep 1824
PRYOR, Jeremiah -- DeKalb Co. Letters of administration to William and John Pryor, 23 December.	STGAZ 29 Dec 1852
PRYOR, Capt. N., sub-agent for the Osage Indians. No date.	BEA 21 July 1831
PTOMEY, Robert died Sunday at an advanced age. Formerly of Bath Co. VA. Presbyterian.	PWH 2 Apr 1845
PUCKETT, Dr. Alfred H., formerly of Perry Co., 10 July.	MORE 17 July 1846

PUGH, Martin -- Montgomery Co. Final settlement by   JEFS 19 May 1827
    Susannah Pugh.

PULLIAM, Drury of Saline Co. died 9 Aug. in his 78th yr.   BRUNS 23 Aug 1849

PULLIAM, Major Elijah R. died at Glasgow Thursday last   BOLT 19 Nov 1842
    in his 28th year.

PULLIAM, H. R. died in the Big Hatchee disaster at Hermann. MORE 11 Aug 1845

PULLEN, John died 5 October in Grundy Co. age 50.   WEPT 11 Oct 1851

PULTE, Dr. Phil A. died 26 Aug. Funeral from his residence MORE 27 Aug 1844
    #10 N. 3rd to Catholic cemetery.

PUTNAM, Charles A., native of Danvers MA and Supt. of the MORE 4 Jan 1854
    St. Louis Public Schools died 2 Jan. age 39.
    Funeral Union Presbyterian Church.

PYATT, James A., 2nd Engineer, died in the Car of   MORE 27 May 1828
    Commerce disaster.

QUARLES, James L., from VA, died 25 October at James   MORE 3 Nov 1819
    Ferry on the Missouri.

QUARLES, Dr. Pryor, late of VA, died in St. Louis Co.   MORE 19 Sep 1821
    on 8 September.

QUARLES, Major Robert died at his plantation in St.   MORE 30 Aug 1827
    Ferdinand Twp. 23 August.

QUARLES, Garret, son of Col. Robert, died at his father's MORE 7 Jan 1837
    home in St. Louis Co. age 25.

QUARLES, Robert, resident of St. Ferdinand Twp., 16 Feb.   MORE 21 Feb 1832

QUICK, Jacob -- Montgomery Co. Final settlement by   JEFS 19 May 1827
    Jacob Groom.

QUIRK, John D., brother of Matthew, died 7 Aug. at the   MORP 8 Aug 1845
    Virginia Hotel in his 24th yr. Philadelphia pls copy.

QUIRK, Michael D. died 5 March.   SWERE 13 Mar 1848

QUISENBERRY, Charles H., son of James S. and Eliza S. of   MORE 17 Aug 1847
    St. Louis Co., killed in New Mexico in
    his 23rd year.

RACE, Henry, a deckhand on the Die Vernes, drowned at   MORE 22 July 1847
    New Orleans 14 July.

RADFORD, Alfred died in Lafayette Co. age (33?).   LEXP 1 Feb 1854

RADFORD, Dr. John B. killed immediately a few days ago in MORE 14 Apr 1843
    Lafayette Co. when a log fell on him at a
    house raising.

RAGSDALE, Richard died yesterday morning in St. Louis.   MORE 29 May 1834

RAISIN, Joseph James died age 25. Resident of St. Louis   SWERE 6 Oct 1845
    for 7 years. Born in Kent Co. MD.

RAMBO, Capt Jacob of Old Mines died in his 48th year. Came MORE 6 Oct 1840
    to MO at age 15, an orphan from KY.

RAMEY, William died in Stonesport, Boone Co. on 22 May age 104. Revolutionary soldier. — MORE 13 June 1845

RAMSEY, Milton died at his home on Clark St. age 28. Lately of Beaver Co. PA. Recently married. — MORE 29 Jan 1844

RAMSAY, Robert, his wife and 3 children killed Saturday last two miles from the old Charrette settlement in St. Charles Co. — MORE 27 May 1815

RANDALL, Charles, native of Fincastle VA, died 26 Jne in his 24th year. Survived by father, 3 sisters. — MORE 29 June 1848

RANDAL, I. killed by lightning Wednesday at the rear of the Missouri Hotel. Pilot of the <u>Michigan</u>. — MORE 10 Oct 1834

RANDAL, John died 14 August. Early settler. Methodist. Left wife, 8 children. — PWH 21 Aug 1841

RANDALL, John J., of Powers & Randall, died 14 June age 24. — MORE 20 June 1837

RANEY, Thomas died recently at his home in Ft. Osage Twp. Late of Lexington KY. Wife, large family. — INJN 10 Oct 1844

RANKIN, Hugh. Funeral from residence of Mrs. Richards (boarding house) to Masonic cemetery. — MORE 11 July 1825

RANKIN, James died in LaGrange 6 November. — CAMP 1 Dec 1848

RANKIN, James F. died 26 Aug. in his 28th year. — PWH 27 Aug 1842

RANKIN, John M. died near Greenfield, Dade Co., 19 Sept. — SPAD 1 Oct 1844

RANKIN, Silas died at Woodville Mills near Boonville in his 31st year 18 Sept. Member Universalist Society. — BORE 26 Sep 1843

RANNEY, Gen. Johnson died in Cape Girardeau. — MORE 28 Aug 1848

RANSON, Ambrose died at Union, Franklin Co. 29 August. Formerly of VA. Petersburg & Lynchburg pls copy. — MORE 12 Sep 1846

RANSON, John F., late of Franklin Co., brother of Evalina Letcher, died in CA 25 May in 28th year. — MORE 2 Sep 1851

RASIN, Joseph J., a clerk, killed on hunting trip Wed. — MORE 29 Sep 1845

RATEIN, John W., late of Baltimore, died Thursday. — MORE 13 Sep 1820

RAWLIN(G)S, John W. (or P.), died near Rocheport 21 Aug. "Left a large family." — BOLT 29 Aug 1840

RAWLINGS, Thomas died in Franklin Co. 12 July of congestive fever. Born Caroline Co. VA 4 Oct 1790. Left wife and niece. — MORE 14 Sep 1844

RAWLINGS, Thomas "one of our oldest and most respected citizens" died 23 October. Large circle of relatives and friends. — MODE 11 Nov 1846

RAY, Col. Benjamin died at Manchester Springs Saturday, late member of the MO legislayure. — MORE 30 Aug 1833

RAY, Henry D., late of Jefferson OH, died 6 April in St. Louis at the home of U. Rasin, age 20. — SWERE 13 Apr 1846

RAY, John, member of the House of Representatives from Ray Co., died in St. Louis 13 October. — SLINQ 14 Oct 1820

READ, Samuel died at his home in Union Twp. (Marion Co.)   PWH 8 Aug 1840
3 August age about 45.

READ, William E. died at his home in Cooper Co. 23 Jan.   COMB 11 Feb 1847

READING, James G. died at his father's home 6 Oct. in   SALT 9 Oct 1841
his 27th year. Presbyterian. Survived by
parents, sisters, brothers.

REARDON, Matthew D. died 12 February in his 63rd year.   MORE 20 Feb 1839

RECTOR, Col. Elias, one of the senators from St. Louis Co.   MORE 14 Aug 1822
in the State Legislature, died Wed.

RECTOR, Col. Wharton, US Army Paymaster, in Van Buren AR.   MORE 24 Feb 1842

RECTOR, Wm. V. Esq., late of MO, died at the home of   MORE 13 Oct 1829
Col. Wharton Rector in Arkansas Territory 16 Sept.

REDDIT, James killed at Valle's Mines in February by   MORE 13 Apr 1826
Patrick Sawer (Sawey or Soy).

REDMON, George W. died near St. Charles age 47.   BEA 20 Oct 1831
Formerly of Clark Co. KY.

REDMAN, William W. -- Montgomery Co. Letters of admini-   FULT 16 Nov 1849
stration to C. C. Redman, 7 November.

REECE, Gird died in New Mexico 1 April, about 35.   STGAZ Nov 1847

REED, Andrew -- Wayne Co. Letters of administration   INP 15 Dec 1826
to H. Carter 14 November.

REED, Isaac, native of MA and citizen of Commerce (Cape   CGWE 1 Sep 1848
Girardeau Co.) 13 years died Tuesday.

REED, Capt. Jacob of St. Louis, of yellow fever 12 Sept.   MORE 25 Oct 1820
Dayton son of Capt. Jacob 9 Sept., New Orleans.   MORE 25 Oct 1820
Milton C. son of the late Capt. Jacob, 30 April   SWERE 10 May 1847
in Shawneetown IL age 38.

REED, James of St. Louis at Galena, Fever River, 17 May.   MORE 27 May 1828

REED, John C. died 28 August at Old Mines, Washington Co.   MORE 10 Sep 1840
age 42. Formerly of Allen Co. KY. Catholic.

REED, John H., formerly of St. Louis, in Pulaski Co. AR   MORE 29 Dec 1845
on 13 December.

REED, Col. Robert, native of Ireland, died 18 June at his   MORE 9 July 1823
home near Cote sans Dessein, Callaway Co., age 67.

REED, Samuel, many years a resident of St. Louis, died in   SWERE 30 Apr 1849
Jackson Co. IA 6 Apr. age 55. Philadelphia pls copy.

REED, William, late of Caswell NC, died in St. Louis 4 Nov.   SLINQ 18 Nov 1823

REED, William died 5 July age about 30.   MORE 13 July 1830

REEDS, William B., in his 21st year, at the home of his   BGRAD 2 Sep 1843
father in Louisville, Lincoln Co., 10 August.

REEL, John -- notice that as a result of his death the   MORE 11 Jan 1838
firm of Reel, Barnes & Co. is dissolved.

REELANT, ___ killed by Indians at Couvre Settlement, St.   MORE 25 Mar 1815
Charles, Sunday.

REESE, David, a shoemaker, died at the home of J. Barclay   MORE 27 May 1839
    on Manchester Rd. 2½ mi. west of St. Louis, age 48.
    Native of Lancaster PA.

REID, Clifton G., formerly of Randolph Co., died at the home   BGRAD 3 Aug 1844
    of John A. Woods in Spencer Twp. (Pike Co.) age 25.

REID, David, native of Scotland, died 23 April in his 67th   MORE 24 Apr 1849
    year. Funeral from his son David's home, Locust-Vine.

REID, Elder William died at the home of his son Gen. S.W.   BOLT 14 Feb 1846
    in Monroe Co. in his 69th year, 16 January. Had
    lived in Madison Co. KY. "A Christian 40 years."

REILLY, John M. died Sunday evening last.   MORE 28 July 1835

REILLY, Michael, age 44, native of Newcastle, Co. Meath,   BEA 9 Feb 1832
    died Thursday; left large family.

REILLY, Michael, died of cholera 29 October.   MORE 30 Oct 1832

REILY, Henry, a merchant, 24 January. Funeral from   MORE 25 Jan 1831
    Mrs. Paddock's.

REINS, Larkin died in Jefferson City 8 September. Left a   JINQ 9 Sep 1841
    large and dependent family.   JEFRE 11 Sep "

REMUS, Frederick K. died 12 June. Left mother, 2 sisters.   MORE 16 June 1848

RENSHAW, Charles T., son of William, yesterday age 22.   MORE 2 Nov 1843

REVEL, Michael, native of Wexford, Ireland, yesterday.   SWERE 22 Jan 1849

REYNOLDS, ___, a young man, shot himself in Saline Co.   BOLT 22 Oct 1842

REYNALS, Dr. Antoine died in St. Charles Monday age 80.   STCHMO 20 Dec 1821

REYNOLDS, Dr. H. died age 28. Resided 4th near Franklin.   MORE 12 May 1849
    Norfolk VA and Louisville pls copy.

REYNOLDS, Jesse D. died Monday age about 50.   PWH 12 Apr 1849

REYNOLDS, Dr. Michael died 9 August age 53. (From the   MORE 15 Aug 1838
    Salt River Journal.)

REYNOLDS, Obadiah died in St. Louis Sunday.   MORE 23 Nov 1826

REYNOLDS, Capt. Otis died 30 Nov. age 39.   MORE 5 Dec 1839

REYNOLDS, Thomas, Governor of Missouri, shot himself   MORE 12 Feb 1844
    in Jefferson City.

REYNOLDS, William of Grundy Co. died 16 June on the   MORE 7 Oct 1850
    way west.

RHEA, William -- Camden Co. Final settlement, Jane Rhea.   JINQ 10 Apr 1845

RHODES, Bradley (Brainley?) age 15 died on the road from   MORE 26 June 1852
    Iowa to Texas.

RHODES, Charles shot and killed in Ralls Co. 8 March by   PWH 23 Mar 1844
    James Fagan of Pike Co.

RHUDAY, Henry / Jesse - Grundy Co. Letters of administration 7 Mar.
    by James M. Howell.   STGAZ 5 May 1848

RHYNE, Joseph -- Montgomery Co. Final settlement, John Hill.   JEFS 19 May 1827

RIBEAUT, John, of Ste. Genevieve, died Friday last in his 35th year.	MORE 29 Apr 1849
RIBELIN, William -- Caldwell Co. Final settlement, J.P. Kern.	LEXP ca 1853-4
RICE, James, "highly respected citizen of Perry Co., died aboard the De_____ (rest illegible).	MORE 29 June 1848
RICE, Michael, a carpenter, killed while working on the Baptist Church Spire.	MORE 17 Aug 1847
RICE, Rev. Samuel Davis died at Hannibal "Sunday last."	MORE 18 Apr 1846
RICE, William, of Co. A., Col. Price's Reg., died at Santa Fe 4 November.	MODE 13 Jan 1847
RICHARDS, Benjamin, a native of Wilkshire, Eng., died 5 November age 42.	SWERE 8 Nov 1847
RICHARDS, Hugh "many years a citizen" died Friday.	MORE 16 July 1838
RICHARDS, Thomas M., a printer, died 12 July age 17. Staunton Spectator please copy.	SWERE 20 July 1846
RICHARDSON, Alford, formerly of Portland ME, died "last evening." Funeral from Ezra Dodge's home.	MORE 13 July 1843
RICHARDSON, James H., assessor for Jefferson Co., died 17 Sept. in his 24th year. Left parents.	MORE 20 Sep 1842
RICHARDSON, John, supposed to have been murdered about 1 July 1836 near St. Francis River. Had recently moved from New Madrid to Arkansas.	SMAD 1 June 1838
RICHARDSON, John Carter of Richmond, Ray Co., died in Cincinnati 8 September.	MORE 18 Sep 1847
RICHARDSON, Skelton, of Franklin Co., died at Gravois. (His estate was filed in Cooper Co.)	MORE 3 Sep 1823
RICKERSON, Asa, many years a resident of St. Louis and formerly of Bedford MA. No other data. (Shown as RICKETSON in Swere, 26 Feb. which says he died at brother's home in New Bedford)	MORE 22 Feb 1849
RICKS, ____, a German, fell from the LaSalle and drowned. Had wife, children in Beardstown IL.	MORE 6 Sep 1844
RIDDELLS, Stephen G. died in Ralls Co. "Tuesday week last."	LEXP 22 Feb 1854
RIDDICK, Col. Thomas F. died in Jefferson Co. last week, many years a resident of this city.	MORE 16 Feb 1830
RIDGELY, Dr. R.G., formerly of Baltimore, died 29 Jan. at Mineral Point WI.	MORE 15 Feb 1839
RIEHL, Nicholas, native of Colmar, France died 9 Sept. age about 41.	MORE 16 Sep 1853
RIELY, Robert died at his home on N. Main St. 29 July.	MORE 1 Aug 1825
RIGGS, J. of Pettis Co. died 8 June 6 mi. west of Ft. Kearney age 45. Left a wife.	MORE 7 Oct 1850
RIGGS, James, Pike Co., run over by wagonload of wood, died.	MORE 4 Oct 1848

RIGGS, Gen. Jonathan died at his home in Lincoln Co. on 20 Jan. in his 46th year. From Campbell Co. KY. Settled first in St. Charles. (Quoted from the Salt River Journal.) — MORE 3 Feb 1834

RIGGS, Samuel, residing about 15 mi. from Independence, killed by lightning 12 July. — MORP 17 July 1845

RIGNEY, Hugh, fireman on the St. Louis, fell overboard and believed drowned. — MORE 25 Aug 1847

RILEY, Ben S., son of Samuel of Cooper Co., died in Sacramento 1 February. — BOBS 29 Apr 1851

RILEY, George -- Ozark Co. Letters of administration to Zachariah and Margaret Riley, 4 Jan. — SPAD 20 Feb 1847

RILEY, J. M. died yesterday age 40. Resided Olive-10th-11th. — MORE 27 Nov 1848

RILEY, Jackson -- Ozark Co. Letters of administration to Robert R.P. Todd, 31 Aug. — SPAD 10 Oct 1846

RILEY, William, 1st Engineer of the Huntress, died Sat. — MORE 17 Aug 1826

RILEY (REILY), John P., funeral from residence of widow at #50 Elm St. Interred Catholic cemetery. (Apparently died elsewhere.) — MORE 9 June 1841

RINDISBACHER, P., miniaturist and landscape painter, died 13 August. — MORE 15 Aug 1834

RINGER, Jonathan, resident of Ray Co., native of OH, died Tuesday in his 40th year. (JEFRE 1 Oct. says native of PA) — JINQ 29 Sep 1842

RISLEY, E., formerly of MO died in Marysville (CA?) on 7 Oct. age 35. — MORE 9 Dec 1851

RISLEY, George of Hartford CT, father of William of St. Louis, died in his 63rd year. — MORE 15 Aug 1846

RITCHEY, Alexander died 8 April in his 63rd year. — WARD 12 Apr 1853

RITTER, William Jr. drowned in a pond in St. Louis Twp. Inquest at home of Jacob Ritter. — MORE 10 July 1848

RIZER, Daniel L. died 19 Sept. age 33. Memphis and Beardstown KY please copy. — SWERE 21 Sep 1846

ROBARDS, William J. of St. Louis, formerly of Shawneetown, died at Shawneetown of a knee wound 30 Jan. age about 50. — MORP 10 Feb 1845

ROBIRDS, Capt. Hardin died yesterday aboard the Grand Turk. — SWERE 28 May 1849

ROBERTS, Isaiah formerly of Norristown PA died 29 April age 30. — MORE 29 Apr 1851

ROBERT, Paul died in Carondelet 24 January. — MORE 9 Feb 1826

ROBERTS, Stephen died Wednesday of wounds from a dirk, inflicted by Finley Hunter. (at Franklin) — MIN 29 Jan 1821

ROBERTS, Saul F., 2nd son of Wm. F. of Potosi, died at the home of John Perry, Perry's Mines, in 22nd year. — MORE 11 Jan 1844

ROBINSON, Rev. Charles S. died at St. Charles 25 Sept. in   MORE 30 Sep 1818
his 36th year. Native of Granville MA, graduate
of Andover Theological Seminary. A missionary.

ROBERTSON, Duncan F. died in Danville 31 Aug. of cholera   FULT 21 Sep 1849
age 65y 3m. Born Lancaster Co. VA, to KY in his
23rd year. Taught school 42 years, member of the
Methodist Church since 1827. Husband and father.
(Father of Rev. W. W. of Fulton)

ROBISON, Edward -- DeKalb Co. Letters of administration   STGAZ 28 July 1848
to Joseph Robison, 12 July.

ROBINSON, George R. -- Montgomery Co. Final settlement   FULT 22 Sep 1848
by John C. Whiteside.

ROBERTSON, Gravron died in Farmington 21 Aug. of typhus.   MORE 10 Sep 1844
Son of Col. and Mary T. (Shelton), formerly of
Compensation, Pittsylvania Co. VA.

ROBINSON, Henry of this city died in Callaway Co. 16 May   JINQ 22 May 1845
(Jefferson City)   age about 46.

ROBINSON, James, an old citizen, died 8 June.   GLWT 12 June 1851

ROBINSON, John -- Gentry Co. Letters of administration   STGAZ 20 Aug 1847
to Elias Robinson 3 August.

ROBERSON, Josiah of Jefferson City, in an infantry   MODE 11 Jan 1847
battalion, died on the way to Santa Fe.

ROBINSON, George, body found in river.   MORE 18 July 1848

ROBINSON, George W. -- Reynolds Co. Letters of admini-   JEM 31 Aug 1852
stration to John Buford, 4 May.

ROBINSON, Garland died at Rocheport 20 Nov. age 38.   MODE 11 Dec 1848

ROBINSON, I., son of Gerard, died of typhoid age ca 22.   MODE 10 Mar 1846

ROBINSON, Capt. James of Manchester died yesterday.   MORE 5 Aug 1840
Funeral from residence of N. E. Janney.

ROBINSON, Capt Jeremiah died at Louisville 23 April. Late   MORE 29 Apr 1839
of the Darr, many years resident of St. Louis.

ROBINSON, Rev. Robert P. died at the home of R. Clayton   MORE 11 July 1835
in St. Louis Co. Late of England, "three years
here," left a disconsolate widow.

ROBINSON, Simon died 10 August age 56.   MORE 11 Aug 1851

ROBINSON, William T. died 6 Sept. in his 34th year. Left   MODE 19 Sep 1848
widow and 5 children.

ROBINSON, Wylie, found dead near Huntsville (Randolph Co.)   MORE 7 Feb 1845
and supposedly murdered.

ROBNETT, George W. died 28 March in his 21st year.   PWH 13 Apr 1844

ROBBINETT, Jesse -- Wright Co. Letters of administration   SPAD 20 Dec 1845
to Jesse Robbinett, 12 December.

ROBNETT, Zephaniah "aged and respected" died 20 July.   PWH 22 July 1843

ROCHEBLAVE, Henry, "a young man of amiable manners, respectability, and usefulness" died Wednesday.   MORE 28 Aug 1818

ROCK, Smith J. -- Gentry Co. Letters of administration to John Huggins, 7 October.   STGAZ 10 Nov 1852

ROE, Robert Augustus, son of John and Martha, died after a fall from a horse. Age 11y 6m. Interred Wesleyan.   MORE 6 Sep 1851

RODGERS, Ezekiel died in Bonhomme Twp 24 March "In consequence of boiling water being poured over his head while he slept, and afterward much beat and bruised." Moses Kenny, the murderer, of Bourbon KY, fled.   MORE 11 Apr 1811

RODGERS, Jonas C. died 19 August in his 21st year.   MORE 20 Aug 1853

ROGERS, Patrick died 1 March age 35.   SWERE 5 Mar 1849

ROGERS, Thomas died 24 June age about 50.   JEFRE 27 June 1835

ROGERS, Williamson died in Franklin Co. in his 49th year, leaving wife, one son, 9 daughters.   MORE 26 Feb 1852

ROHER, Jacob, MD died of consumption 21 March age 35.   MORE 22 Mar 1851

ROHRBACKER, Charles drowned at Loutre Island 18 April age 36. From Hermann, Gasconade Co. Widow inquiring if his body had been found.   MORE 9 May 1840

ROLLINS, Dr. A. W. died in Richland, Boone Co. of paralysis 9 Oct. in his 62nd year. Formerly of Richmond KY.   MORE, 8 & 10 Nov. 1845

ROLLS, Capt. Daniel, member of the MO Legislature from Pike Co., died at Col. Benton's on 30 October.   MORE 8 Nov 1820

ROSE, Hugh, age 47, died last night. Schenectady pls copy.   SWERE 14 May 1849

ROSE, Lewis died in St. Ferdinand Twp. Tuesday.   MORE 3 Sep 1823

ROSE, Mathias died at his home in St. Ferdinand Twp. on 5 July.   MORE 11 July 1834

ROSE, Stephen died at Big Prairie Twp., New Madrid -- (ROSS) "legislator, husband, father."   INP Nov 1822

ROSS, Abner S. died Saturday morning in his 28th year.   MORE 20 Mar 1837.

ROSS, Charles, formerly of Washington D.C., now of St. Louis Co., died 3 July at W. H. Brantner's home.   MORP 9 July 1845

ROSS, James -- Gentry Co. Letters of administration to Archibald Ross, 10 November.   STGAZ 11 Dec 1846

ROSS, Capt. John, late of Newburyport MA, died 31 Oct. at the home of William Allen.   MORE 2 Nov 1848

ROSS, Thomas P. died of cholera at Palmyra.   MORE 28 June 1833

ROSS, William C., son-in-law of Dr. Hart, drowned in the Missouri River 19 March. Here about 3 years, formerly of Fauquier VA. (Boonville)   WEM 21 Mar 1839

ROSSMAN, John B. -- Chariton Co. Final settlement by William Ballentine.   BRUNS 4 Nov 1847

ROURKE, Michael Esq. died 21 Sept. age 38. Member of the Board of Aldermen, in St. Louis since 1818. Native of Co. Kildare. Wife, 2 children.   SOV 22 Sep 1832

ROUSSIN, Etienne died in Richwoods, Washington Co. on   MORE 5 Feb 1833
    24 January age 66.

ROWE, Christopher died age about 20. Funeral from home of   MORE 18 June 1849
    his father-in-law Wm. Flanagan, 15th and Pine.
    Interred Catholic cemetery.

ROWE, Patrick died 14 June age 35. Native of Ireland.   MORE 15 June 1849
    Lived at 9th and Mullanphy. Interred Cath. cemetery.

ROWLAND, Alfred, age 32 died Friday. Formerly of NY.   MORE 5 July 1836

ROY, John B. died 18 May in his 70th year.   STGAZ June 1852

ROY, William died in Hannibal 12 March at the home of   PWH 18 Mar 1847
    O.H.P. Lear, in his 27th year.

ROYCE, Norton D. died about 15 August 1845. Estate notice.   STGAZ 26 Sep 1845
    Age about 30, stout, born in OH.

RUBEY, Dr. Robert C. of St. Louis Co. died in Columbia   WEM 13 June 1839
    on 30 May.

RUBY, John F., 14, died at his father's home, Independence.   INJN 12 Sep 1844

RUCKLE, Peter died yesterday in his 62nd year. Lived 4 mi.   MORE 4 Jan 1853
    from St. Louis on Manchester Rd. Baltimore and
    Cincinnati, please copy.

RUDISCEALE, John died in Jackson (Cape Girardeau Co.)   MORE 19 Jan 1853
    leaving wife and children.

RUE, ___ "a poor drunk fell dead on the road to Linneaus."   BRUNS 19 July 1849

RUGGLES, Abijah died 26 Feb. age 30, resident of St. Louis   SWERE 3 Mar 1845
    for 7 years, formerly of Brighton MA.

RUGGLES, Martin, Whig candidate for the legislature from   MORE 7 Aug 1840
    Washington Co., died 3-4 days before the election.

RULAND, Capt. John died near St. Charles 1 Jan. age 59.   MORE 3 Jan 1849
    Lived on Morgan St., St. Louis. Catholic cemetery.

RULE, Press G. died at Newport, Franklin Co.   MORE 3 Aug 1830

RUNDLETT, Maj. John died near St. Louis yesterday. In   MORE 1 Sep 1836
    St. Louis several years, formerly of NH.

RUPE, Gilead died near Lexington 2 December age 75, "A   BRUNS 23 Dec 1847
    pioneer companion of Daniel Boone."

RUSSELL, James R. -- Montgomery Co. Letters of admini-   NERA 23 Sep 1841
    stration to A. B. Snethen, 9 August.

RUSSELL, John J. of Cole Co. died on the Little Blue River   MORE 7 Oct 1850
    6 June. Left wife and 4 children.

RUSSELL, Richard died yesterday age 27.   SWERE 30 Apr 1849

RUSSELL, John, a carriage maker in Lexington, died 3 Dec.   LEXP 10 Jan 1855
    Late of MD.

RUSSELL, Robert -- Montgomery Co. Notice to his heirs,   BGDB 17 May 1845
    all over 21 (named in article).

RUSSELL, Ignatius died 28 Feb. age 23. Formerly of MD.   MORE 1 Mar 1841

RUSSELL, Richard accidentally shot by a playful Mrs. McGilvery
who thought the gun was not loaded. He was a well-
respected man, in the business of raising goods   MORE 2 Mar 1840
from sunken vessels.

RUSSELL, Gen. Robert S. died at the home of his son-in-law   MORE 24 Jan 1842
Judge Freeland in Callaway Co. 6 Jan. in his 80th
year. A Revolutionary soldier. Emigrated from VA
about 50 years ago, settled near Lexington till
1835. Only surviving child of Gen. Wm. Russell, an
officer at Point Pleasant. Left an aged wife, mother
of all his children. Married 55 years. Member of the
Church of Christ.

RUSSELL, William died in Washington Co. 3 February.   MORE 12 Feb 1852

RUTGERS, Arend died yesterday at a very advanced age.   MORE 20 Mar 1837

RUTHERFORD, Hamilton died 16 March age (?35). Resided   MORE 17 Mar 1853
at 224 7th St. Interred Bellefontaine.

RYAN, Joel Z. -- Montgomery Co. Letters of administration   FULT 17 Aug 1849
to Thomas Perry 13 August.

SADLER, Samuel died in the hospital age 25. Born in VA,   MORE 20 June 1840
in St. Louis one year.

SAILOR, Emanuel -- Montgomery Co. Final settlement by   FULT 4 Aug 1848
James Sailor.

ST. CYR, Francis Fonville died in Florissant 14 March,   MORE 26 Mar 1839
age about 45.

ST. CERRE, Narcissus, missing about 3 weeks and feared   MORE 30 Nov 1809
dead. Suffered from epileptic fits. Ca 14 or 15.

ST. GEMME, L. B. died at Fredericktown 23 Feb. He left   MOAR 5 Mar 1840
four infant children.

ST. VRAIN, Charles died Thursday last. (prob 21 Oct)   MORE Oct 1834

ST. VRAIN, Capt. Jacques DeHault Delassus de, died   MORE 26 June 1818
Monday evening last.

SALEY, Lambert died 28 November.   SOV 29 Nov 1834

SALLY, James Sandford, son of Edward, died age 16.   FULT 25 Aug 1848

SALTONSTALL, Guerdan F., late of Howard Co., died in   MORE 25 July 1851
Marietta OH 24 July.

SAMSON, Rev. Ashley died 19 October at the home of Mrs.   BOLT 24 Oct 1840
Hughes near Fayette. Late of Cornwall VT.

SAMS(?), Benoni -- St. Clair Co. Final settlement by   OSIN 25 Dec 1852
U. L. Sutherland.

SAMUEL, Jamison died in Hannibal 10 Sept. in his 49th yr.   PWH 21 Sep 1848

SAMUEL, Robert L. died of cholera in Palmyra.   MORE 28 June 1833

SAMUEL, Shelton of Randolph Co. died 15 November.   MODE 24 Nov 1847
Interred by I. O. O. F.   BRUNS 25 Nov "

SANDERLIN, James, a printer, died in Jefferson City.   BRUNS 21 June 1849

SANDERS, Samuel D. died in Sarcoxie 10 January.	MORE 25 Jan 1853
SANDERS, William C., formerly of Mansfield OH. Age 28.	SCOMB 29 Nov 1840
SANDERSON, Lewis of Co. M., Col. Price's Reg., died at Santa Fe 8 November.	MODE 13 Jan 1847
SANDERSON, T. of Chariton Co., in Col. Price's Reg., died on the way to Santa Fe.	MODE 13 Jan 1847
SANDLIN, James -- Wayne Co. Letters of administration to Polly S. Sandlin and Lemuel Ketrell.	JASO 2 Jan 1838
SANFORD, Alexander Esq. died at Owens Station 13 Feb.	SWERE 21 Feb 1848
SANFORD, R.H. died near Ashley 24 Aug. age about 43.	MORE 26 Aug 1843
SANFORD, William Y. died at his home in St. Charles Co. 19 July in his 46th yr. From Hampshire Co. VA.	MORE 27 July 1842
SANFORD, Major Henry B. died 28 January.	MORE 29 Jan 1844
SANGUINET, Charles Sr. died Sunday last at advanced age.	MORE 9 Oct 1818
SANSBURY, Reason died 9 Sept. in his 57th year. Left wife and large family near Jefferson City.	JINQ 19 Sep 1844
SAPPINGTON Hartley of St. Louis Co., in his 58th year.	BRUNS 31 Mar 1849
SAPPINGTON, John died Sunday morning at Gravois in the 63rd year of his age, survived by nearly 30 children and grandchildren.	MORE 16 Sep 1815
SAPPINGTON, John Jr. died 1 April in his 42nd year.	MORE 4 Apr 1851
SAPPINGTON, Samuel Jr., late of Philadelphia, died 14 Aug.	MORE 15 Aug 1844
SARPY, Gregoire died last Saturday at an advanced age.	MORE 17 May 1824
SATERFIELD, James, a teamster, died in the Santa Fe country.	MODE 13 Jan 1847
SAUGRAIN, Dr. Anthony died Thursday night in 57th year.	MORE 24 May 1820
SAUNDERS, Christopher died Tuesday, "many years a much respected citizen."	MORE 19 Nov 1835
SAUNDERS, David, a passenger, killed in the Car of Commerce explosion.	MORE 27 May 1828
SAUNDERS, John -- Chariton Co. Letters of administration to Ann Saunders.	BOLT 5 Sep 1840
SAUNDERS, Samuel (and wife) died of cholera at Harrisonville.	LEXP 2 Aug 1854
SAVAGE, James H. died at his home near Plattsburg 8 Nov. in his 35th year.	GLWT 18 Nov 1852
SCALES, Charles W. of Linn Co. died 18 Aug. in his 22nd year. Brother of the wife of Judge C.C.P. Hill.	MODE 8 Sep 1847
SCALES, Joseph Sr. -- Chariton Co. Letters of administration to Wm. C. Woodson 13 September.	BOLT 9 July 1842
SCALES, M.D. died of consumption at Brunswick, age about 50 -- just returned from CA.	GLWT 19 May 1852?

SCHAUMBOURG, Judge C. W. (and his 2-year-old son Charles) died the same day. Interred Episcopal cemetery. (Wife and mother shown as Orleana.)   MORE 26 June 1849
" 27 "

SCHEPERS, Theodor -- Montgomery Co. Letters of administration to Gerhard & John Schepers, 8 Dec.   HERMWOCH 23 Dec 1853

SCHOLZER, William, "a German" died very suddenly 5 Sept.   PWH 13 Sep 1849

SCHRAEDER, Francis committed suicide in the office of Bryan Mullanphy, where he was employed.   MORE 8 June 1839

SCHROEDER, Charles died 2 Oct. age 50. Philadelphia please copy.   MORE 4 Oct 1847

SCHUESSLER, Valentine, a German drayman kicked by a horse, not expected to survive.   MORE 6 Aug 1845

SCIELE, ___ killed by lightning in St. Charles at the home of Dr. Thompson.   MORE 23 Aug 1845

SCOFIELD, E.M. of Willock's Co. died in Santa Fe.   MODE 13 Jan 1847

SCOTT, Dr. Arthur of Keytesville died Tuesday. Born in Ireland, "graduate London," practiced 12-15 years in Brunswick, had a partial stroke 3 years ago. Buried by Masons.   BRUNS 30 Dec 1848
His 2nd eldest son, Charles Arthur, died 18 March age 11.   BRUNS 24 Mar 1849

SCOTT, Charles I., formerly of Washington Co. VA, died 9 Feb. at the home of his brother William, age 30. Funeral from St. George's Church.   SWERE 12 Feb 1849

SCOTT, Dr. Charles R. of Fayette died of cholera 11 May, having just returned home from VA.   BRUNS 19 May 1849

SCOTT, George B. died in Jasper Co. near Carthage 6 Feb. Native of Bourbon Co. KY, came to MO in 1838.   MORE 19 Feb 1844

SCOTT, James, a merchant at Franklin, died Tuesday.   MIN 15 Mar 1827

SCOTT, James -- Chariton Co. Letters of administration to Hardin Scott.   BRUNS 20 Apr 1848

SCOTT, Joel, a returning Californian from Dade Co., died on the Saranak at the mouth of the Arkansas. Left wife and 8 children.   STGAZ 21 Jan 1852

SCOTT, John, age 64, died 9 April. Lived 11th-Washington.   SWERE 16 Apr 1849

SCOTT, John Sr. died at his home near Potosi 26 July in the 109th year of his age.   MORE 22 Aug 1839

SCOTT, King B. murdered in Lexington and his brother-in-law John C. Lester tried for the crime.   MORE 15 Dec 1845

SCOTT, Moses died 20 August.   MORE 20 Aug 1823

SCOTT, Samuel "a worthy and much respected young man" died Friday last.   MORE 19 Aug 1828

SCOTT, Robert M. of St. Joseph died at Coloma, El Dorado Co. CA age 20y 5m 17d.   MORE 17 Nov 1850

SCRUGGS, Thomas, age about 22, died of cholera 8 Oct.   JEFRE 12 Oct 1833

SCUDDER, John W. Esq., of Boonville, died Sunday last.   MIN 5 Aug 1822

SEAVER, Norman, a merchant, died 12 May. (Of the firm   MORE 14 May 1838
    of Stone, Seaver, and Busch, Boston.)

SEAY, _____ died 27 July.   COMB 30 July 1846

SEELY, _____ died 22 Oct. at the missionary station near   STCHMO 3 Jan 1822
    the Great Osage village.

SEELY, Peter, of Jefferson City, in an infantry battalion,   MODE 13 Jan 1847
    died on the way to Santa Fe.

SEGER, Cornelius V. killed by lightning Sunday while   MORE 20 July 1841
    inside his house, on the Mississippi across
    from Col. Lewis Bissell. Western NY pls copy.

SEIXAS, Charles, a marble cutter formerly of NY, working   MORE 7 Sep 1841
    in St. Louis and New Orleans, died 26 Aug. in NO.

SELBY, Edward K. died in St. Louis 11 November.   MORE 12 Nov 1835

SELLERS, Benjamin died in his 45th year 3 October.   MORE 6 Oct 1845
    Lebanon OH please copy.

SERSFIELD, John, of Co. F., Col. Price's Reg., died in   MODE 13 Jan 1847
    or on the way to Santa Fe 26 October.

SESSANT, Amable died in St. Ferdinand 25 Jan. in his   MORE 29 Jan 1853
    84th year.

SETTLE, Andrew J., son of John and Nancy, died at Old   MORE 3 May 1847
    Mines 16 April age 21y 16d.

SEXTON, George, a former resident of Boone Co., died in   MORE 14 Mar 1852
    Kansas MO 7 March age 75.

SEXTON, Isham B. died yesterday at his home on Oak St.   MORE 21 Dec 1839
    leaving widow and large circle of friends.

SEWELL, W.B. of Lafayette Co. died 7 June on the Little   MORE 7 Oct 1850
    Blue River age 46. Left wife, 5 children.

SEYMOUR, Albert, son of Jesse and Elizabeth, died in his   MORE 13 Oct 1845
    17th year. Funeral from the Missouri Hotel.

SHACKELFORD, Col. John "one of our oldest citizens" died   PWH 14 Oct 1847
    Thursday last.
        Walter son of Col. John died Tuesday.   PWH 12 Feb 1845

SHACKELFORD, Judge Thomas, of Saline Co., died of cholera   MORE 20 June 1835
    in St. Louis on returning from a trip to
    Nashville. In his 59th year.

SHACKFORD, John Esq., Sergeant of Arms, US Senate, "one   MORE 17 Aug 1837
    of our oldest and most respected citizens"
    died at the home of Gen. Nathan Ranney.

SHACLEFORD, Dr. William P. died at the residence of his   SPAD 26 Sep 1846
    brother Dr. G.P. Formerly of Springfield,
    now of Franklin Co. AR. Visiting his brother.
    Left widow and 4 children.

SHANAHAN, Thomas, native of Co. Kilkenny, died 1 Feb age 32.   SWERE 7 Feb 1848

SHANNON, Capt. Alfred, funeral to be held from Mrs. Bacon's.	MORE 1 May 1849
SHANNON, Jacob of Marion Co. died in Frankfort KY at the home of William Shannon, 12 Nov., age about 60.	PWH 1 Jan 1846
SHANNON, James M. died in Lewis Co. 22May in his 28th yr.	PWH 24 June 1847
SHANNON, John P., a writer, died "a day or two ago."	MORE 12 June 1847
SHANNON, Robert died at the home of Mrs. Melinda Shannon 9 April age about 18.	PWH 12 Apr 1849
SHANNON, William D. of Ste. Genevieve died Sunday at the residence of John Walsh in St. Louis.	MORE 29 Dec 1835
SHAON, David died 25 Dec. in his 32nd year. Left wife and (one child? children?)	JINQ 31 Dec 1840
SHARP, _____ died of cholera 9 October.	JEFRE 12 Oct 1833
SHARP, _____ died of cholera 28 June.	FULT 6 July 1849
SHAW, Dr. Benjamin died in Ste. Genevieve 18 March.	SWERE 28 Mar 1849
SHAW, John died "in this place" Sunday night.	MIN 18 Sep 1824
Robert, son of John, died in Franklin Monday.	MIN 13 Nov 1821
SHAW, Jesse committed suicide near Bowling Green.	MORP 2 Sep 1845
SHAW, Lyman B., merchant, died 8 October.	MORE 9 Oct 1845
SHAY, Thomas died 29 January age 24.	SWERE 5 Feb 1849
SHEARMAN, Levi died age 38. Bridgeport CT and Columbia SC please copy.	MORE 14 Jan 1852
SHEETS, Joseph, died 12 December leaving wife and several children. (Two of his children had died in the previous week.)	MORE 13 Dec 1824
SHELBY, Capt. William died Sunday last.	LEXP 10 May 1854
SHELL, Henry, son of Michael decd., died at the home on Waters of Caney 27 October age 31.	JASO 27 Oct 1838
SHEPARD, Charles died Wednesday last.	MORE 9 Oct 1818
SHEPARD, Charles O., formerly of Northampton MA, age 19.	MORE 12 Aug 1844
SHEPHERD, Chauncey drowned 26 December as he and 3 sons were bringing wood down the Missouri on a raft.	MORE 4 Jan 1841
SHEPHERD, James died 20 Sept. in his 62nd year.	BOLT 27 Sep 1845
SHEPPARD, Robert, son of James, died in Jackson 1 Jan. age about 25.	MORE 19 Jan 1853
SHEPHERD, Samuel, of Howard Co., died in Liberty, Clay Co. on 16 Sept.	MIN 26 Sep 1828
SHERMAN, David died at Hickory Grove, his residence, in Warren Co. on 29 Jan. in his 62nd year. Native of VT, later NY, came west about 1818.	MORE 10 Feb 1844
SHERMAN, Isaac Jr., native of Bridgeport CT, died 19 May age 48. In St. Louis 3 years.	MORE 1 June 1849

SHIELDS, Thomas -- Ripley Co. Final settlement by   SPAD 9 Jan 1847
           James Kinnard.

SHIELDS, William -- Greene Co. Letters of administration SPAD 28 Jan 1845
           by James Rennard (later Kinnard) 6 Feb.

SHIPLEY, George Abel, only son of Mrs. Ann C. of St. Louis, MORE 11 Nov 1851
           died 12 Sept. en route to Santa Fe.

SHIPP, Samuel died at the home of Dr. Wm. Morris, Manchester,
           9 March. Funeral from home of Capt. Lewis Bissell. MORE 11 Mar 1843

SHOBE, Jesse, son of the late Abraham of Darst Bottom, St.
           Charles, died at the home of Enoch Matson in   MORE 2 Aug 1844
           Pike Co. age 54 on 26 July.

SHOBE, Robert -- Montgomery Co. Lemuel Price, adm.   JEFS 19 May 1827

SHORE, Thomas, formerly of Petersburg VA died 7 Dec. in   MORE 8 Dec 1847
           his 57th year. Resided 5th and Carr.

SHORT, John died in Franklin 17 December.   MIN 1 Jan 1821

SHRADER, Otho, one of the Supreme Court judges of the   MORE 16 Nov 1811
           territory, died in Ste. Genevieve.

SHRODES, Capt. Andrew of the *Herald*, in St. Louis 12 Dec. MORE 13 Dec 1831

SHRYER, William, proprietor of the Beverly Hotel, died   MORE 12 Sep 1853
           age 55. Louisville and Maryland please copy.

SHURLDS, William Henry, eldest son of Judge Shurlds, died MORE 14 Oct 1843
           yesterday. Presbyterian cemetery. Age 14.

SIGLEY, John, age 52, died in Carondelet 22 June.   MORE 30 June 1852

SILVERS, William -- DeKalb Co. Final settlement by   STGAZ 22 Dec 1852
           Thomas Smith.

SIM, A. died 28 September. (Of St. Louis.)   MORE 30 Sep 1836

SIMMONDS, J.M.W. of Franklin Co. died 24 June on the   MORE 7 Oct 1850
           North Fork of the Platte age 17.

SIMONDS, Moses H. -- Gentry Co. Letters of administration STGAZ 10 Mar 1848
           to Daniel Saunders 17 January.

SIMONS, Benjamin age 35 died 12 Jan. "Carriages at the   MORE 13 Jan 1852
           2nd Baptist Church."

SIMONDS, John, age 72 "many years past the Harbor   MORE 7 Sep 1839
           Master" died last night.
           His brother Joseph died at Fitchburg MA ae 75. MORE 30 Nov 1839

SIMONS, Linus, stage driver for Fink and Walker, killed   MORE 4 Sep 1845
           by lightning 26 Aug. on St. Charles Road.

SIMPSON, Edward, late of Howard Co., died of smallpox   MORE 19 Jan 1843
           in the St. Louis vicinity 29 December.

SIMPSON, Erasmus died in St. Charles Co. in his 69th   MORE 24 Sep 1840
           year on 19 September.

SIMPSON, Hugh G. "a young gentleman in the store of   MORE 11 Dec 1839
           T. S. Rutherford." No other data.

SIMPSON, Joseph, a merchant at Franklin, died 12 January. MIN 8 Feb 1828

SIMS, William, son of Hon. L.H. of Greene Co., died on 11 Oct. age about 22.   COMB 29 Oct 1847

SINCLAIR, Anthony, late of Philadelphia, died age 52.   SWERE 24 Apr 1848

SINCLAIR, John of Boone Co. died in Sacramento 1 Sept.   MORE 26 Nov 1851

SINGER, Joseph Henderson, son of Dr. Singer of Trinity College, Dublin, died 24 Oct. age 21. Cincinnati, please copy.   MORE 26 Oct 1851

SINNICKSON, Robert J. of Erwin & Sinnickson died in his 24th year. Formerly of Salem NJ.   MORE 25 Jan 1839

SISK, Austin, of Co. L., Col. Price's Regiment, died in or on the way to Santa Fe 29 October.   MODE 13 Jan 1847

SISSON, John age about 53 died in Ashley (Pike Co.) 15 Sep. Left "disconsolate widow and large family."   BGDB 20 Sep 1845

SITTON, Eldridge G. -- Montgomery Co. Letters of administration to G.G. Sitton, 23 November.   MORE 9 Dec 1851

SITZE, Michael -- Stoddard Co. Letters of administration to Jacob Sitze.   JASO 30 Mar 1838

SIZEMORE, Jordan -- Montgomery Co. Letters of administration to James C. Fox.   MORE 2 Apr 1836

SKEEL, Dr. Samuel of Carondelet died 26 Sept., for many years an eminent practitioner in Jefferson Co.   MORE 27 Sep 1851

SKELLY, Robert of DeWitt died Saturday week, Canadian by birth, in Carroll Co. for 10 years. Left wife and child. Pulmonary consumption.   BRUNS 16 Mar 1848

SKIDMORE, Andrew A. -- DeKalb Co. Letters of administration to James M. Skidmore, 28 November.   STGAZ 7 Dec 1853

SKILES, James Jr., formerly of Bowling Green KY, died 15 Dec. in his 24th year.   MORE 17 Dec 1844

SKINNER, Curtis age 56 died yesterday at his home in St. Louis Co. Funeral from residence of T. Polk.   MORE 3 Oct 1842

SKINNER, John -- Montgomery Co. Final settlement by John Skinner.   BEA 17 Mar 1831

SLAFTER, John F. of St. Louis died aboard the <u>Revenue Cutter</u> en route from St. Peters to St. Louis. Norwich VT please copy.   SWERE 1 Nov 1847

SLAVEN, William, formerly of the Brunswick area, committed suicide in the Ohio River below Louisville 12 May.   BRUNS 1 June 1848

SLAYBACK, A.L., attorney-at-law, died in Lexington 19 Aug.   BRUNS 2 Sep 1848

SLOANE, Davis R. died at his home in Perry Co. age 43. Left wife. Virginia papers please copy.   MORE 22 Dec 1843

SLOAN, Dr. Samuel C., M.D., died at Palmyra 25 April. Born 1796 in Pulaski Co. KY, graduated Transylvania. Married Pocahontas Harrison, dau/Robert (late of Fayette Co. KY), settled in Palmyra 1828. Left widow, 4 children. Ruling elder, Presb. Church.   MORE 17 May 1841

SLOAN, Samuel L. died 16 June in Cape Girardeau town, in   SMAD 20 Apr 1838
    his 30th year. Native of Iredell NC, to MO 1832.

SLOAN, ___ killed by his father-in-law ___ Armstrong   MORE 23 May 1839
    in Callaway Co. "last week."

SMALL, David, formerly of Mason Co. KY, died at his home   MORE 23 May 1844
    in St. Louis Co. age 67y 74 4d. Maysville pls copy.

SMALL, Capt Joel died age 35y 10m. New Orleans pls copy.   MORE 28 Mar 1851

SMALL, Dr. Nelson died at the home of his mother 18 July   MORE 1 Aug 1851
    in his 28th year.

SMEAD, Ezra murdered by John McCoy. Reward by sheriff.   STCHMO 26 Aug 1820

SMILEY, Samuel died at his home in Lincoln Co. 7 Jan.   MORE 29 Jan 1844

SCHMIDT, ___ a German died "at our landing" last   BRUNS 25 May 1848
    Sunday while bathing.

SMITH, Andrew died in Howard Co. 11 October age 61, a   BOLT 17 Oct 1840
    pioneer of Missouri, resided in this county 30(?)
    years -- patriot, soldier, Christian.

SMITH, ___, "an inoffensive citizen of this place"   MORE 21 Apr 1819
    stabbed by Lege, a Canadian.

SMITH, Abraham, hanged by mob at Fredericktown 6 Aug.   MORE 2 Oct 1844

SMITH, Antoine died in Florissant age 83.   MORE 13 Aug 1853

SMITH, Birden G. -- DeKalb Co. Final settlement   STGAZ 29 June 1853
    by S. A. Bell.

SMITH, Chamness Jr. died in Calumet Twp. (Pike Co.)   BGRAD 14 Dec 1844
    30 June. Formerly of VA. Left wife, child.

SMYTHE, Charles, formerly of Toronto, died age 28.   MORE 6 June 1851

SMITH, Chauncey died very suddenly of cholera at   MORE 19 Aug 1834
    Herculaneum "many years highly respected etc."

SMITH, Christopher -- Chariton Co. Letters of admini-   BRUNS 28 Oct 1847
    stration to J.R. Horsely (pub. adm.) 30 Sept.

SMITH, Dalzell died of bilious fever 19 Sept. in his 30th   MORE 30 Sep 1845
    year. Born in St. Louis, moved to Athens with
    his family two years ago.

SMITH, Daniel C., a passenger, killed in the Car of   MORE 27 May 1828
    Commerce disaster.

SMITH, Edward of Moniteau Twp., Cole Co. died 9 Oct.   JEFRE 12 Oct 1833
    of cholera.

SMITH, Frederick M. died Sunday morning age 30.   MORE 26 Jan 1836

SMITH, Garry died Monday last.   MORE 1 Aug 1844

SMITH, George, of Weston -- of the firm of Smith, Bedford   BRUNS 19 July 1849
    & Tootle -- died at St. Joseph Sunday.

SMITH, Hiram drowned in the Mississippi 20 May. Formerly   MORP 22 June 1845
    of Iowa, lately of Bellefontaine, St. Louis Co.

SMITH, Isaac, killed in Car of Commerce disaster; passenger.   MORE 27 May 1828

SMITH, Jacob, Notary Public, died 31 Mar. in 68th year.   MORE 1 Apr 1851

SMITH, James, supposedly from St. Charles, died 7 Dec.   SWERE 13 July 1846
at Ft. William, Nebraska Territory.

SMITH, James of Platte Co., in an infantry battalion,   MODE 11 Jan 1847
died on the way to Santa Fe.

SMITH, James S., a blacksmith living 4 miles from Paris,   MORE 2 June 1847
Monroe Co., killed by lightning.

SMITH, John B.N., formerly cashier of the Bank of St. Louis,
died at his home near the city Thursday.   MORE 4 Sep 1822

SMITH, Dr. John Davidson died at his summer retreat in   MORE 15 Oct 1838
Clark Co. age 70. (Resident of Concordia LA.)

SMITH, John J., a teamster, died in Mexico 3 November.   MORE 20 Dec 1847
Native of PA, lived in St. Louis 6 years.

SMITH, John J. of Gentry Co. died 11 June on the South   MORE 7 Oct 1850
Fork of the Platte age 26. Wife, 2 children.

SMITH, Joseph Calvert of St. Louis died near the Humboldt   MORE 1 Nov 1850
River 7 August in his 22nd year.

SMITH, Lewis, fireman, died in the Car of Commerce tragedy.   MORE 27 May 1828

SMITH, Merriwether Skelton died from injuries received in   MORE 24 Feb 1851
ferryboat explosion. Funeral, Christ Church.

SMITH, Oliver C., native of Rohobeth MA, died last   SLINQ 27 Oct 1821
Sunday age 29.

SMITH, Peter Sydney, formerly of Nottaway Co. VA, died   JINQ 15 Aug 1845
Sunday evening last age 26.

SMITH, R. Kennon, late of Nottoway VA, died at the home   JINQ 28 Sep 1843
of his brother P. Sydney 7 September.

SMITH, Reuben, second son of Gen. Thomas A., Saline Co.,   MORE 31 Mar 1843
died in Williamsburg VA 27 Feb. age 20y 4m.

SMITH, Samuel, recently of KY, died 4 September. (His   MORE 1 Nov 1836
wife Serena died 31 Aug. near Alexandria LA.)

SMITH, James, eldest son of the late Gen. Thomas, died in   MORE 3 Feb 1851
Saline Co. 14 January in his (35th?) year

SMITH, "Trout" youngest son of the late Thomas of Saline   MORE 19 Feb 1851
died 18 Nov. on the voyage from Canada to
Panama, age about 24.

SMITH, Major Thomas F. died in Bonhomme Twp. 7 December.   MORE 8 Dec 1843
Funeral from his farm to the Catholic Church.

SMITH, Weathers died in St. Francois Co. at the home of   MORE 20 Aug 1842
his father James W. 13 August in his 26th year.
Left wife, father, 2 brothers, 2 sisters.
Lexington KY please copy.

SMITH, William, of J. & W. Smith, yesterday age 33. Funeral   MORE 12 Aug 1842
from his home on Franklin Avenue to the burying
ground of Col. John O'Fallon.

SMITH, William, a merchant, died "Sunday last."   MORE 4 Oct 1817

SMITH, William, formerly of Clorty, Lancashire Eng., died   MORE 12 Oct 1844
       Friday 4 Oct. age 56.

SMITH, William died of cholera in Palmyra.   MORE 28 June 1833

SMOOT, R. L., only son of Middleton, died 26 March on the   CAMP 13 Apr 1849
       Gen. Jessup en route from New Orleans.

SNELL, Tavner died at his home in Marion Co. age about 45.   PWH 4 June 1842

SNELL, William died in Howard Co. 27 Sept. in his 70th y.   BOLT 1 Oct 1842

SNIDER, James Esq. "old and respected" died this morning.   GLWT 5 June 1851

SNEIDER, William died in Hannibal 8 September.   HANT 9 Sep 1852

SNYDER, Virgil, only son of Jeremiah and Eleanor, died   BRUNS 16 Aug 1849
       at Princeton MO age 15.

SNYDER, ____, a young man killed by fall from a horse.   BOLT 8 Feb 1845

SODOWSKY, Ephraim died of bilious pleurisy 29 July in   PWH 8 Aug 1840
       his 15th year.

SODOWSKY, Jacob died Tuesday evening, age about 50.   PWH 29 Aug 1840

SOLLE, Richard L. -- Gentry Co. Final settlement by   STGAZ 8 June 1853
       John C. Williams.

SOLOMON, Samuel D. died at Carondelet Saturday last.   MORE 15 Mar 1831

SOMMERS, John, insane, killed by a fall from an attic   MORP 7 Nov 1845
       window in a public house below So. Market.

SOULARD, Anthony Esq. died last Tuesday.   MORE 14 Mar 1825

SOUTHACK, Joseph, son of the late Col. Francis, for 12   MORE 8 Aug 1851
       years resident of St. Louis, died Sandwich MA.

SPACE   John, murdered at Hazelrun Mines, Ste. Genevieve   MORE 7 June 1810
(SPAHR)   Dist. Native of Holland. Peter Johnson suspected.

SPALDING, Dr. Asa, late of Flushing NY, died in his 52nd   MORE 23 Oct 1845
       year. Resided #44 N. 6th.

SPALDING, James L., city fireman, formerly of Cincinnati.   MORE 11 June 1849

SPALDING, Josiah Esq. died 14 May. Funeral Christ Church.   MORE 15 May 1852

SPALDING, Patrick died yesterday in his 70th year.   LEXP 8 Nov 1854
       Resident of Lexington for 6 years.

SPALDING, T.J. of St. Charles killed in the explosion of   MORE 20 May 1839
       the George Collier 80 mi. below Natchez.

SPANN, Aaron -- Dallas Co. Final settlement by   SPAD 20 Dec 1845
       Armstrong Conner, d/b/n.

SPEARS, Chrisman died 13 Jan. at the home of Joseph Custer   MORE 14 Jan 1834
       in Lincoln Co., age 26. Son of John, Fayette Co. KY.

SPEARS, Lieut. Edward killed in a battle with Indians   MORE 27 May 1815
       near Fort Howard, with others of Capt. Craig's Co.

SPEED, Joseph Mason, oldest son of John M., Jr. of Jefferson
       Co. KY, died 16 November in his 37th year.   MORE 11 Dec 1832

SPEED, Thomas Penticost, age 14 years, died 31 July near   BEA 21 Aug 1831
    Herculaneum. Son of John, Jr., late of near
    Louisville KY.

SPENCER, Alexander shot, stabbed and scalped 3 miles from   MORE 10 June 1815
    St. Charles on the road to Cuivre last Sunday.

SPENCER, Harlow died Wednesday last.   MORE 30 Aug 1833

SPENCER, Henry Jr., native of St. Louis, died 14 January   MORE 25 Jan 1849
    in New Orleans, in his 27th year, of cholera.

SPENCER, James P., member of the Board of Aldermen, died   MORE 12 Aug 1837
    Thursday night last.

SPENCER, Lee -- Grundy Co. Letters of administration   BRUNS 19 May 1849
    to Andrew W. Temple 1 May.

SPENCER, Loren Esq., member of the St. Louis Bar and   MORE 4 May 1847
    Recorder of Land Titles. No date or age.

SPIERS, Samuel B. -- Montgomery Co. Letters of admini-   MORE 11 Oct 1831
    stration to Lewis and Susan Spiers.

SPRINGER, Thomas, formerly of Oldtown MO, died 20 July   MORE 31 July 1850
    in Sacramento City.

SPRINGER, William J. son of Rev. John W. died yesterday   MORE 12 June 1852
    age 23.

SPROAT, Spencer C., formerly of Philadelphia, died 4 July   MORE 5 July 1841
    in his 25th year. Friends of Harrison L. Sproat
    invited to funeral, Myrtle near Main. Interred
    Presbyterian cemetery.

SPROULE, George, many years a resident of St. Louis, died   MORE 22 Mar 1848
    at Wheatfield, Fermanagh Co., Ire. 21 December.

SQUIRES, William -- Gentry Co. Final settlement by   STGAZ 1 Dec 1852
    Paschal Robinson.

STACKHOUSE, William, late engineer of the *Argus*, died   BEA 15 Sep 1831
    at the home of John Gaines.

STAFFORD, Michael drowned near Cape Girardeau, body found   MORE 14 July 1842
    on 8 July. Certificate of naturalization date
    1 Aug. 1840, St. Louis, found on body.

STALEY, David died in Indian Creek Twp., Pike Co., age 40.   BGRAD 15 July 1843

STALLARD, George, believed to be of St. Charles Co., died   MORE 25 Feb 1852
    7 Jan. at Virgin Bay, Nicaragua Lake.

STALLCUP, Col. George died at the home of his father,   SPAD 14 Feb 1846
    James, in Taney Co. 2 February.

STAND (STEAD), Joseph, steamboat casualty, Lexington. Age 29.   MORE 4 July '42

STANDEFORD, Shelton died 21 Aug. in the Salt Creek neigh-
    borhood.   BOLT 29 Aug 1840

STANPHILL, David -- Dallas Co. Final settlement by   SPAD 30 Aug 1845
    John H. Aikens.

STANPHILL, Sneed -- Dallas Co. Letters of administration   SPAD 30 Aug 1845
    by John H. Aikens 6 August.

STARK, ___ died "Tuesday morning last" in an accident. MORE 16 Nov 1816
    He was from Bourbon Co. KY.

STARK, Col. Cyrus died 10 Sept. at his mother's home. PWH 17 Sep 1846
    Born Bourbon Co. KY, to MO in 1839.

STARK, William died yesterday "deeply regretted" etc. MORE 24 July 1822

STAUKING, John died in St. Louis "about a year ago." MORE 5 June 1849

STEARNS, Joseph, a merchant, died 22 September. SWERE 23 Sep 1844

STEEN, _____ died Monday evening. MORE 24 July 1822

STEEN, Christopher -- Wright Co. Letters of admini- SPAD 15 Apr 1845
    stration to Christopher Steen, 22 March.

STEINBECK, Daniel, "old and respected" merchant of Cape INP Feb-Mar
    Girardeau, died en route home from Baltimore.   1825

STEPHENS, John B., wife and two children killed by John MIN 4 June 1821
    Duncan on 13 Dec.; he was executed at MORE 10 Jan 1821
    St. Michaels, Madison Co.

STEPHENS, Joseph L. died of cholera at Palmyra. MORE 28 June 1833

STEVENS, Richard -- Montgomery Co. Letters of admini- FULT 6 July 1849
    stration to Hiram A. Stevens 28 April.

STEVENS, William P. -- Wayne Co. Final settlement by INP 15 Dec 1826
    John Shoemaker.

STEVENSON, George R. killed by Frederick A. Bemis MORE 5 Oct 1843
    "last spring."

STEPHENSON, Hugh M. died 3 March age 28. MORE 10 Mar 1829

STEPHENSON, James -- Montgomery Co. Letters of admini- MORE 14 May 1823
    stration to Micajah Owsley.

STEPHENSON, Nicholas -- Montgomery Co. Final MORE 30 Aug 1831
    settlement by T. D. Stephenson.

STEPHENSON, Dr. Samuel died in St. Louis age about 34, at PWH 29 Apr 1847
    the residence of C. A. Lord. Formerly of
    Portland ME, late of West Ely.

STEPHENSON, Hon. William died at his home in Pike Co. MORE 10 July 1840
    15 June in his 73rd year, late of VA. Presiding
    Judge of the Pike Co. Court.

STERIGERE, David, Judge of the 9th Judicial District of MO MORE 27 Sep 1843
    died at his home in Washington, Franklin Co.,
    Sunday 24 September.

STERNE, _____, son of Charles Esq. of Carroll Co., formerly MODE 16 Dec 1846
    of Howard Co., accidentally shot himself at
    Hensley's Mill.

STERNE, Capt. John died 27 July at the home of J. L. MORE 31 July 1840
    Quisenberry, Pleasant Hill. Formerly of VA.

STERNS, William, of Co. G., Doniphan's Reg., died in MODE 13 Jan 1847
    early January in Santa Fe.

STEWART, Dr. Abraham died at Hannibal 11 Oct. In his profession "upward of 20 years." Originally an army surgeon. Left wife, 2 children.   MORE 17 Oct 1834

STEUART, Charles, formerly of Erie PA, died Wednesday at Florissant age 56.   MORE 30 Sep 1834

STEWART, George -- Dallas Co. Letters of administration to Hardin Payne & Ruthy Stewart, 13 Feb.   SPAD 11 Mar 1845

STEWART, Joshua -- St. Clair Co. Letters of administration to Mary Ann Stewart 5 August.   OSIN 9 July 1853

STEWART, Levi D. -- Dallas Co. Letters of administration to John Evans 26 October.   SPAD 15 Nov 1845

STEWART, Robert died 6 Oct. in his 40th year. Citizen of Palmyra 16 years.   PWH 19 Oct 1848

STIBBS, Christopher died 2 May age 72. Funeral from home of N. Childs, Jr. Interred Methodist cemetery.   MORE 3 May 1849

STIBBS, William Oland, younger son of Christopher, died at his father's home of an inflammatory sore throat, age 23y 5m 7d. Late of NY.   MORE 7 Nov 1836

STICKLAN, Abiel -- Reynolds Co. Letters of administration to Benjamin F. Johnson 21 June.   STEGPD 9 July 1853

STILL, Joseph killed by Indians at Boone's Lick.   MORE 18 Mar 1815

STILL, William killed by a falling limb, Audrain Co.   PWH 16 Jan 1841

STINE, Jacob R., formerly Collector, died 8 Oct. in St. Louis Co. Funeral Centenary Ch. Methodist cemetery.   MORE 8 Oct 1846

STIRMAN, Alfred died "this week." A Mason, member of the Christian Church, left wife and 3 children.   PWH 25 Sep 1844

STITH, Benjamin W., Sheriff of Lewis Co., died 15 Feb. of pneumonia in his 46th year.   PWH 25 Feb 1847

STOCK, Frederick died of cholera 13 July.   MORE 14 July 1851

STODDARD, John H., son of Dr. John, a printer, died in New Orleans 28 September.   MORE 21 Oct 1834

STOKES, William Esq. died at the home of John O'Fallon.   MORE 3 Sep 1823

STONAM, William -- DeKalb Co. Final settlement by Andrew Sherard.   STGAZ 4 Feb 1852

STONE, Daniel E. died at Rochester MO 27 October, age about 33.   STGAZ 23 Nov 1853

STONE, Jacob killed on the *Banner*, age about 15.   MORE 3 Oct 1834

STONE, John F. Esq. died in Boone Co. "a few days ago," member of the late State Convention. A young man.   MORE 31 Mar 1846

STONE, Thomas C. died at the home of his father, William, 23 March age 19. Formerly of Madison Co. KY.   COP 2 Apr 1842

STONE, William -- Taney Co. Letters of administration to Martha Stone, 12 April.   SPAD 20 Apr 1847

STORK, H. N., died in Boonville where he had resided for more than 5 years on 10 October. — BOLT 18 Oct 1845

STOREY, Cornelius -- St. Clair Co. Final settlement by Joseph Storey. — COMB 11 Apr 1846

STORY, Joseph -- St. Clair Co. Final settlement by James P. Dunnica. — OSIN 18 Jan 1851

STOUTENBERG, John Newton died age 23y 4m. Formerly of NY. — MORE 18 July 1851

STRACHAN, David, native of Ireland, died 30 June. Interred Presbyterian cemetery. — MORE 1 July 1847

STRACHAN, William, native of Perthshire, Scotland died 19 May. Interred Presbyterian cemetery. — MORE 20 May 1848

STRACZER, Matthias died 10 October age about 33. — PWH 15 Oct 1842

STREBEC, Fred, native of Germany and resident of St. Louis for 7 years, died 29 May in his 28th year. Lived on Locust betw 2-3rd. Catholic cemetery. — MORE 30 May 1844

STREET, Alfred died yesterday age 26. — SWERE 17 Dec 1848

STREET, John drowned when the ferry sank at the Savannah Landing. — STEGPD 21 May 1853

STREETT, William G. died at the residence of Kennedy Streett age 28. Interred Judge Walton's cemetery. — MORE 9 May 1849

STREMKI, Ferdinand William died Friday last. — MORE 6 Mar 1832

STREUWE, Herman Rudolph died a8 April. Member I.O.O.F. — MORE 30 Apr 1849

STRICKLAN, Abel -- Reynolds Co. Letters of administration to Isabel Stricklan. — POT 20 Sep 1849

STRICKLAND, Abiah -- Reynolds Co. Letters of administration to John C. Strickland, Exr. — MORE 19 Nov 1845

STRODE, William F. died 16 April age 45. — SLAM 18 Apr 1845

STROTHER, George F. Esq. died Saturday last, formerly of Culpepper VA. Interred Episcopal cemetery. — MORE 30 Nov 1840

STUART, Judge Alexander, of St. Louis Co., died in VA. — MORE 22 Jan 1833

SUBLETTE, John C. of Lewis Co. reported lost in the sinking of the *Eliza*. — COP 11 Nov 1842

SUBLETTE, Milton G. died at Fort William, River Platte, on 5 April. — MORE 16 June 1837

SUBLETTE, William L. of St. Louis died in Pittsburgh on 23 July. — MORE 1 Aug 1845

SULLIVAN, J. D. of Mercer Co. died at Ft. Laramie on 2 July age 32. Left wife, 3 children. — MORE 7 Oct 1850

SULLIVAN, Col. John C. died in St. Louis Co. Monday. — MORE 3 Aug 1830

SULLIVAN, _____ died of cholera at Palmyra. — MORE 28 June 1833

SULLIVAN, William Esq., one of the judges of the county court, died 7 Sept. in his 44th year. Native of VA, to St. Louis 1801. Left large family. — MORE 12 Sep 1820

SUMMERFIELD, Edward Esq., lately from Missouri, formerly   MORE 10 Sep 1833
    of Georgia, died near Chicago 26 August.

SUMMERS, _____ of Liberty, Clay Co. blew himself up   COMB 29 Apr 1847
    with gunpowder on account of pecuniary embarrass-
    ment and threatened ruin. Age about 23.   MODE 21 Apr 1847
    "Mental condition indicated."

SUTHERLAND, J. C., a government teamster of St. Louis,   MORE 11 June 1847
    died of dysentery in New Orleans.

SUTOFF, John Theodore. A body believed to be that of this   MORE 12 Nov 1841
    man was taken from the river and the public
    administrator took over the estate.

SUTTER, John W. died in Scotland Co. 8 March age about 68.
    Native of Shelby Co. KY.   PWH 16 Mar 1848

SUTTON, Oliver of Saline Co. died of bilious fever at   MORE 7 Oct 1850
    Chimney Rock on 20 June, age 16.

SUYDAM, C. B., late of St. Louis, died in Sacramento   MORE 18 July 1853
    on 3 June age 30.

SWAIN, John E., formerly of Uniontown PA, died 4 Sept.   SLDU 5 Sep 1846

SWARTZOTT, J. D., a printer on the Springfield Whig,   BRUNS 10 Feb 1849
    died at Jefferson City 5 Feb. age 19.

SWEARINGEN, James, native of Jackson Co. MO and formerly   MORE 7 June 1853
    of Jefferson Co. VA, died in Grason TX in
    his 35th year on 4 April.

SWEENEY, Philip, native of Co. Tyrone, died 15 Sept.
    age 26.   MORE 16 Sep 1853

SWEENEY, Arthur M., formerly of Dallas Co. MO, died in   MORE 18 Jan 1852
    Nevada 5 Nov. age 26y 8m.

SWEENEY, James died yesterday morning age 70 at the home   MORE 25 Mar 1839
    of Joseph Charless, with whose family he had
    lived for 27 years.

SWIFT, Capt. J. N. died 6 April at his residence on   OSIN 16 Apr 1853
    Grand River.

SWINDLER, James -- Chariton Co. Letters of administration   BRUNS 2 Feb 1848
    to T. T. Elliott, 2 December.

SWINFORD, Dr. Samuel died near Lone Jack 24 June.   LEXP 5 July 1854

SWINNEY, William H., formerly of Glasgow, died near   GLWT 14 Apr 1853
    Georgetown, CA 1 Feb., age 23y 15d.

SWITZLER, Michael died at Brunswick 14 Oct. age 56. He   GLWT 21 Oct 1852
    had just returned from CA by way of the Isthmus,
    took sick in St. Louis, and died in Brunswick at
    the home of his son William H. The disease
    resembled cholera.

SYMONDS, James Esq. "late colonel of the US Army." No date.   MORE 14 July 1816

TABEAU, Jacques died at Portage des Sioux 30 Apr. age 103.   MORE 27 June 1811
    Survived by wife age 100; married 80 years.

TAID, John A. drowned when the ferry sank at Savannah Landing. STEGPD 21 May 1853

TALBOT, Haile of Loutre Island, Montgomery Co., died 31 Aug. in his 76th year. Born in VA, served in the Revolution. First to KY, then to MO 1810. MORE 9 Sep 1828

TALIAFERRO, Francis died near Louisiana, Pike Co., on 9 Jan. age 56. SALT 16 Jan 1841

TANNER, Ralph Jackson, son of Edward, 21 Feb. age 14y 10d. MORE 22 Feb 1852

TARGEE, T. B. killed in St. Louis by the explosion of a building blown up to check the spreading fire. BRUNS 31 May 1849

TARR, ____ (brother of B.F.) died of cholera, St. Joseph. BRUNS 21 June 1849

TARR, B. F. of Brunswick drowned recently off the *Independence*. His family arrived in San Francisco. STGAZ 11 May 1853

TATE, Lite S. of Canton died in Texas. Brother-in-law of Stephen Cooper, now in CA. MORE 14 May 1849

TAYLOR, Archibald Ritchie died Wed. at the home of his brother in his 43rd year. Native of VA, lately of New Orleans. MORE 29 Jan 1833

TAYLOR, Benjamin Jr. -- Stoddard Co. Letters of administration to Lawson Taylor 18 September. JASO 13 Oct 1838

TAYLOR, Colby H. died in Lincoln Co., at Westport, in July. MORE 26 Aug 1848

TAYLOR, George V. of Ripley Co. died 11 June. MORE 24 June 1852

TAYLOR, Jeremiah died 21 May in his 76th year. Baptist. PWH 25 May 1848

TAYLOR, Johnston -- Montgomery Co. Final settlement by Isaac Fulkerson and William Hayes. JEFS 19 May 1827

TAYLOR, Joseph -- DeKalb Co. Letters of administration to Isaac N. Shambaugh (d/b/n) 1 August. STGAZ 17 Aug 1853

TAYLOR, Moses, late Justice of the Peace. (No other data.) MORE 12 Mar 1851

TAYLOR, Daniel age 95 died at Danville 27 August. From nw NC, Revolutionary soldier. Baptist. MORE 5 Mar 1841

TAYLOR, Edward died at the home of his father, John H., near Florissant. Late of Galena IL. MORE 2 Sep 1837

TAYLOR, John H., native of Donegal, many years resident of St. Louis. Philadelphia please copy. MORE 25 Nov 1844

TAYLOR, Nathaniel of Marion Co., in Lt. Col. Willock's command, died on the way to Santa Fe. MODE 13 Jan 1847

TAYLOR, Philip, merchant, died Wed. after a long illness. MORE 21 June 1833

TAYLOR, Raymond, 2nd cook (of St. Louis) killed in the *Big Hatchee* explosion at Hermann, 23 July. STGAZ 15 Aug 1845

TAYLOR, Robert R. died in Jackson, Cape Girardeau Co. MORE 19 Jan 1853

TAYLOR, Theodore, a printer who apprenticed on the *Argus*, thrown from horse and killed near Manchester. MORE 1 Nov 1841

TAYLOR, Zachariah -- Chariton Co. Letters of administration to Thornton Rucker, 12 Oct. MIN 9 Nov 1826

TAYON, Francis died Tuesday last.   MORE 24 July 1818

TYON, Hubbard, killed near Fort Howard on the Lower Cuivre
    ferry in a skirmish with Indians. Capt. Craig's Co.   MORE 27 May 1815

TEASLY, George, a Revolutionary soldier, died in St.   SLAM 13 Mar 1846
    Charles age 90.

TILLIER   Rudolph, a native of Berne, Switzerland, died "a   MORE 6 Sep 1810
(TELLIER) few weeks ago" at his farm near Belle Fontaine.

TEMPLETON, William, died in his 62nd year 15 September.   MORE 19 Sep 1845
    Wheeling VA please copy.

TERRELL, Justus died 6 February age 42.   SLINQ 3 Mar 1821

TERRY, William, Co. E., Col. Price's Reg., died at   MODE 13 Jan 1847
    Santa Fe 5 November.

TESSON, Francis C. died 2 November. Native of St. Domingo
    and past 20 years resident of St. Louis.   MORE 4 Nov 1839

TESSON, Pierre died Wednesday morning last.   MORE 20 Feb 1818

TEVIS, Henry L. died 29 March in his 33rd year. Lived on   MORE 30 Mar 1853
    8th betw Pine-Chestnut. Louisville and
    Philadelphia, please copy.

THIELE, Ferdinand C. died Saturday.   MORE 19 Sep 1853

THIELL, Joseph -- notice that in consequence of his death   MORE 3 Feb 1838
    the firm of Murray, Thiell is dissolved.

THOLOZAN, John E. age 68 died at his home Thursday. Lived   SWERE 26 June 1848
    on 7th betw Walnut-Elm. Buried on his farm
    on Gravois Road.

THOMAS, Charles E. drowned Monday; body found.   MORE 26 Sep 1846

THOMAS, David D., of Delaware Co. PA, died at the home   MORE 12 Sep 1840
    of his brother-in-law Dr. Richard J. Harvey
    9 September age 38.

THOMAS, David, late of Woodstock VT, died 25 July age 24.   STCHMO 29 July 1820

THOMAS, Major Granville P. died at Jefferson City Saturday.   BRUNS 3 Feb 1849

THOMAS, Hartman, member of the German Musical Assn.,   MORE 17 Jan 1840
    died yesterday. Lived on Market St.

THOMAS, John P., for many years a resident of Frankfort KY,   MIN 5 Jan 1833
    died in Columbia at the home of his son Robert
    on 31 Dec. age 72.

THOMAS, Martin Esq. died 13 Sept. in his 53rd year.   MORE 14 Sep 1848
    Funeral from St. Xavier's Church.

THOMAS, Peter died at Ste. Genevieve 26 Sept., leaving   MORE 9 Oct 1832
    widow, 2 sons, 3 brothers in MD. Born in Chester
    Co. but relatives didn't know which state.

THOMAS, Sidney, a printer, died 28 January age 34. Native   SWERE 5 Feb 1849
    of Plymouth MA, in St. Louis 10 years.

THOMAS, William L. -- Chariton Co. Final settlement by   BRUNS 12 July 1849
    Jesse Brooks.

THOMPSON, Alexander P. died 12 March age 27y 10m 6d.   MORE 12 Mar 1846
    Funeral from home of his brother-in-law,
        James Yeatman.

THOMPSON, Charles G. died 15 April in Greene Co. Left   SPAD 2 May 1846
    wife and one child.

THOMPSON, Colden W. died in Clay Co. 7 October, son of   MODE 4 Nov 1846
    Nero and Elizabeth of Howard Co. age 20y 4m 11d.

THOMPSON, David died Wednesday age 78. Funeral from home   SWERE 26 Mar 1849
    of A.J. Lammey, 133 N. 7th.

THOMPSON, George; John Bauer sentenced to death for his   MORE 21 Apr 1838
        murder, Ste. Genevieve.

THOMPSON, John died 6 October at the home of Fulton   MORE 1 Nov 1839
    Thompson near Auburn MO.

THOMPSON, Capt. John accidentally shot by a sentinel   MIN 24 Sep 1822
    at Richmond Wednesday night.

THOMPSON, John S., eldest son of John B. Esq., died in   MORE 14 Oct 1847
    his 18th year. Late of Charleston SC.
    Interred Episcopal cemetery.

THOMPSON, John W., former sheriff of this county, died   MORE 25 Oct 1820
    Wednesday evening last.

THOMPSON, Mason died Monday last at the home of Francis   BOLT 26 Sep 1840
    Shields near Fayette. Recently of Garrard Co. KY.

THOMPSON, Montgomery M. died 11 Sept. at the home of Wm.   MORE 4 Nov 1844
    Boxley, St. Louis Co. Late of Hanover Co. VA.

THOMPSON, Oliver late of Edinburgh died age 25.   MORE 15 May 1851
    Cincinnati please copy.

THOMPSON, Reanos -- St. Clair Co. Final settlement by   OSIN 28 May 1853
    Elizabeth Thompson.

THOMPSON, Royal Esq. died 20 November age 45 at his home   CGWE 1 Dec 1848
    12 miles from Jackson.

THOMSON, Thomas Tucker, resident of St. Louis, died at   MORE 6 Aug 1853
    the home of his uncle in Kane Co. IL age 21, on
    28 July. Cincinnati and New York, please copy.

THOMPSON, Dr. William P. died at Trenton, Grundy Co., on   MODE 11 Dec 1848
    21 November of inflammation of the brain. Native
    of VA, had been in the legislature of that state
    and in the War of 1812. One of the earliest
    settlers in Grand River Country.

THOMPSON, William died age 45. Funeral from his home,   MORE 7 Dec 1851
    5th St. New York please copy.

THORNHILL, Bluford died of cholera in Lincoln Co.   BRUNS 2 Aug 1849

THORNTON, Col. John died at his home in Clay Co. on   MODE 10 Nov 1847
    24 October age 61.

THRASH, Richard, volunteer in Doniphan's Regiment, died   MODE 28 July 1847
    in Monterey 13 July in his 19th year.

THRALL, Logan A., son of Augustus and Louisa, died in his 18th year on 24 November.	COP 16 Dec 1842
THRELKELD, Benjamin Jr. died 2 April age about 16.	STGAZ 14 Apr 1852
THUIN, Paul M., lately of Montreal, died 4 October age 23.	SLINQ 14 Oct 1824
THURMAN, G. A. of Pettis Co. died 10 June, 80 miles west of Fort Kearney, age 27.	MORE 7 Oct 1850
THURMAN, R. W. died of cholera at Castle Bluff on Platte River, between June 7-16. Late of Lynchburg VA.	FULT 27 July 1849
THURSTON, J. C., student in the medical department of St. Louis University, died 6 Jan. age 29.	SWERE 8 Jan 1849
THURSTON, James C. died 14 July age 28.	MORE 15 July 1841
TIBBELS, Henry. Funeral notice, from Morgan & 7th Sts. to the Methodist cemetery.	MORE 28 July 1840
TICE, Jacob, late of St. Louis, died in San Francisco 13 June age 45.	MORE 18 July 1853
TIERNAN, Owen of St. Louis died in Jefferson City 3 October age 30.	JINQ 5 Oct 1843
TIERNAN, Paul died yesterday at the home of Thos. Reyburn.	SWERE 7 Aug 1848
TIERNAN, Peter died in Washington Co. 26 June, age about 60.	MORE 18 Aug 1840
TIERNAN, William died of consumption 12 Nov. in his 68th year. Native of Gillinstown, Co. Meath. Resided St. Charles Road. Member of the Hibernian Benevolent Assn. Funeral from the Cathedral; interred Catholic cemetery.	MORE 13 Nov 1844
TIERNEY, John died as a result of a fall from a horse.	MORP 22 July 1845
TIFFANY, Otis, a merchant from Baltimore, died Saturday.	MORE 4 Sep 1822
TILDEN, Richard Swift died 21 January age 58. Funeral from the Church of the Messiah.	MORE 23 Jan 1852
TILFORD, Alfred A. died Wednesday in his 26th year.	MORE 25 Sep 1843
TILTON, _____, a trader at the Mandans, killed by an Aracari.	MIN 27 Mar 1824
TILTON, Col. William P. died at Ft. Gibson 16 October.	MORE 9 Nov 1838
TILL, Henry, a deckhand on the Hannibal, drowned between Cape Girardeau and Commerce.	MORE 8 June 1846
TIMON, James Jr. died Monday last. Age 25.	SOV 5 Jan 1833
TINKER, Edwin H., funeral to be preached 3rd Sabbath in May by Rev. J. W. Campbell at the home of Dr. Tinker, father of Edwin.	SALT 23 Nov 1839
TINSLEY, William H. died 27 September. (His wife died the same day and an infant daughter had died 19 Sept.) They were lately from VA.	BGRAD 30 Sep 1843
TINSLEY, William -- Camden Co. Letters of administration to William P. Tinsley 13 January	JEM 27 Jan 1852

TISDALE, Richard K. -- Chariton Co. Final settlement   BRUNS 24 Mar 1849
    by V. Harper.

TISON, Albert died at his home in St. Louis Co. on   MORE 27 Jan 1835
    20 January in his 70th year.

TESSIER, Nicholas Gabriel, native of France, died   MORE 12 Aug 1834
TISSIER   Sunday last.

TITCOMB, Samuel died yesterday. Funeral from home of Mrs. MORE 21 June 1842
    Shallcross, 5th below Pine and Olive. Interred
    Presbyterian cemetery.

TITSWORTH, John G. Jr. died in Cooper Co. 14 October.   BORE 17 Oct 1843

TITTLE, Lemuel P. of Marion Co. died in Wheeling VA   PWH 23 Oct 1841
    6 October in his 48th year.

TODD, Howard, of Howard Co., died 5 June on the Little   MORE 7 Oct 1850
    Blue River age (?20?)

TODD, Merryman D. died of congestive fever 17 August.   PWH 21 Aug 1841

TODD, Roger North died in Columbia 11 April in his   PWH 30 Apr 1846
    49th year.

TODD, William died Friday 10 September, " a native of   MORE 18 Sep 1813
    Ireland who had been sometime blind."

TOLSON, George B. died Saturday age about 46.   MODE 23 Sep 1846
    (Obituary this date refers to him as "Major")   " 7 Oct 1846

TOLSON, William, a Revolutionary soldier, died 10 Aug.   BOLT 17 Aug 1844
    in his 89th year.

TOMB, David, veteran of the Revolution, died in Pike Co.   MORE 24 Sep 1839
    13 September age 77.

TOMPKINS, John, age about 14, son of William M. Esq.,   SWERE 12 Aug 1844
    thrown from a horse and killed Monday last.

TOMPKINS, Judge, of Cole Co., died at his home 7 April.   MODE 29 Apr 1846
    One of the oldest members of the Bar in MO,
    early settler Boonslick country. Many years
    Chief Justice of the Supreme Court.

TONCRAY, Francis L. Funeral notice.   MORE 20 July 1851

TONTOUP, Henry, a fireman, died 25 September.   SWERE 28 Sep 1846

TOOLEY, James -- Chariton Co. Letters of administration   MIN 30 Sep 1825
    to John Tooley.

TOOLEY, William D., a printer, died at Jefferson Barracks. MORE 25 Aug 1848

TORODE, John died at the home of Presley Cordell in St.   BOLT 17 Jan 1846
    Louis 29 December. Formerly of Fayette.

TOWLER, Joseph died 7 June in his 19th year, the third   PWH 11 June 1842
    child his parents have recently lost.

TOWN, Ephraim, a merchant many years. Funeral from home   MORE 14 June 1849
    of D. W. Dixon, Esq.

TOWNSEND, Benjamin died 5 Sept. in St. Louis Twp. in his   MORE 7 Sep 1853
    37th year. Native of Green Twp. PA. (sic)

TOWNSEND, Jeremiah A., formerly of Alton, died 15 Oct.   MORP 16 Oct 1845
in his 45th year.

TRABUE, Joseph B., late of Dover MO, oldest son of   MORE 2 Apr 1845
G. W. of Glasgow KY, died in his 25th year on
27 March in Louisville.

TRACY, Elza, age 59, died 2 November. Emigrated from   MODE 11 Nov 1846
Garrett Co. KY in 1832. Wife, large family.
Dorastus, son of Elza and Emaliah, died
4 November age 22.

TRAXID, Daniel of Pettis Co. died at Crab Creek 16 June   MORE 7 Oct 1850
(TRAXILL) age 4-? Wife, 4 children.

TRIBBLE, George Jr. was fatally shot by Dr. W. W. Freeman   COGL 10 Dec 1847
while hunting near Spencerburg, Pike Co.

TRIMBLE, James T. of Randolph Co., recently returned   GLWT 3 Mar 1851
from CA, drowned in Boonville.

TROTTER, Isaac P. died 24 July.   SWERE 31 July 1848

TRUDEAU, Dr. John M. F. died 22 August.   MORE 23 Aug 1853

TRUESDELL, James M. died in Texas Co. 5 January age 35.   MORE 15 Feb 1849
Lexington KY please copy.

TRUESDELL, Nathan died at the home of his son in   MORE 9 Apr 1846
Central Twp. (St. Louis Co.) 26 March in his
84th year. Revolutionary soldier.

TSCHIPPAT, Jacob died Monday "age 50 or 60."   BRUNS 16 Sep 1848

TUCK, James killed near Warsaw MO by Mr. Nowel.   MORE 21 Apr 1841

TUCKER, Joseph of Cooper Co. died on the Red River near   WEM 21 Nov 1839
Alexandria LA on a horse-trading expedition,
age 24y 8m 20d, on 24 October. Left widow and
infant. Cumberland Presbyterian.

TURK, Thomas J. of Polk Co. shot and killed Thursday near   BORE 27 Aug 1844
his home by Isom (Isham) Hobbs. He was the third   BOLT 24 "   "
member of his family shot down in the road; his
father and brother were shot from ambush. Hobbs
had apparently been a good friend of the family.

TURNAN, Owen died Tuesday at the National Hotel. To be   JEFRE 7 Oct 1843
interred in St. Louis.

TURNBULL, Benjamin L. killed in a warehouse fire at   MORE 2 Sep 1839
Laurel and Vine.

TURNER, Benjamin died at the home of his father near   BOLT 20 July 1844
Glasgow Wednesday last.

TURNER, Dr. John S., age about 22, died of consumption   MODE 26 Jan 1848
at the home of Paul Christian, Randolph Co. 11 Jan.

TURNER, Richard E., son of Talton, died in his 23rd year.   BOLT 10 Jan 1846

TURNER, Talton T., son of Thomas, formerly of Saline Co.,   MORE 29 May 1853
died in California 13 April age 17y 5d.

TURPIN, William R., formerly of Pike Co., a merchant,   MORE 2 Sep 1834
died Saturday last.

TUTT, Col. John of Cooper Co. died 22 July age 67. A native of Culpepper Co. VA. BRUNS 12 Aug 1848

TUTT, Joseph died 16 July in his 27th year at the home of Porter Jackman, Fayette. Methodist. Formerly of VA. BOLT 26 July 1845

TUTT, Lewis G. died at the home of his father 5 miles from St. Joseph. STGAZ 26 Sep 1845

TUTTLE, David W. died Sunday night last. MORE 27 Oct 1819

TUTTLE, James -- Montgomery Co. Final settlement by Nicholas W. Tuttle. MIN 27 Aug 1831

TWITTY, John R. -- Wayne Co. Letters of administration to Ambrose W. Twitty & James McCourtney, 20 Feb. MORE 23 Mar 1846

TYLER, C. K. died of cholera 3 July in his 21st year. MORE 4 July 1851

TYLER, Joseph, age about 40, died 25 June. MORE 26 June 1851

TYLER, Richard, died at Port William, Franklin Co., 15 October, of nervous fever. MORE 22 Oct 1845

TYREE, John "supposed to be from St. Louis" died in the _Moselle_ disaster at Cincinnati. MORE 1 May 1838

UHL, Jesse -- Gentry Co. Letters of administration to William Steel, 10 February. STGAZ 2 June 1848

UNCAPHER, Andrew "an honest and good man" died 16 July. JEFRE 23 July 1842
UNCAPHER, Adam died 16 July. JINQ 21 July 1842

UPDIGRAFF, John K. died yesterday. Methodist. Baltimore please copy. MORE 18 Aug 1843

USHER, Caton -- Chariton Co. Letters of administration to John C. Cavanaugh & Wm. Fleetwood, 8 Feb. James H., son of Caton, died 27 Feb. age 23y 11m. Baltimore and Philadelphia, please copy. BRUNS 17 Feb 1849
MORE 10 Mar 1843

VACHARISSA, Louis, died (no date). Lived 212 S. 2nd. MORE 11 June 1849

VALLE, Jean Bte. Jr. died at Ste. Genevieve. MORE 7 Feb 1837

VALLENTINE, William, former resident of St. Louis, drowned at Niagara Falls. MORE 26 Dec 1810

VALINDINGHAM, E., a teamster, died in Santa Fe country. MODE 13 Jan 1847

VALLE, Francois died in Ste. Genevieve 30 July. MORE 1 Aug 1851

VALLE, Louis died in Ste. Genevieve 24 September. MORE 27 Sep 1833

VALOIS, John B. D. died Tuesday evening. SOV 22 Aug 1834

VALOIS, Francis died 21 May in his 68th year, leaving a large family. MORE 24 May 1833
Francis X oldest son of Francis died 24 May. MORE 31 May 1827

VANBEBER, Isaac died in Montgomery Co. 30 Sept. Born 1771 in Greenbrier Co. VA, settled 20 miles above St. Charles in 1799. (This gentleman had a very long obituary.) MORE 9 Oct 1840

VAN BERGEN, Martin died 25 July.   MORE 26 July 1833

VAN BETTER, Franklin of Ray Co. died at Ash Hollow on   MORE 7 Oct 1850
        13 June of diarrhoea, age 19.

VANDERCOOK, Russell A., son of Maj. Vandercook and grand-   MORE 3 Sep 1839
        son of Gen. Eddy of NY, died at the home of
        Thomas Clark Esq., St. Ferdinand, 20 miles from
        St. Louis, on 24 August. Late of Pottstown,
        Rensslaer Co., NY.

VAN KIRK, John -- Chariton Co. Letters of administration   MIN 1 Feb 1826
        to James Ryan.

VANLANDINGHAM, Holland, son of Lewis, died Tuesday in his   PWH 23 Dec 1843
        30th year. Left wife, 2 small children.

VAN LOMMEL, Rev. John, S.J., died in Florissant.   MORE 26 Feb 1833

VANNOY, John W. died in Canton 23 Aug. at the home of his   CANE 25 Aug 1853
        brother, S.P. Vannoy, age 15.

VANNOY, John died Friday morning last.   PWH 30 Jan 1841

VAN QUICKENBORNE, Charles Felix, S.J. at Portage des Sioux.   MORE 26 Aug 1837

VAN SWEERELDT, Rev., 10 May. Interred at St. Stanislaus   MORE 11 May 1841
        near Florissant.

VASHON, Capt. George, sub-agent for the western Cherokee   MORE 9 Feb 1836
        Nation, died at the Seneca Indian agency west
        of the Mississippi 31 Dec. age 50.

VASQUEZ, Benito died in St. Louis Co. 12 Feb. age 67.   MORE 20 Feb 1847

VASQUEZ, Benito "departed this life on Saturday 17 Feb."   MORE 22 Feb 1810

VASQUEZ, Joseph died 17 May age 62.   SWERE 22 May 1848

VAUGHN, David L. of Clarksville MO died 22 Dec. on board   SWERE 1 Jan 1849
        the <u>Missouri.</u> Interred at Ely J. Lourdine's
        place on Cow Island, 16 mi. below Memphis.

VENABLE, Dr. H. S. of Saline Co., formerly of Richmond KY,   BOLT 23 May 1846
        died 5 May in his 54th year.

VERDIN, Nicholas, a fireman, died 16 Dec. Funeral from   SWERE 17 Dec 1848
        home of Dr. James Verdin, 3rd & Walnut.   MORE   "

VERNER, William P. of Potosi died 14 April in his   MORE 22 Apr 1852
        20th year. Pittsburgh please copy.

VERNOY, Elijah died 27 Oct. in Marion (Co.?) Born in NC,   JEFRE 5 Nov 1836
        en route to visit relatives in Johnson Co.

VETT (VEST? VEIT?) Joseph died on the way west 7 May   MORE 7 Oct 1850
        age 32. From St. Louis.

VICLE, Loderick A. late of Michigan City IL died   MOAR 7 Apr 1840
        3 April age 38.

VINALL, Jacob P., missionary to the Indians, died at   MORE 22 Dec 1819
        Belle Point, military post on the Arkansas,
        24 Oct. "Newspapers eastward please copy."

VIVION, Preston died at Greenville, Saline Co., on 20 Sep.   BOLT 3 Oct 1840
        of congestive fever. Left wife, 4 small children.

VOGH, William committed suicide by hanging. Native of NY, butcher at the market house in Christy's Addition. MORE 23 June 1841

VOULLAIRE, Jean Francois, native of Guadaloupe, died age 49. Funeral from home on Franklin Ave to the Catholic cemetery. MORE 2 Sep 1846

WADDLE, Armstead died in Peno Twp., Pike Co. 16 Dec. age about 55. BGDB 27 Dec 1845

WADDELL, Carr B. died 13 Sept. age 45. (Testimonial) LEXP 17 Sep 1844

WADDELL, James died yesterday of apoplexy. MORE 10 Apr 1837

WADDELL, Samuel died Thursday in his 30th year, of the firm of James Waddell & Co. Formerly of Baltimore. MORE 24 July 1832

WADE, Horatio died at 6pm 10 Aug. age 52. Residence on Vine known as Merchant's Exchange. Formerly of Philadelphia. MORE 11 Aug 1838

WAGNER, Theodore missing since February and believed murdered. Lived in the German settlement on Brazo Creek in Perry Co. Family from Saxony. Age 22. Bloody coat found near Grand Tower. MORE 15 Oct 1840

WAGGONER, William died at his father's home 1 Mar. in his 23rd year. CAMP 9 Mar 1849

WAHRENDORFF, Charles died Saturday in the 42nd year of his age. (An obituary the following week.) MORE 30 Aug 1831

WAINWRIGHT, Ellis died Tuesday in his 40th year. Lived in St. Louis 17 years. Wife, several children. Pittsburgh please copy. MORE 17 May 1849

WALDEN, Joseph P. died at the home of his father in Howard Co. 21 October, age 15. BRUNS 4 Nov 1848

WALDEN, Maj. William died 9 Dec. in Platte Co., age 45. Late of Weston, formerly of Woodville VA. BRUNS 30 Dec 1848

WALDO, L.L. (brother to Capt. David) of Howard Co. assassinated in the Taos massacre. MODE 31 Mar 1847

WALES, James R., son of Orin and Mary, died 17 Sept. age 23. NY and MA please copy. MORE 18 Sep 1846

WALKER, Dr. David V. died last Friday. MORE 12 Apr 1824

WALKER, Green of Morlan (Marion?) Twp. age about 40 died of cholera 6 October. JEFRE 12 Oct 1833

WALKER, Jesse, a Revolutionary soldier, died in Howard Co. age 100y 7m 21d. BRUNS 17 Mar 1849

WALKER, John died in Commerce MO 5 Dec. in his 64th year. Native of Wilmington DE. MORE 11 Dec 1840

WALKER, Dr. John of St. Louis died in Illinoistown Sun. MORE 27 Aug 1833

WALKER, Nathan, formerly of Onondagua Co. NY, died on 14 Oct. when a bank of earth where he was working caved in on him. MORE 21 Oct 1828

WALKER, Philip -- Ripley Co. Letters of administration to James B. Smith. STEGPD 3 Oct 1852

WALKER, Richard died at the home of his son Tandy on   PWH 18 May 1848
    Friday last. "One of our oldest citizens."

WALKER, Robert of Scott Co. died 11 June "100 miles this   MORE 7 Oct 1850
    side of Ft. Kearney age 33. Left wife, children.

WALKER, Samuel, brother of Major R.B., formerly of   MORE 22 Oct 1848
    Troy NY. Interred Jefferson Barracks cemetery.

WALL, S.D. -- Wright Co. Pub. adm. took over estates.   SPAD 31 May 1845
    W.

WALLACE, Andrew "a pioneer" died in Cooper Co. 7 Sept.   LEXP 27 Sep 1854
    age 62.

WALLACE, Hugh, formerly of Culpepper Co. VA, late of KY,   MORE 14 July 1829
    died Friday in his 21st year.

WALLACE, John S. died in Chariton Co. Thursday in   GLWT 21 Aug 1851
    his 50th year.

WALLS, John died Monday.   MORE 7 Aug 1822

WALSH, Bartholomew died Friday in his 93rd year.   MORE 13 Aug 1833

WALSH, James died 13 July age 45. Funeral from home on   MORE 15 July 1841
    St. Charles St. to the Catholic cemetery.

WALSH, John J. died 23 May of consumption, age 36. Funeral   MORE 25 May 1837
    from home of brother Patrick. Catholic cemetery.

WALSH, William died yesterday age 18, son of Patrick Esq.   MORE 26 Nov 1839
    Funeral from father's home. Catholic cemetery.

WALSH, Joseph W. Esq., Clerk of the St. Louis Court of   MORE 26 Sep 1842
    Common Pleas, died 23 Sept. in his 32nd year.
    Resided 3rd & Plum. Catholic cemetery.

WALTER, Peter died Tuesday night (cholera epidemic).   MORE 30 Oct 1832

WALTER, W. died last Sunday. (Given name possibly
    Washington.)   MORE 24 Aug 1826

WALTON, Thomas C. of Chariton Co. died 20 March.   BOLT 26 Mar 1842

WALTON, Washington. Shown in Pulaski Co. with Wilson   JEFRE 30 Sep 1837
    A. Bell as administrator and in
    Wright Co., Robert N. Martin adm.   MORE 4 Mar 1842

WANTON, James died, date not clear, probably of cholera.   BEA 18 Oct 1832
    "Many years a resident." Native of Ireland.

WARD, John died in Bonhomme Twp., St. Louis Co. 24 Oct.   MORE 2 Nov 1826

WARD, John -- St. Clair Co. Letters of administration to   BORE 24 Oct 1843
    John Ward 5 September.

WARD, John died of congestive fever.   MORE 19 May 1836

WARD, John Jr. -- St. Clair Co. Petition to sell real   OSIN 18 Jan 1851
    estate by George Preston.

WARD, Justin died 2 Nov. at his home near the Arsenal.   MORE 5 Nov 1836
    Left wife and child. Age 25.

WARD, Richard, late of St. Louis, died in Carrolton IL.   MORE 10 Oct 1834

WARD, William, resident of the Fayette vicinity, died 9 Jan. BOLT 13 Jan 1844
at an advanced age. Early-day emigrant.

WARD, William M. of Campbell & Ward died in Wellington MO MORE 27 May 1851
"last Sunday week."

WARRANCE, William L., youngest son of William of St. Louis SWERE 15 Nov 1847
died 29 Oct. at Gretna, opposite New Orleans,
age 32. Philadelphia please copy. (Another son
Ambrose White ae 10y 11m died 23 June 1836) SCOMB 24 June 1836

WARREN, Jesse D., late of Rodney MA, died 19 July. SWERE 20 July '46

WARREN, John -- DeKalb Co. Letters of administration STGAZ 20 Apr 1853
to A. H. Skidmore, 7 April.

WARREN, Thomas of Ray Co. died at the Upper Crossing of MORE 7 Oct 1850
the Platte 18 June, age 22.

WARREN, William, died at his home in Greene Co. 15 Nov. SPAD 19 Nov 1844

WASELER, Amos, land agent, died in St. Louis 9 June. SLINQ 10 June 1822

WATERS, ____ of Linnaeus, merchant, late of Boone Co., BRUNS 11 May 1848
committed suicide Thursday.

WATERS, Andrew Jackson, formerly of Baltimore, died MORE 25 Sep 1839
23 Sept. age 25.

WATERS, John, a fireman, a young man, whose funeral had a MORE 29 Feb 1844
"large crowd." Date and cause of death not shown.

WATERS, Freeman died in Jefferson Co. 2 April age 33. MORE 10 Apr 1849

WATERS, George Washington, son of late Capt. G.W. and MORE 16 Nov 1847
Letitia, Jefferson Co., died 9 Nov. age 14.

WATHEM, Henry A. died 26 April in his 28th year. MORE 28 Apr 1852
Interred Catholic cemetery.

WATHEN, George W. died 4 May in his 23rd year. Survived MORP 9 May 1845
by mother, brother, sisters.

WATKINS, John died 11 Sept. of bilious fever, age 59, MORE 19 Sep 1845
his son John died 14 Sept. of inflammation of
the bowels. Lexington please copy.

WATSON, Edward W. died of congestive fever 8 Aug. in his MORE 9 Aug 1839
23rd year. Son of the senior editor of the
Missouri Argus. Lived Corner 3rd & Myrtle.

WATSON, John, father of James M., died about 4 miles east SALT 1 Aug 1840
of Bowling Green age about 70.
James son of James M. Esq. died in Calumet Twp. BGRAD 10 Aug 1844
9 August age 19.

WATSON, John died at the home of his brother R. D. MORE 2 Oct 1851
2 October age 59.

WATSON, Col. Thomas of Linn Co. died "three weeks since." MORE 20 Apr 1847
Pioneer of Chariton Co., representative first in
the legislature, then the senate.

WATT, James, formerly of St. Louis, died in Calcutta MORE 1 Jan 1849
in July.

WATTS, Francis died in Calumet Twp, Pike Co. Tuesday last age about 50. "Old and respected" etc. — BGDB 5 Apr 1845

WATTS, Col. Henry, senator from Lincoln and Montgomery Cos. died a few days since at his home near Louisville, Lincoln C. — MORE 19 Aug 1839

WATTS, Solomon A. died 5 Sept. in his 31st year. Funeral from the Missouri Hotel. Baltimore please copy. — MORE 6 Sep 1847

WAYLAND, John W., formerly of Madison Co. VA, died 31 July age 39. — BOLT 10 Aug 1844

WEAVER, Hammond Randall, youngest son of John and Rebecca, died age 22. Formerly of Baltimore. Interred Bellefontaine. — MORE 18 July 1851

WEAVER, Jacob, clerk for VonPhul and Magill, found shot after a fire. Age 22. Father a house painter. Came to St. Louis from Washington City 3 years ago, lived on Oak St. (Four men were subsequently executed for his murder -- MORE 10 July 1841) — MORE 19 Apr 1841

WEAVER, J. died in the Moselle disaster, Cincinnati. — MORE 1 May 1838

WEBB, Cuthbert, formerly of Fayette Co. KY, died 21 Nov. in his 43rd year. — BORE 12 Dec 1843

WEBBER, Matthew died in Potosi 12 Jan. age 42. Native of England. Left two small children. — MORE 20 Jan 1853

WEBSTER, Calvin, formerly of Haverhill MA, died 21 May age 20. Left mother and sister. — MORE 2 June 1842

WEBSTER, Daniel son of Ira and Ann of Hartford CT, age 17. — MORE 14 Dec 1844

WEBSTER, John died of typhus 30 Sept. in his 39th year. Native of Lincolnshire, Eng.; in St. Louis 5 yrs. — MORE 7 Oct 1834

WEIGHTMAN, William Sr., formerly of Washington City, died 8 Nov. in his 55th year. — MORE 12 Nov 1846

WEIL, Isaac, a young man, native of Germany, brother-in-law of S. Oberdorfer, Brunswick merchant. — BRUNS 28 June 1849

WELBOURNE, James C., formerly of Worcester Co. MD, died Saturday last in St. Louis Co. — MORE 5 Apr 1841

WELCH, Charles, funeral from home of his brother Edward, Marion and Berry. — MORE 17 Dec 1846

WELCH, James, body found in the Mississippi. — SWERE 9 Sep 1844

WELCH, James Craft died near Hickory Grove, Warren Co. in his 25th year, 1 Aug. Former member of the Philadelphia Bar. — MORE 12 Aug 1847

WELCH, Solomon died 7 Nov. at Santa Fe. In Co. M. of Col. Price's Regiment. — MODE 13 Jan 1847

WELSH, Thomas F. died age 42. Lancaster PA please copy. — MORE 12 Apr 1852

WELSH, Dr. J. W., only son of Gen. James of the East India Co., died 12 Sept. New York please copy. — MORE 14 Sep 1846

WELDON, John -- Chariton Co. Letters of administration to James Wells, 6 March. MIN 28 Mar 1828

WELLING, W. P. Hunt, son of Charles and Elizabeth, died in Jackson 30 Dec. age 13. MORE 8 Jan 1853

WELLINGTON, William W., native of Templeton MA, died in his 25th year Tuesday. Funeral from the home of George C. Anderson, Esq. MORE 13 Oct 1842

WELLMAN, H. W., MD, of MO died at Panama 3 March. MORE 3 May 1853

WELLS, Charles died at Bolivar MO in his 44th year, late of St. Louis. MORE 20 Jan 1846

WELLS, Elihu, from Chenango Co. NY died Wednesday of a bilious fever, age 23 (25?). MORE 28 Aug 1818

WELLS, George N. of Lincoln Co. killed by lightning when riding horseback to see a sick friend 14 June. PWH 28 June 1849

WELLS, Japhtha Esq. "a young man of fine promise" died in Warrenton 11 November. MORP 22 Nov 1845

WELLS, Nicholas age 60 died 11 Feb. in Louisville, Lincoln Co. Native of KY, settled in MO 28 years ago. Methodist. (His wife died a week earlier.) BGRAD 17 Feb 1844

WELLS, Hyman G. died in Franklin Co. 17 November. Son of the late Edward of Hartford CT. MORE 21 Nov 1845

WELLS, Col. Samuel of St. Charles died age 70. Had been a member of the legislature in both KY and MO. Left widow and 11 children. BEA 30 Sep 1830

WELLS, William E. -- Montgomery Co. Final settlement by John D. Anderson. FULT 30 Mar 1847

WELTON, Major Moses died in Osage Co. 28 Jan., age nearly 70. "Husband, parent." MORE 13 Feb 1847

WERNER, B., a watchmaker in Jefferson City but recently of St. Louis died 29 June. MORE 4 July 1851

WEST, James died 1 Jan. in his 37th year. Resided on Spruce betw 5th-6th. MORE 3 Jan 1849

WEST, James R. of Johnson Co. died in Mexico. COMB 16 Dec 1847

WEST, Stephen of MO died in Sacramento age 24. MORE 29 May 1853

WESTON, David died 5 Oct. age 34. Born in Kingston, Plymouth Co. MA. In St. Louis 12 years. Funeral 1st Congregational Church. Presbyterian cemetery. MORE 6 Oct 1845 MORP "

WESTON, John, a German deckhand, drowned from the New Haven. MORE 7 Sep 1846

WETHERILL, William H., a resident 5 years, died in his 58th year. Cincinnati, Philadelphia pls copy. MORE 14 Apr 1847

WETMORE, Maj. Alphonso died 13 June in his 56th year. Interred Episcopal cemetery. MORE 15 June 1849

WETZEL, William, for many years a mail contractor, died Tuesday last. MORE 20 Aug 1835

WHALEN, Bartholomew died at the house of John Geiger in Herculaneum 29 July; landed ill from steamboat. Had lived in Troy MO and Beardstown KY -- had a sister and brother near there. (But later stated that he had no relatives.) Also mentioned Davis Co. KY.   MORE 18 Aug 1837

WHALEY, Capt. Edward died 4 August in his 77th year. Came to MO 1822, formerly of KY.   PWH 16 Aug 1849

WHALEY, Volney died Thursday night last age 40. Left wife and several children.   PWH 11 Jan 1849

WHALEY, Stephen C. died at Woodville Mills near Boonville 24 Sept. in his 37th year.   BORE 26 Sep 1843

WHARTON, Dr. J. J. died in St. Louis 14 Dec. age 31, late of VA. Funeral Union Hotel to city graveyard.   MORE 15 Dec 1838

WHEELER, Amos, Land Agent, died Sunday last.   MORE 12 June 1822

WHEELER, Capt. Chester died at Marthasville 9 Jan. after an illness of 37 hours. (His wife died the same day, no mention of cause.)   MORE 24 Jan 1832

WHEELER, John B. age 55 died 29 Nov. near Manchester. At an early age he moved from Albemarle Co. VA to Mason Co. KY, and then to MO.   SWERE 3 Dec 1848

WHEELER, John E. -- Montgomery Co. Final settlement by George W. Wheeler and Madison Jones.   BGRAD 20 May 1843

WHEELER, R. P. or Edward P. of the firm of Wheeler & Weddinghaus. Probably cholera.   MORE 23 Oct 1832

WHERRY, Joseph A., Register of C.O., St. Louis, died yesterday. Funeral from late residence on 7th St.   MORE 14 Feb 1843

WHERRY, Mackey died at Memphis on his way up from New Orleans on 3 August.   MORE 5 Aug 1828

WHERRY, Daniel Boon, youngest son of Mackey (one of the earliest American settlers in St. Louis) died in Osage Co. 3 June.   MORE 12 June 1844

WHIPPLE, Samuel H. died in Warsaw 17 September.   SPAD 27 Sep 1845

WHISTLER, Capt. Charles, late of St. Louis, died in Louisville KY on 5 January.   MORE 25 Jan 1831

WHISTLER, Major John died at his home at Bellefontaine Wednesday age 71; of the US Army.   MORE 8 Sep 1829

WHITAKER, John, for several years resident of St. Louis, died suddenly in Cincinnati 12 April age 52. Formerly of Bradford, Yorkshire, England.   MORE 21 Apr 1845

WHITBY, Augustus E. age 48y 2m 2d died 8 March at his Canton residence. Left widow, 4 children.   CANE 16 Mar 1854

WHITE, B. H., convicted of the murder of Mr. Adams in Ray Co., to be executed 13 August.   MORE 29 July 1841

WHITE, Duff G. died 30 Sept. at the residence of his father, Col. John P., in St. Louis Co. Richmond *Whig* please copy.   MORE 10 Oct 1842

WHITE, Gen. Greene died Sunday last while discharging his duties as deputy sheriff. Left wife, 3 small children.	JEFRE 19 Aug 1843
WHITE, Capt. Isaac died in St. Louis 20 May age 53. Was a captain under Gen. Harrison, 1812. To St. Louis 1818.	MORE 25 May 1841
WHITE, Capt. James M. died 25 Sept. age 48. Interred in the Episcopal cemetery.	MORE 26 Sep 1846
WHITE, James K. died Thursday. Left wife and six small children.	PWH 9 Oct 1845
WHITE, Jefferson recently murdered in Macon Co. by Oliver P. Magee, who fled.	MORE 30 Jan 1849
WHITE, Joseph M. died at the home of his brother, Dr. White, Saturday. Arrived 2-3 weeks ago with wife. Noted jurist.	MORE 21 Oct 1839
WHITE, Noble, of Co. Cavan, Ireland, died at the Hospital 11 March age 33.	MORE 14 Mar 1849
WHITE, Robert L. -- Chariton Co. Public administrator took over his estate.	BRUNS 26 Jan 1848
WHITE, Samuel died yesterday age 60 years.	INJN 24 Oct 1844
WHITE, William -- Chariton Co. Letters of administration to John Tooley and Charles P. Tooley.	MIN 7 June 1827
WHITE, William M. died at Lafayette Co. 19 October, a resident of Howard Co.	MODE 21 Oct 1846
WHITEHEAD, George W. -- Montgomery Co. Final settlement by Dougald F. Stevens.	MORE 31 Dec 1847
WHITEHEAD, Judge Robert of Jefferson Co. died 30 July.	MORE 23 Aug 1839
WHITEHEAD, Thomas drowned from the Polar Star Sunday last at St. Joseph. Body sought.	STGAZ 12 Apr 1854
WHITESIDE, Francis -- Montgomery Co. Final settlement by John C. Whiteside.	MORE 23 Mar 1830
WHITESIDES, John -- Chariton Co. Letters of administration to John Jr. and Sarah, exrs.	BRUNS 19 May 1849
WHITFIELD, W. G., Juror in the US Court in St. Louis, died suddenly yesterday. Age about 45. Lived at 5th & Myrtle. Interred Methodist cemetery.	MORE 12 Apr 1843
WHITLEDGE, Gen. Thomas B. died in Pike Co. "about two weeks since" age 33.	BGRAD 1 June 1844
WHITLOCK, Andrew S., late of St. Louis, native of VA, died at the home of Henry Yeatman Esq. in Nashville. Richmond VA please copy.	MORE 16 Aug 1842
WHITMAN, Nathan Jr. died of consumption 4 January. Philadelphia please copy.	MORE 5 Jan 1846
WHITAKER, Benoni "respected citizen" died Thursday.	SALT 14 Dec 1839
WHITTAKER, James died at the Sulphur Springs Sunday evening, 2 September, age 30.	MORE 4 Sep 1832
WHITTAKER, Mark -- Bates Co. Final settlement by Job Richardson.	SPAD 4 July 1846

WHITTENBURG, Joseph, a printer of Cape Girardeau, died recently.	MORE 17 Aug 1830
WITTENBURG, John W. of Co. A., Col. Price's Regiment, died 11 November at Santa Fe.	MODE 13 Jan 1847
WICKHAM, William of VA died in his 21st year. Funeral from home of Major R. Graham.	MORE 12 May 1851
WIGGIN, Joseph, a St. Louis merchant, died 3 September on passage from New Orleans to Boston.	MORE 27 Oct 1819
WIGGINS, John Shackford, only son of Samuel, died in Cincinnati age 18 years.	MORE 13 Dec 1842
WIGGINTON, John L. died in Boone Co. 26 September in 78th? year.	MORE 20 Oct 1851
WILBANKS, Thomas drowned himself at one of the wharves on Sunday last.	MORE 13 Apr 1830
WILCOX, Dr. Daniel P., a representative of this county, died 10 February.	MIN 19 Feb 1831
WILCOX, Horace, resident of South St. Louis, died 9 Nov. age 33.	MORE 11 Nov 1839
WILCOX, Joseph -- Dallas Co. Letters of administration to Ruth Wilcox 3 March.	SPAD 11 Mar 1845
WILCOX, Lazarus died in Boone Co. 23 October.	MIN 7 Nov 1835
WILEY, John Jr. of Palmyra died Saturday in St. Louis.	MORE 20 June 1837
WILEY, John O. -- Chariton Co. Letters of administration to F. S. Hix 25 November.	BOLT 18 Jan 1845
WILFORT, Simon died in Jackson, Cape Girardeau Co., on Wednesday last in his 25th year.	MORE 19 Jan 1853
WILGUS, Charles T. died aboard the _Collier_ on 30 April in his 30th year. (His 11-m-old son Charles Powell died 1 May.) Funeral for both at 2nd Presbyterian Church, interment Bellefontaine.	MORE 2 May 1853 " 3 May "
WILHOIT, T. H. of Benton Co., in Col. Price's Regiment, died on the way to Santa Fe.	MODE 13 Jan 1847
WILKERSON, Henry -- Chariton Co. Final settlement by John Montgomery and Martha Wilkerson.	MIN 29 June 1826
WILKINSON, Brannick, of Livingston Co., died 4 February in his 78th year.	BRUNS 24 Feb 1848
WILKINSON, John "a respectable citizen and early settler." Died Thursday.	MORE 11 Sep 1841
WILKINSON, Capt. Walter of Perry Co. "a man of irreproachable character" died in St. Louis Sat.	MORE 20 Feb 1837
WILLARD, E. H., a former auctioneer, found murdered.	STGAZ 28 July 1852
WILLARD, Francis, a deckhand, accidentally shot himself at St. Mary's Landing. Buried Chester IL.	MORE 8 June 1841
WILLERS, Major John died 20 Dec. at the home of Benj. Emmons in St. Charles. Family in Baltimore. Here 5-6 wks.	STCHMO 3 Jan '22

WILLIAM, Philip, a German, committed suicide Sunday. He was melancholy since the death of his wife in Louisville about six months ago.   MORE 16 Sep 1845

WILLIAMS, _____ "an Englishman of industrious habits" died suddenly Tuesday, supposedly of apoplexy. Age 42.   MORE 28 Aug 1818

WILLIAMS, Anthony T. -- Montgomery Co. Letters of administration to Thomas J. Williams 1 November.   BGRAD 21 Dec 1844

WILLIAMS, Charles S. (or W.), consort of Mary, died at Hillsboro 17 October of congestive fever.   MORE 30 Oct 1844

WILLIAMS, Edmund -- Dallas Co. Letters of administration to Elizabeth Williams, 21 March.   SPAD 8 Apr 1845

WILLIAMS, Elias died in Pike Co. 5 September age about 45.   BGRAD 9 Sep 1843

WILLIAMS, Elisha died of cholera at Palmyra.   JEFRE 4 July 1835

WILLIAMS, Humphrey died in Buffalo Twp. (Pike Co.) Friday age 23.   BGRAD 7 Oct 1843

WILLIAMS, J. of Chariton Co. died 2 July at Chimney Rock age 80 (?).   MORE 7 Oct 1850

WILLIAMS, Joseph of Taney Co. died 100 miles west of Ft. Kearney 13 June age 50. Wife, six children.   MORE 7 Oct 1850

WILLIAMS, James C., son of Notely C. Williams of MO, died in Loudon Co. VA 7 October.   MORE 17 Nov 1843

WILLIAMS, John, late of Oneida Co. NY, died "in this town" 27 August age 74.   STCHMO 12 Sep 1821

WILLIAMS, John H. -- Thomas H. Coots was indicted for his murder in Warsaw, Benton Co.   MORE 7 June 1845

WILLIAMS, Capt. John W. died 30 July in Warren Twp., Marion Co.   PWH 5 Aug 1843

WILLIAMS, John L. died yesterday of an affliction of the liver. Funeral from the home of Mrs. Turpin, St. Charles St. Presbyterian burying ground.   MORE 31 July 1837

WILLIAMS, John, 2nd mate, killed in the _Persian_ explosion on 7 November.   MORE 14 Nov 1840

WILLIAMS, Rev. Louis died in Gasconade Co. 16 Nov. in his 54th year at the home of James Walton. Baptist.   MORE 23 Nov 1838

WILLIAMS, Luther G. died at the home of John Fagg on 10 March in his 23rd year.   BGDB 14 Mar 1846

WILLIAMS, Robert P. died 22 April in his 63rd? year. Funeral from St. Paul's Church.   MORE 23 Apr 1851

WILLIAMS, Samuel died last Saturday.   MORE 30 July 1823

WILLIAMS, Samuel died in Chariton 11 August. Member of the MO legislature. Left widow and several children including a son Henry.   MIN 28 Aug 1821

WILLIAMS, Sebastian died in Randolph Co. 12 September in his 39th year. (His wife died 5 days earlier.) Left three small children.   MODE 22 Sep 1847

WILLIAMS, Stephen -- Montgomery Co. Letters of administration to Anthony T. & Rebecca Williams 31 Oct.   SALT 28 Nov 1840

WILLIAMS, Capt. Thomas B., age 30, died near Richmond on 3 July.   MIN 19 July 1834

WILLIAMS, Uriel (Uriah) died Wednesday last "old and worthy citizen."   BOLT 30 Oct 1841

WILLIAMS, William died at the home of Lewis Vanlandingham 2½ miles from Palmyra on 12 January. Formerly of Warren Co. KY, once in Callaway Co. Family in Newton Co.   PWH 16 Jan 1841

WILLIAMS, Capt. W. L. died yesterday in his 53rd year. Funeral from his home, 33 N. Main.   MORE 8 Mar 1841

WILLIAMSON, George died 17 October age 42. Native of Carrick-on-Shannon, Leitrim.   MORE 20 Oct 1851

WILLS, Charles M. of Boone Co. died in New Orleans on 8 March while en route to California.   MORE 1 Apr 1851

WILSON, Major Abiel died 7 July, formerly of NH. He was interred with Masonic honors.   SLINQ 14 July 1821

WILSON, Dr. Andrew died at St. Charles 26 April in his 58th year. Native of NY, to MO when young, more than 30 years in St. Charles. "Good and practical" physician. Left wife and children.   MORE 5 May 1842

WILSON, David Henry, son of Pleasant Esq. of Fayette, died in St. Louis age 17.   MORE 15 Feb 1851

WILSON, Major George died 26 January at his residence 13 miles from St. Louis in his 74th year. Born in Scotland.   MORE 7 Feb 1821

WILSON, Thomas F., youngest son of the late James of Philadelphia, died at Jefferson City en route to St. Louis 28 December.   MORE 3 Jan 1839

WILSON, John L. stabbed and killed at Warsaw by Thomas H. Coats (possibly a duel).   BOLT 8 Mar 1845

WILSON, Rev. Joshua of the Methodist Church died at Marysville 17 April.   MORE 12 June 1851

WILSON, Singleton W. of St. Louis died in Louisville KY on 1 March.   SWERE 9 Mar 1846

WILSON, Thomas age 43 died in St. Charles 13 June. Formerly of Deckertown NJ.   STCHMO 27 June 1821

WILSON, Samuel and son died of cholera in Palmyra.   MORE 28 Jan 1833

WILSON, / WILLSON - Clark Co.   William G. died 31 January 1843.   PWH 4 Feb 1843
William J. letters of administration to J. S. Hening 9 October.   PWH 21 Oct 1843
(William G.'s adm. was Ephraim L. Wilson -PWH 25 Feb.)

WILSON, William Henry, eldest son of Barton S., died 12 June age 17. Lexington and Paris KY and Jacksonville IL please copy. COMB 17 June 1847

WILSON, Zachariah, note to unknown heirs. He had married Sarah Ann Adams about 1824; she died March 1827 leaving an infant who died the following month. Wilson died in 1836. MORE 9 Jan 1837

WILT, Andrew, brother and partner of Christian, died on Wednesday night last age 26. MORE 18 Aug 1819

WILT, Christian died Monday evening last "came to town a youth about ten years ago." MORE 29 Sep 1819

WILTBANK, Charles, formerly of Philadelphia, died 1 July in his 27th year. MORE 4 July 1846

WIMER, Jacob died 22 December. MORE 23 Dec 1836

WINBURN, Henry, of New Franklin, died 17 March age 72. BOLT 26 Mar 1842

WINDHAM, ____ and his daughter shot, axed, and their house set afire. He lived long enough to describe his assailant. MORE 25 Nov 1834

WINDSOR, Henry R., formerly of western NY, died 24 August age 23. A printer, recently married. MORE 26 Aug 1843

WINLOCK, George "one of our oldest inhabitants" died 13 Oct. Born Stafford Co. VA 7 June 1783. PWH 18 Oct 1849

WINGFIELD, Charles died in Johnson Co. 27 June age 56 of inflammatory rheumatism. Formerly of Albemarle Co. VA, to Johnson Co. 1836. LEXP 8 July 1845

WINGO, Samuel D., sheriff of Shannon Co., shot and killed 31 August by ____ Moyres. MORE 18 Sep 1843

WINTERS, William, late of the District of Arkansas. MORE 30 May 1812

WISDOM, James, froze to death in Randolph Co. 24 October. Left home of neighbor and drove into a pond while intoxicated. BOLT 4 Nov 1843

WISE, Jacob found dead under a bridge of the River des Peres. Missing since 3 Aug. Lived in Central Twp. MORE 11 Aug 1843

WISE, William of Palmyra, late of KY, died in St. Louis 16 May. FREEP 23 May 1833

WITCHER, Ephraim -- Montgomery Co. Letters of administration to George Crews, 9 March. BGDB 4 Apr 1846

WITHERS, Julius died near Fayette 10 Aug. in his 35th yr. GLWT 14 Aug 1851

WITHERS, Rolla M. died 25 July age 37. Cincinnati and Covington please copy. MORE 26 July 1853

WITT, Capt. E. B. died 24 February. MIN 27 Feb 1829

WITTEN, Thomas C. -- Kinderhook (Camden) Co. Letters of administration to Nancy Witten and L. D. Pinkston, 7 February. JINQ 24 Feb 1842

WITTY, Godfrey -- letters of administration to the public administrator, 27 December.   BRUNS 10 Feb 1849

WOLF(F), George died in St. Louis and an inquest was held. First report said he had d.t.s and it was a "visitation of God." Later gave name as George W., residence S. Main, cause of death apoplexy.   MORP 23 July 1845
" 24 "

WOOD, Abner died at the home of Benj. Jones 21 May; many years resident, native of NY. Latter part of his life blind.   MORE 2 June 1829

WOODS, Absolom T. of Ray Co. killed "some time ago." Isaac Renfro convicted of the murder.   MIN 10 Apr 1824
" 2 July 1825

WOOD, Adam C. died 7 August age 54. Born in Madison Co. KY, to Howard Co. MO in 1817.   BRUNS 16 Aug 1849

WOODS, Major Andrew died in Jackson Co. 16 June; left wife and 4 children in St. Charles and 3 brothers in Nashville. Many years in the fur trade.   MORE 3 July 1832

WOOD, Andrew -- DeKalb Co. Letters of administration to Nancy and Abraham Wood, 6 March.   STGAZ 15 Mar 1854

WOOD, Henry died in Manchester 4 September, age 36. Formerly of Newport RI.   MORE 6 Sep 1841

WOOD, Ebenezer H. -- Gentry Co. Letters of administration to Jesse Gay, 27 August.   STGAZ Sep 1847

WOODS, George D., son of Major Michael, died in Boone Co. 27 March age 14.   MIN 20 Apr 1833

WOOD, John B. -- Daviess Co. Letters of administration to Andrew McHaney 5 June.   MOAR 20 Aug 1838

WOOD, John S. of Jackson Co. died at "Creek" (on the way west). Date not shown. Wife, 2 children.   MORE 7 Oct 1850

WOODS, Joseph "most respected citizen" died yesterday.   BEA 6 Apr 1830

WOODS, S. P. decd. -- St. Clair Co. Petition to sell his real estate. George Reese, adm.   OSIN 18 Jan 1851

WOODS, Silas -- Chariton Co. Final settlement by Henry M. Duncan.   BRUNS 7 Oct 1848

WOOD, Thomas died 6 Sept. in his 28th year. Lived on 8th St. between Locust-St. Charles.   MORE 7 Sep 1847

WOOD, Thomas died at his residence in Franklin Co. in his 63rd year 21 August.   MORE 29 Aug 1851

WOOD, Thomas, formerly of Green Co. PA, died 7 March in Bonhomme Twp.   MORE 21 March 1846

WOODBRIDGE, Horace P., native of St. Louis, died at Keokuk 27 July age about 45. Hartford CT please copy.   MORE 30 July 1851

WOODBURN, William Esq. died 14 November in his 54th year. Lived at Collins and Ashby. Methodist cemetery.   MORE 15 Nov 1847

WOODSON, Richard -- Chariton Co. Final settlement by John M. Bell.   BOLT 4 Mar 1843

WOODSON, Stephen Austin died 5 April in Jefferson Co. in his 24th year. Left widowed mother, 5 sisters and brothers. Buried Herculaneum. MORE 21 Apr 1847

WOODWARD, Thomas Emmet died at the residence of his father George Esq. near Richmond MO 17 November 1839. A horse he had just bought threw him onto a fence post. He was born in Lexington KY 31 Oct. 1821. MORE 22 Jan 1840

WOOLL, Francis, late of St. Louis, died in New Orleans 26 February age 23. SWERE 19 Mar 1849

WOOLBRIDGE, John, a carpenter, died 13 Aug. of bilious fever. Native of Rockingham Co. VA. MORE 16 Aug 1833

WOOLERY, Lawrence died near Palestine, Cooper Co., 9 April age 100. WEM 18 Apr 1839

WOOLF, George, eldest son of George Sr., died 12 Nov. in his 18th year. MORE 14 Nov 1842

WOOLFOLK, Norben, late of Lincoln Co., died at Potosi WT (Wisconsin?) a few days ago. Louisville pls copy. MORE 17 Mar 1841

WOOLFOLK, Dr. R. H. died of cholera in Lincoln Co. BRUNS 2 Aug 1849

WOOLFOLK, Dr. John died Tuesday last. MORE 29 Aug 1834

WOOLFORT, Adam died Thursday last in his 45th year. MORE 15 Feb 1817

WOOLFORT, Ezekiel accidentally drowned Tuesday morning in an accident that took several other lives. MORE 16 Nov 1816

WORREL, Franklin A., of Carthage MO, killed at Warsaw in Mormon disturbances. MORE 19 Sep 1845

WORTH, Christian found drowned near Boonville 22 Sept. Thought to have a brother in New Orleans. MORE 2 Oct 1843

WRIGHT, Amos -- Gentry Co. Letters of administration to George W. Birch 14 April. STGAZ 5 May 1852

WRIGHT, Edward of St. Louis died in Galena 11 Sept. age 42. SLDU 12 Oct 1846

WRIGHT, James of Taney Co. died 17 June 160 miles west of Ft. Kearney, age 28. MORE 7 Oct 1850

WRIGHT, James G. died 1 Feb. in Warren Twp. (Marion Co.) PWH 10 Feb 1848

WRIGHT, Dr. John C. died Saturday morning last of congestive fever. PWH 7 Aug 1841

WRIGHT, John J. died 16 July. BEA 21 July 1831

WRIGHT, John D. -- Taney Co. Letters of administration to William Pierce and Sarah B. Wright 1 June. JINQ 27 July 1843

WRIGHT, Joseph of Boone Co. died in CA 24 December. MORE 1 Apr 1851

WRIGHT, Henry died at his home in Montgomery Co. 14 Aug. age 46. NH and MA papers please copy. MORE 28 Aug 1843

WRIGHT, M. Jarvis died at Philadelphia 23 August, for the past 6 years a resident of St. Louis. MORE 3 Sep 1841

WRIGHT, Richard J. died at the home of his brother Uriel. PWH 4 June 1842

WRIGHT, Robert Esq. died in New London, Ralls Co. 6 Oct. MORE 14 Oct 1844
of congestive fever. Left wife, 3 children.

WRIGHT, Rev. Thomas died at the house of David Armour, a INP 13 Feb 1825
Methodist member and teacher near 18 years.
Buried near McKendree Chapel.

WRIGHT, Major Thomas died Sunday evening last. US Army. MORE 11 Nov 1834

WRIGHTMAN, William died 5 March at the home of B. Collins, MORE 7 Mar 1821
in the 35th year of his age.

WYATT, Joseph -- Montgomery Co. Letters of administration STCHMO 21 Mar 1822
to John Wyatt (settle with John Wyatt Jr.
living near Pinckney.)

WYATT, Thomas W. of Morgan Co. (may be IL) drowned near MORE 18 July 1846
Alton. In Capt. Zabriskie's Co. of Volunteers.

WYMER, Charles and child died of cholera in Palmyra. MORE 28 June 1833

WYNN, Thomas of Moniteau Co. killed "about two weeks ago" MORE 14 Nov 1848
by his brother Nat. Both drunk.

YAGER, Thomas B. died in Randolph Co. 11 May age 62. GLWT 29 May 1851

YALE, B. B. of Louisiana MO died Saturday age about 30. SWERE 2 Apr 1849

YANCEY, Col. John of Saline Co. died 16 Oct. "Old, worthy." MODE 4 Nov 1846
(BOLT 31 October gives John S.)

YEATS, David died Friday evening last. MORE 13 Aug 1833

YATES, George died 7 October of cholera, age about 50. JEFRE 12 Oct 1833

YATES, James, a Jesuit, at St. Louis University 1 Feb. SOV 9 Feb.1833

YATES, Thomas J. R. died of dysentery 8 Oct. age 34. MORE 11 Oct 1847
Baltimore and Cambridge please copy.

YEATS, Thomas D. died 27 June age 25. MORE 29 June 1852

YELDER, _____ a Dutch shoemaker and his wife killed by a MORE 7 Mar 1844
Negro belonging to the estate of Philip
Coontz (Coonce) near Herculaneum. Their
infant slightly injured.

YOACHUM, Jacob Sr. -- Taney Co. Letters of administration SPAD 15 Nov 1845
to Michael Yoachum 4 November.

YOACHUM, William murdered by Alpha P. Buckley in MORE 23 July 1838
Jackson County 5 July.

YOSTE, Joseph died 3 Jan. near St. Charles Ferry, age 29. MORE 5 Jan 1820

YOSTI, Emilien died Wednesday night last age 78. MORE 17 Apr 1818

YOSTI, Louis died 11 April age 62y 11m 24d. Lived MORE 13 Apr 1852
near St. Charles.

YOUNG, Aaron H. died 9 October at his home in St. Louis Co. MORE 11 Oct 1837
Formerly of Fayette Co. KY.

YOUNG, Leonard W., son of Aaron and Theodosia, died MORE 13 Jan 1835
1 January age 21.

YOUNG, Capt. Benjamin died in a cholera epidemic.   MORE 6 Nov 1832

YOUNG, George W. S. of St. Charles died 28 August in   MORE 7 Sep 1853
    New Orleans.

YOUNG, Harry killed by a slave of G.H. Kennerly in an   SWERE 2 Sep 1844
    affray aboard the Nimrod.

YOUNG, Henderson died 23 July. Born in TN in 1808, came   LEXP 16 Aug 1854
    to MO in 1833. Married Doshea Callaway, daughter
    of Rev. T. Buried Machpelah cemetery.

YOUNG, Hiram drowned en route to St. Louis from Galena   BEA 13 Oct 1831
    "a short time since." Notice concerning lost
    note by his partner Robert R. Young.

YOUNG, Dr. James E. age 35 died 5 March in St. Louis Co.   MORE 6 Mar 1839
    James Milton, age 34, in St. Louis Co. 15 years,   " 13 Mar
    left widow, 4 babies, mother, 2 sisters.

YOUNG, James H. "aged and respectable" died Sunday last.   PWH 13 Aug 1845

YOUNG, Dr. M. G. died Friday morning last.   STGAZ 26 Oct 1853

YOUNG, John, native of PA, died 4 Sept. in St. Louis.   STCHMO 12 Sep 1821

YOUNG, John A. of St. Michaels died Tuesday in St. Louis.   SLINQ 8 Sep 1821
    Native of PA, came to St. Louis in fall of 1816.

YOUNG, Joseph died Friday 15 September.   MORE 18 Sep 1837

ZANTZINGER, Richard A. of the 2nd Reg. US Artillery died   MORE 6 Jan 1842
    at Planter's House 4 January.

ZIEFEL, Francis died 1 April age 29.   SWERE 3 Apr 1848

ZOECKLER, Louis died 20 Sept. age about 33.   MORE 22 Sep 1847

ZUMWALT, Jacob -- Montgomery Co. Final settlement by   MORE 13 Dec 1831
    Lewis Crow.

++ ++ ++ ++ ++ ++ ++

www.ingramcontent.com/pod-product-compliance
Lightning Source LLC
Chambersburg PA
CBHW020652300426
44112CB00007B/344